SAMUEL JOHNSON AND THE CULTURE OF PROPERTY

Kevin Hart traces the vast literary legacy and reputation of Samuel Johnson. Through detailed analyses of the biographers, critics and epigones who carefully crafted and preserved Johnson's life for posterity, Hart explores the emergence of what came to be called 'the Age of Johnson'. Hart shows how late seventeenth- and early eighteenth-century Britain experienced the emergence and consolidation of a rich and diverse culture of property. In dedicating himself to Johnson's death, Hart argues, James Boswell turned his friend into a monument, a piece of public property. Through subtle analyses of copyright, forgery and heritage in eighteenth-century life, this study traces the emergence of competing forms of cultural property: a Hanoverian politics of property engages a Jacobite politics of land. Kevin Hart places Samuel Johnson within this rich cultural context, demonstrating how Johnson came to occupy a place at the heart of the English literary canon.

KEVIN HART is Professor of English and Comparative Literature at Monash University in Melbourne, Australia. He is the author of *Trespass of the Sign* (1990), *A. D. Hope* (1992), and editor of *The Oxford Book of Australian Religious Verse* (1994). He is a Fellow of the Australian Academy of Humanities.

SAMUEL JOHNSON AND THE CULTURE OF PROPERTY

KEVIN HART

CAMBRIDGE
UNIVERSITY PRESS

PUBLISHED BY THE PRESS SYNDICATE OF THE UNIVERSITY OF CAMBRIDGE
The Pitt Building, Trumpington Street, Cambridge CB2 1RP, United Kingdom

CAMBRIDGE UNIVERSITY PRESS
The Edinburgh Building, Cambridge, CB2 2RU, UK http://www.cup.cam.ac.uk
40 West 20th Street, New York, NY 10011–4211,   USA http://www.cup.org
10 Stamford Road, Oakleigh, Melbourne 3166, Australia

© Kevin Hart 1999

First published 1999

Printed in the United Kingdom at the University Press, Cambridge

Typeset in Baskerville 11/12.5pt [VN]

A catalogue record for this book is available from the British Library

Library of Congress Cataloguing in Publication data

Hart, Kevin, 1954–
Samuel Johnson and the culture of property / Kevin Hart.
p.   cm.
Includes bibliographical references and index.
ISBN 0 521 65182 4 (hardback)
1. Johnson, Samuel, 1709–1784 – Knowledge – Economics.   2. Property –
Social aspects – Great Britain – History – 18th century.
3. Literature and society – Great Britain – History – 18th century.
4. Intellectual property – Great Britain – History – 18th century.
5. Cultural property – Great Britain – History – 18th century.
6. Boswell, James, 1740–1795.   Life of Samuel Johnson.   7. Great
Britain – Civilization – 18th century.   8. Biography as a literary
form.   9. Economics in literature.   I. Title.
PR3537.E25H37   1999
828'.609–dc21   98-45599
CIP
ISBN 0 521 65182 4 hardback

Contents

Economic acts

'There is nothing which so generally strikes the imagination, and engages the affections of mankind, as the right of property.' So declares William Blackstone, the first Vinerian Professor of English Law at the University of Oxford, in his magisterial *Commentaries* (1765–69). Property, he goes on to say, is 'that sole and despotic dominion which one man claims and exercises over the external things of the world, in total exclusion of the right of any other individual in the universe'.[1] Having gone so far, he is moved to open the Bible, citing Genesis 1: 28, which he calls 'the only true and solid foundation of man's dominion over external things'.[2] It is rare to find Blackstone evoking the imagination or expressing such a sense of awe. And yet it is understandable here: for he is confronting the ground and abyss of his great theme. The laws of England, as gathered and ordered by him, are at heart an affirmation and elaboration of the right to property.[3]

That property is a natural right, established at the level of the individual rather than the State, is the burden of John Locke's eloquent remarks on the subject in his *Two Treatises of Government* (1690). To say that his theory of property was influential would be a tepid understatement; it formed a horizon for all discussions of law and society in eighteenth-century Britain, including Blackstone's lectures.[4] No student of the age can be unaware of Locke's bold central contention: 'Though the Earth, and all inferior Creatures be common to all Men, yet every Man has a *Property* in his own *Person*. This no Body has any Right to but himself. The *Labour* of his Body, and the *Work* of his Hands, we may say, are properly his. Whatsoever then he removes out of the State that Nature hath provided, and left it in, he hath mixed his *Labour* with, and joyned to it something that is his own, and thereby makes it his *Property*.'[5] Thus Locke; and the tradition of liberalism – or, if you prefer, possessive individualism – that largely derives from him will add as a coda that only a natural right, underwritten by God, can truly serve as an absolute ground for regulating social life.[6]

Fiercely protected by the law, property in turn kept watch over the world of political power in eighteenth-century England. Only those men who held land with a taxable value of at least 40s per annum were eligible to vote in parliamentary elections. And only those men who held considerable tracts of landed property could seek to contest a seat or borough. This latter measure came onto the books in 1710 when, after many delays, the Commons finally passed an 'Act for Securing the Freedom of Parliaments', 9 Annæ c. 5, which required an elected candidate to own land yielding at least £600 above reprizes per annum for a country seat and £300 above reprizes per annum for a city borough.[7] The Tories had been calling for such a measure for some time, and their reasons for doing so were perfectly cogent. In the decades following the Glorious Revolution, the country gentlemen had been forced to accommodate themselves to a new political order. Whatever their attachments may have been to the divine right of kings and indefeasible hereditary succession, let alone to James II or, later, the Old Pretender, they had little choice but to endorse William III as King *de facto* and to protect their interests as best they could. The Tories' 'ideology of order', as H. T. Dickinson calls it, was under threat from the men of the City who, if circumstances allowed, could upset the old hierarchies with the power bought by their new-found wealth. It was necessary to prevent them from gaining a quick admittance to the third estate.[8]

Only those men of substantial property would have the commitment to the country required to govern wisely, the Tories argued, and only those men would have the leisure to attend conscientiously to the work of legislature. It was as though they were quoting directly from James Harrington's *Oceana* (1656):

> For dominion personal or in money, it may now and then stir up a Melius or a Manlius, which, if the commonwealth be not provided with some kind of dictatorian power, may be dangerous, though it have been seldom or never successful; because unto property producing empire, it is required that it should have some certain root or foothold, which, except in land, it cannot have, being otherwise as it were upon the wing.[9]

Speculators, traders and small squires would have to be excluded from government. When one thinks of the many financiers who made and lost fortunes over the course of the century, let alone the calamities consequent on the bursting of the South Sea Bubble in 1720, the concerns of the Tories come into sharp focus. Yet from the viewpoint of those with no or little land, including those whose family estates had been heavily mortgaged in the recent war to pay land tax, it must have seemed as though the Glorious Revolution had never happened. In terms of parliamentary representation, at least, one might have been forgiven for thinking that one 'sole and despotic dominion' had replaced another.[10]

This thought should encourage us to disentangle questions of parliamentary representation from questions of landed property. By the middle decades of the eighteenth century business men, minor gentry and political radicals were all muttering against the current system of parliamentary representation. In the 1740s London merchants complained they were subject to a disproportionately high amount of land tax: their interests would be better served, they thought, by eliminating rotten boroughs and creating new seats in London and other commercial centres.[11] Twenty years later the same group found themselves disadvantaged by government restrictions on trade with the American colonies. The brief period of living in harmony with the ministry, under the leadership of William Pitt, must have seemed like a pleasant dream. Now things were very different, but there were few opportunities for effective displays of discontent. One came in the crisis of 1768–69 when John Wilkes repeatedly attempted to represent first London then Middlesex in the Commons. He received vigorous support from disgruntled merchants; and when, after the third by-election, he was declared unable to be elected, the government was beleaguered with grievances from craftsmen and tradesmen.[12]

The commercial classes gave little or no encouragement to the radicals, however, and it is easy to see why. By and large the political radicals distrusted the new world of floating debt, international trade and paper credit. Consider Thomas Hollis (1720–74), for instance. James Boswell called him a 'strenuous Whig', thinking no doubt of his republicanism.[13] To be sure, Hollis was an extremist in advocating the dissolution of the monarchy of Great Britain, but the right to property was never in question for him: he looked to the powerful landowners for national leadership. Had he lived a further twenty years, Hollis would certainly not have enjoyed all of Edmund Burke's *Reflections on the Revolution in France* (1790). In particular, the vision of the dauphiness at Versailles in all her beauty and glory would have repulsed him. Yet he would not have disagreed completely with the sentiments of a passage like this one:

Nothing is a due and adequate representation of a state, that does not represent its ability, as well as its property. But as ability is a vigorous and active principle, and as property is sluggish, inert, and timid, it never can be safe from the invasions of ability, unless it be, out of all proportion, predominant in the representation. It must be represented too in great masses of accumulation, or it is not rightly protected. The characteristic essence of property, formed out of the combined principles of its acquisition and conservation, is to be *unequal*.[14]

Hollis and Burke: the conjunction reminds us that in eighteenth-century Britain even people from distant parts of the political spectrum could agree on the importance of landed property for the continued health of the nation.

As the century wore on, two developments aided the financiers and merchants rather more than the radicals. There had been members of the Commons with family backgrounds in commerce as early as George I's first parliament, and over the years the proportion of non-élite parliamentarians increased.[15] Bankers and merchants purchased and entailed landed property to secure their futures and those of their descendants; and one consequence was that, by the last decade of the century, the old-style country gentlemen were a minority in the House.[16] At the same time, the British economy was growing; and as the country's wealth became increasingly tied to credit and commerce, political power began to respond to personal as well as real property. The inevitable reference point is Adam Smith's *The Wealth of Nations* (1776). His definition of property may have been more narrow than Locke's which extended to 'life, liberty and estate', but if one steps back far enough one can make out the philosopher standing behind the economist.

Another tireless advocate of merchants, Daniel Defoe, would have been pleased by what had happened in the decades after the *Review*; but it must be remembered that not even he doubted that stable government of the realm ultimately depended on freeholders of property:

The *Freeholders* are the proper Owners of the Country: It is their own, and the other Inhabitants are but Sojourners, like Lodgers in a House, and ought to be subject to such Laws as the Freeholders impose upon them, or else they must remove; because the Freeholders having a Right to the Land, the others have no Right to live there but upon Suffrance... And I make no Question but Property of Land is the best Title to Government in the World...[17]

We think of Defoe as a supporter of liberty, and so he was. If we ask what the word meant to him, though, we learn something important about what the old rallying cry 'Liberty and Property!' often meant in practice. 'Pray, what is Liberty – But a Freedom to possess Property, a Liberty to enjoy it, and a Right to defend it – And this is so much the Priviledge of an *English* Man, that no Human Power can, without a Crime to forfeit it, or a Consent to yield it, divest him of it – If it can, ye may wipe your Mouths with *Magna Charta*, Claim of Right, and all the Laws hitherto to defend them.'[18]

Defend the English man's right to property the Laws certainly did. From the Restoration to the death of George III about 190 capital offences were added to the books, most of which concerned crimes against property.[19] We can read these figures as the grim record of a society violently protecting the rights of its élite, often with cruelty, and to a large extent we are obliged to do so. Yet these figures also tell us that the notion of property was in flux, expanding in several directions at the same time. Ronald Paulson is right to point out that property is not to be accommodated by any single or simple polarity. It is variously contrasted with the human, liberty and ability; and these shadings have different intensities in different contexts.[20] And Peter Linebaugh is also correct to argue that in the eighteenth century the concept of property changes in four distinguishable though hardly distinct ways: how it is produced, how it is used, how it is valued, and how the laws pertain to it.[21] To take just one example, although a very important one, all these changes in the notion of property are caught up in the long and often heated debate that finally resulted in the modern understanding of intellectual property.

Three events are of particular significance in this debate. In 1709 Parliament passed the 'Act for the Encouragement of Learning', 8 Annæ, c. 21, often known as the Statute of Anne, which ended the free-for-all in the book trade that had been unleashed since the Licensing Act had been allowed to lapse in 1694. It was now clearly affirmed that literary works were the personal property of the author or bookseller, and a term of copyright was set at twenty-one years for books already in print, and at fourteen years for new titles (extendable to twenty-eight years, if the author was alive at the end of the first term). Less than clear, however, was whether the Statute of Anne merely bolstered a common law understanding of literary property, in which case copyright would be perpetual, or whether it was by itself the whole law, in which case copyright would be limited. The matter remained unresolved until the case of *Millar* v. *Taylor* (1769), when the Court of the King's Bench affirmed that copyright was perpetual. The decision was in effect for just five years. For in the landmark case of *Donaldson* v. *Becket* (1774), the House of Lords voted in favour of limited copyright. With this decision authors, rather than booksellers, became the owners of copyright. It was the beginning of what people were beginning to call the 'Golden Age of Authors'.

In late seventeenth- and early eighteenth-century Britain, then, we see the emergence and consolidation of a rich and diverse culture of property. It is not my intention to describe or explore it further. Historians of British economics, literature and politics have already done so in illuminating detail, especially in recent years, and I will be drawing on their work in the chapters that follow.[22] My concern is with one man who participated in this culture and in some respects has come to stand for it: Samuel Johnson. That he wrote with strength and originality on many of its features – agriculture, economics, forgery, land, law and literary property – may not be as well known as it deserves to be, and these writings will be of interest to me. But they are not my main focus, which is given in the title of this introduction. In coining the expression 'economic acts' I have not wished to signal a sympathy with economic reductionism or an attempt to draw parallels between language and money.[23] Rather, I would like the expression to identify those actions in which something is appropriated and/or expropriated: economic logic, not economism, is the issue.[24] Sometimes these acts concern real, personal or literary property. Sometimes they do not: for as Blackstone and others before him knew, the right to appropriation is distinct from the right to property. Whether it is historically or logically distinct is a matter that divides Marxists from non-Marxists, and I do not propose to debate the question here. Suffice it to say, though, that sometimes these acts straddle the line dividing the two kinds of right.

In each chapter Samuel Johnson is linked in one way or another to James Boswell, and in explaining why I do this I can also give a better idea of my concern. Certainly some explanation is necessary, for scholars of eighteenth-century British writing are far more cautious now about associating these two writers than we were even a generation ago. In 1951 Bertrand H. Bronson expressed what many had felt, that Boswell's 'Flemish portrait' of Johnson had fundamentally affected the ways in which we respond to him. 'Johnson has come down to us in a double tradition', he suggested. 'Like any other author, he exists for us in his works. But he exists also like a character in one of our older novels, and on the same level of objectivity and familiarity.'[25] Johnson had become a split figure, writer and talker, with Boswell ultimately responsible for the scission. More than that, Boswell divides Johnson only to appropriate his idiom: after all, the proper name 'Boswell' has come to stand for the *Life of Johnson,* and therefore for Johnson the talker. A writer's idiom, usually a mark of singularity, is here taken by another, made proper and profitable to him. So much so that the biographer is raised by many readers above his subject: the annex becomes larger (and certainly more comfortable) than the original house. The movement is a familiar one: what seems secondary and supplemental can displace the primary figure; the excessive becomes successive. And equally customary is the irritation such movements cause among the votaries of the primary figure. For some Johnsonians it is well nigh impossible to mention Boswell without a certain sharpness of tone.

Given Bronson's assumptions, it would seem that the best way to recover the true Johnson, the challenging writer, is to read what he wrote and what his contemporaries wrote about him. Certainly we have more information about Johnson, his early years in particular, than was available to Boswell.[26] We have a fine edition of his letters, a growing complete edition of his works, and a better sense of his canon; we have Frances Burney's journal and letters, along with other memoirs; there is all the genealogical research of Aleyn Llyll Reade, diverse biographies, and all the many contributions that explore aspects of Johnson's reading and writing.[27] When we take all this into account we see that Boswell's perspective on Johnson was not the only one, or perhaps always the most telling one. It is also true that, with the recovery of his journals and letters, we know far more about Boswell than could have been imagined a century ago. When the research edition of the journals is complete we will know even more. Marshall Waingrow's edition of the original manuscript of the *Life of Johnson* already gives invaluable insights into Boswell's writing habits.[28] In reading these documents and editions along with his books we can identify several layers of Boswell's self-mythologising, one copious seam of which consists of his relationship with Johnson.

So Johnson and Boswell were far less hand in glove than was once thought. If this gives Johnsonians a tonic satisfaction, it also causes them a flicker of anxiety now and then. For Johnson has been extricated only at the cost of revealing a Boswell who competes for our attention. This revelation occurs in two main stages. First, there is a change of sympathy: Macaulay vilifies Boswell in his famous review of J. W. Croker's 1831 edition of the *Life,* but the biographer is rehabilitated by the editions of Birkbeck Hill, Chauncey B. Tinker and Frederick A. Pottle.[29] Second, there is a change of genre: the great biographer takes a step to the side, allowing the supreme diarist to stand in the spotlight. The transformation of Boswell is not without problems: high claims for his drama of the self do not persuade those who were not in the first place charmed by that self in the *Life*. Reading the journals we repeatedly see an elastic conscience being stretched to its limits then suddenly snapping back, bringing terrible remorse. One might wonder whether this makes for art of a high order, as Frederick Pottle contends, or merely a record of 'self-absorption and mediocrity of mind', as Claude Rawson judges.[30] Yet it is a debate about Boswell, and for once 'Boswell' does not stand for 'Johnson'. The new-found independence of both writers means that their relationship must be rethought, both in itself and as received in literary history. In part this project requires us to examine Boswell's diverse appropriations of Johnson, and in part it invites us to study the desire to expropriate Boswell from the reading of Johnson. Both acts mark 'Samuel Johnson' as a particular kind of property.

To regard Boswell's writings on Johnson as 'economic acts' is to acknowledge complex acts of appropriation and expropriation that are managed there. Also, though, it is to attend to Boswell's biographical style: his promised frugality – 'to explain, connect, and supply' – as set against his many excesses. Boswell positions himself to be as passive as possible with respect to Johnson: not to speak after his subject's death, as other biographers do, but to let his subject present himself in his own words. Inevitably, this passivity becomes a mastery: the *Life* preserves a memory of Johnson and programmes it for future generations, so effectively in fact that it is often taken to be *the* memory of Johnson. If various meanings may be drawn from the word 'economic' at different moments of this study, the same is true of 'acts'. Usually the word denotes simply a deed or an exploit. On occasion, though, its legal sense is brought into the foreground; while at other times, the word evokes the theatre. It is not irrelevant that Boswell the lawyer was also Boswell the theatre goer and mimic.

Samuel Johnson and the Culture of Property begins by pondering how Boswell makes Johnson into a monument, a piece of public property, and ends by meditating on what escapes all monumentalisation, that cluster of repetitive appropriations we call 'everyday life'. In between I examine how the decades in which Johnson lived have come to be economised in his name, forming an 'Age of Johnson', and how Boswell's *Life* becomes a kind of property in nineteenth- and twentieth-century arguments about biography and editing. Boswell's second major Johnsonian work, the *Journal of a Tour to the Hebrides*, becomes the focus in two chapters. In the first I analyse the play of subordination and exchange in Johnson's transit of Caledonia, paying attention to how a politics of money engages a politics of land. And in the second I turn to examine Ossian and Johnson as competing forms of cultural property.

I began formulating the questions that now shape this study when lecturing on eighteenth-century English literature at the University of Melbourne in 1986, and over the years many people have helped me in a variety of ways.

This book came to life slowly and in many places. Different sections of the first chapter were given as papers in the Department of English at the University of Melbourne and at the American Society for Eighteenth-Century Studies, East-Central Division, held at Georgetown University in Washington, DC in 1996. One part of the second chapter was read at the colloquium of the Department of English, the University of Sydney, and another part at the colloquium of the Department of English, Northwestern University, Evanston, in 1998. A portion of the third chapter was presented to meetings of the Departments of English at Monash University, Melbourne, and Case Western Reserve University in Cleveland. A draft of chapter four was read at a staff seminar of the Department of English at the Australian National University, Canberra, and a slightly different version of this paper, which included material from chapter five, was presented at the eighth David Nichol Smith Seminar, held at Monash University in 1990. One part of the fifth chapter was read at the colloquium of the Department of English, La Trobe University, Melbourne, and another part was presented at the staff–postgraduate seminar of the Centre for Comparative Literature and Cultural Studies at Monash University in 1997. Finally, pages from chapters one and three were presented at the 1993 and 1994 Annual Meetings of the Johnson Society of Australia, both held in Melbourne. I am grateful to all those who contributed to the discussion of these papers and, in several cases, offered useful suggestions.

A truncated version of the first chapter appeared as 'Johnson as Monument' in *The Critical Review*, 34 (1994) and a highly compressed statement of chapters four and five was published as 'Economic Acts: Johnson in Scotland' in a special number of *Eighteenth-Century Life*, 16, ns 1 (1992). My thanks to the editors of both journals: Richard Lansdown and Clive Probyn respectively.

I would like to thank the Australian Research Council for a large grant which enabled me to consult books and manuscripts in libraries in England and the United States. It is a pleasure to acknowledge the help given to me by librarians over the last decade. In Australia: Deakin University Library, and Monash University Library. Particular thanks are due to Richard Overell of the Rare Books Room at the Monash University Library. In Britain: the British Library in London, and the Johnson Birthplace Museum in Lichfield. In the United States: the Bieneke and Stirling Libraries of Yale Univesity, the Widener and Houghton Libraries of Harvard University, the Howard W. Gunlocke Rare Book and Special Collections Room of the Lauinger Library of Georgetown University, the New York Public Library, the Special Collections Room of the Vassar College Library, and the Law Library Reading Room and the Rare Books and Special Collections Room of the Library of Congress, Washington, DC. I am grateful to the University of Nottingham library for granting me permission to quote from William Burke's letter of 26 July 1779 to the Duke of Portland (Pw F 2149). Most of this study was written while on study leave from Monash University in the first semester of 1994 and in my term as a Visiting Professor at Georgetown University in 1996–97. I am obliged to friends and colleagues at Monash for letting me go and at Georgetown for letting me come.

When I started to outline this study first Megan Collins and then Bridget Bainbridge served as research assistants, and their dedication and skill saved me much time and many pains. Harold Bloom, Ian Donaldson, Paul Kane, Paul Tankard and Stephanie Trigg each read portions of the typescript and offered valuable advice and encouragement. John W. Byrne, Robert Crawford, David Matthews, Robert DeMaria, Alvaro Ribeiro, SJ, Stuart Sherman and Gordon Turnbull kindly found information or material that I could not otherwise obtain, and Rachel McClellan of the 'Boswell Factory' in the Stirling Library at Yale gave me every assistance when I was investigating uncollected works by James Boswell. Michael Suarez, SJ read the entire manuscript and made many useful comments. It is pleasant to remember that, when I taught at the University of Melbourne, Robin Grove first invited me to lecture on eighteenth-century literature and, in doing so, allowed me to develop the ideas elaborated in this book. My thanks to all.

My largest debt is to my wife, Rita Hart, who tolerated me spending an excessive amount of time at home and away reading and writing on Johnson. The book is dedicated to my daughters, Sarah and Claire, who were born while this study was in progress and have had to live with it in one or more rooms of the house, almost as another member of the family.

CHAPTER I

The monument

One day, so the story goes, Samuel Johnson and Oliver Goldsmith visited Westminster Abbey together. As they passed through the south transept and came upon Poets' Corner they viewed the tombs and memorials there – Chaucer's, Spenser's, Shakespeare's, Milton's, and all the others – and Johnson quoted an apt line from Ovid: *Forsitan et nostrum nomen miscebitur istis*, 'It may be that our name too will mingle with those' (*Life*, II, 238). Later in the day, they passed Temple-bar where the impaled heads of the rebel Scotch Lords were a grisly reminder of the Forty-Five, and Goldsmith slyly whispered the line back to Johnson with a different emphasis, *Forsitan et nostrum nomen miscebitur ISTIS*, 'It may be that our name too will mingle with THOSE'. Part of the pleasure in reading this little story lies in knowing that Johnson, not Goldsmith, was proved right, that whatever real or imagined Jacobite sympathies they may have had both writers kept their heads. After Goldsmith died in 1774 and was buried in the Abbey, Johnson wrote his epitaph – in Latin, because 'he would never consent to disgrace the walls of Westminster Abbey with an English inscription' (*Life*, III, 85). And on his deathbed, ten years later, he asked Sir John Hawkins 'where he should be buried; and on being answered, "Doubtless, in Westminster-Abbey", seemed to feel a satisfaction, very natural to a Poet' (*Life*, IV, 419).

In this story we see Samuel Johnson, the monumental man of letters, wishing to be a monument. We catch him on an unspecified day, though certainly after 1759 or so when he met Goldsmith who was then a Grub Street hack just emerging from obscurity. Johnson is in his early fifties. It is a day long after the Drury Lane performance of his tragedy *Irene*, years after the publication of his poems 'London' and 'The Vanity of Human Wishes', after the appearance in various forms of his periodical essays the *Rambler* and the *Idler*, and, most recently, after the release of his oriental tale *Rasselas* (1759). For various ordinary reasons of the day none of these works bears Johnson's name on its title page, and gathered together they do not represent anything like all that he has published.[1] He does not always sign, and does not always sign 'Samuel Johnson'. None of his writing has made him wealthy or even financially secure. If the visit to the Abbey is set later than 1762, though, he has accepted a pension of £300 a year from George III, which for the first time in his life frees him from toiling for the booksellers but which also brings him a considerable amount of censure from the press.[2] Certainly the walk to Poets' Corner occurs after the publication of his *Dictionary* (1755). The dense papers of the *Rambler*, completed in 1752, have mostly earned him deep respect from those who have discovered their author but it is the *Dictionary* that has made him famous at home and abroad. There he does sign, famously, 'Samuel Johnson, A.M.' Here is a man who, as his admirers boast, has done for English in nine years what it took forty members of the Académie Française forty years to do for French. His literary fame is set firmly on national pride and has some of the lustres of heroism.

With the benefit of hindsight, literary historians with a taste for periodisation will place this day firmly within 'the Age of Johnson', an expression which tempts the lips but which conceals a world of competing literary, social and political values. Yet the ground for this name and age was already being laid during Johnson's lifetime. In 1755, the year of the *Dictionary* and amidst strong feeling against the French, David Garrick was quick to see his former teacher as a national hero. In a poem he exclaims, 'And Johnson, well arm'd, like a hero of yore, / Has beat forty French, and will beat forty more'.[3] Just before the *Dictionary* was published, Lord Chesterfield, Johnson's cool patron, was entreated by Robert Dodsley to warm to his role. His lines in *The World* are all elegance:

Toleration, adoption, and naturalization have run their lengths. Good order and authority are now necessary. But where shall we find them, and at the same time the obedience due to them? We must have recourse to the old Roman expedient in times of confusion, and choose a dictator. Upon this principle, I give my vote for Mr Johnson to fill that great and arduous post. And I hereby declare that I make a total surrender of all my rights and privileges in the English language, as a free-born British subject, to the said Mr Johnson during the term of his dictatorship.[4]

Johnson as *dictator*? Chesterfield was writing with tongue almost in cheek, thinking of the *Dictionary* (both words derive from the Latin verb *dicare*), yet Johnson had already made a bid for the authority of Mr

Rambler who calls himself 'dictatorial' (Yale, v, 319).[5] In a letter of 1759 Tobias Smollett referred grudgingly to 'that great CHAM of literature, Samuel Johnson' (*Life*, I, 348).[6] And that same year Goldsmith, writing in *The Bee*, drew a flattering portrait of Johnson being praised by the old coachman of 'The Fame Machine'. After admitting several notables to his carriage, the coachman sees 'a very grave personage' who, on closer inspection, turns out to have 'one of the most good-natured countenances that could be imagined'. 'The Rambler!', the coachman cries, 'I beg, sir, you'll take your place; I have heard our ladies in the court of Apollo frequently mention it [the periodical] with rapture . . .'.[7] Several years later, in 1767, James Boswell, writing to Giuseppe Baretti, fulsomely characterises their mutual friend as 'the illustrious Philosopher of this age Mr Samuel Johnson',[8] using 'philosopher' as Johnson had defined it, as 'a man deep in knowledge, either moral or natural'.[9] This high praise was publicly confirmed in 1775 by the University of Oxford when in the diploma declaring Johnson Doctor of Laws he is referred to as '*in Literarum Republicâ PRINCEPS jam et PRIMARIUS jure habeatur*' (*Life*, II, 332). When Bishop Percy said that Johnson's conversation 'may be compared to an antique statue, where every vein and muscle is distinct and bold', his simile perhaps went further than depicting the man's talk and hinted that he was a living classic (*Life*, III, 317). There is no need for a 'perhaps' with Boswell. In his *Journal of a Tour to the Hebrides* (1785), an image of the classic was well and truly in place. There Johnson's living countenance is described as 'naturally of the cast of an ancient statue, but somewhat disfigured', an observation which quietly yet forcefully naturalises his friend's cultural authority (*Tour*, 18).[10]

That memoir and the later *Life of Samuel Johnson* (1791) are nowadays held responsible for fixing a popular and inadequate conception of Johnson, which they surely have done and still do, despite the many pleasures they offer. An uncritical reading of Boswell will yield a Johnson who is indeed a monument, frozen in old age, well-known and honoured, the centre of an adoring circle. Yet Boswell begins his *Tour* by giving us a glimpse of Johnson's fame as it stood then, before the biographer's books had started to shape it. He remarks that 'Dr Samuel Johnson's character – religious, moral, political and literary – nay his figure and manner, are, I believe, more generally known than those of almost any man' (*Tour*, 16). Needless to say, it is a deft rhetorical justification for what is to follow, but it is not empty rhetoric. It is worth noting how Boswell teases out the elements in his expression 'the illustrious Philosopher of this age'. Johnson's mind, he suggests, powerfully encompasses a wide range of human concerns – religious, moral, political, and literary – so wide in fact that he might be said to embody a general sense of his times. But Boswell's implicit claim goes further than this. It is not only that Johnson is an intellectual representative of the age but also that his 'figure and manner' are familiar idiosyncrasies, of interest with such a man, that can and should be recorded in detail.

We see here how Boswell begins to separate Johnson's work from his life: on the one hand we have his writings, and on the other his personal oddities. There is some point in the distinction, but before dwelling on it I would look elsewhere. Boswell is captivated by Johnson's character and genius, his scope as well as his strength, and these can be grasped partly from his writings and partly from his actions and conversations. In the *Dictionary* Johnson defines 'character' (in the relevant sense) as 'personal qualities; particular constitution of the mind', and 'genius' (again, in the relevant sense) as 'a man endowed with superior faculties'. Writing, for Johnson, was not a natural consequence of his character or his genius. The idea would have struck him as cant. 'The true Genius', he wrote in later life, 'is a mind of large general powers, accidentally determined to some particular direction'.[11] For Johnson, being a writer was a result of having to make a choice of life that best suited his abilities and situation. He may have written on political, moral and religious themes, and some of these compositions may have been of immense value (as Boswell thought they were), but his writings about these themes do not exhaust his literary character. His acts and conversation are eloquent testimony to that, as his friends and admirers well knew.

Boswell was not the only one to prize Johnson's character but thanks to the success of his biographies he has become the most important to do so. Then as now others placed a stronger stress on his writings. Thus Richard Brocklesby, one of the doctors who attended Johnson during his last illness, offered 'to take a share to the amount of 4 or 500£ to build him up the noblest and handsomest monument in a handsome and intire edition of his own works, for we thought they were better and more lasting materials than any monument of brass or Stone in Westminster Abbey'.[12] It is the old Horatian boast, *exegi monumentum aere perennius*, neatly turned as a compliment to a dying friend. Certainly in the past this patient had obliquely cast a cold eye on funereal pomp. In *Rasselas* Imlac surveys the Great Pyramid of Cheops and says, 'I consider this mighty structure as a monument of the insufficiency of human enjoyments. A king, whose power is unlimited, and whose treasures surmount all real and imaginary wants, is compelled to solace, by the erection of a pyramid, the satiety of dominion and tastelessness of pleasures, and to amuse the tediousness of declining life, by seeing thousands labouring without end, and one stone, for no purpose, laid upon another.'[13] Imlac is not Johnson, nor is the Great Pyramid a monument in the Abbey, yet Johnson's desire to be remembered there does not exclude an awareness of the vanity attending that desire. Even more to the point, that patient knew well enough how delusive literary fame could be. It is a theme that runs throughout his writings, especially the *Lives of the Poets* and the *Rambler*. 'To raise "monuments more durable than brass, and more conspicuous than pyramids", has been long the common boast of literature; but among the innumerable architects that erect columns to themselves, far the greatest part, either for want of durable materials, or of art to dispose them, see their edifices perish as they are towering to completion, and those few that for a while attract the eye of mankind, are generally weak in the foundation, and soon sink by the saps of time' (Yale, IV, 200).[14]

In the end, Johnson was memorialised both by statues and by an edition of his writings. In 1796, with money raised by the Friends to the Memory of Dr Johnson, an imposing monument by John Bacon with an inscription by Samuel Parr was erected in St Paul's. The choice of the Cathedral rather than the Abbey where Johnson was buried was urged by Sir Joshua Reynolds with the support of Edmund Burke. A contrast between the two places had been on Reynolds's mind at least since 1781 when he was visiting Flanders and Holland. New sculptures erected in the Abbey, he wrote then, 'are so stuck up in odd holes and corners, that it begins to appear truly ridiculous: the principal places have been long occupied, and the difficulty of finding a new nook or corner every year increases. While this Gothic structure is encumbered and overloaded with ornaments which have no agreement or correspondence with the taste and style of the building, St Paul's looks forlorn and desolate, or at least destitute of ornaments suited to the magnificence of the fabric.'[15] Other statues of Johnson were later raised in Lichfield and London.[16] Meanwhile, Sir John Hawkins had been employed by the London booksellers to prepare an edition of the *Works*, which was duly published in 1787, in eleven volumes octavo, to be supplemented by four more volumes from 1787 to 1798.[17] From the very beginning, Johnson has been remembered by two kinds of monuments: statues of the man to admire in public places, and thick volumes to contemplate in libraries. This is not merely a consequence of his literary abilities receiving due recognition; it is part and parcel of conceiving Johnson as a national hero, of almost mythic proportions. It is important to recognise, right at the start, that while Johnson is a canonical figure of English literature this is not the sole ground and origin of his cultural standing. He is one of those writers – like Dante, Goethe and Shakespeare – whose monumentality exceeds his canonicity.

The line between canonicity and monumentality is neither simple nor singular and sometimes cannot be traced at all. But usually it can be followed for a while. To begin with, despite my invocation of Dante, Goethe and Shakespeare, the category I have in mind is not restricted to the highest figures of a national canon: Robert Burns is a wonderful poet but his wider significance rests on his monumentality. Poems like 'Holy Willie's Prayer', 'To a Louse' and 'A Red, Red Rose' may rightly appear in all kinds of anthologies but the statues of the poet and the clubs dedicated to his name concentrate social forces which the poetry conducts. Monumentality and canonicity sometimes converge and sometimes diverge, even in the one reputation over a long enough period. There are writers who attain both and then substantially lose one: Alexander Pope has become more and more entrenched in the canon yet his monumentality has all but faded, while Ossian is now a grim monument mouldering outside the canon. And there are writers who become canonical without ever having gained a sense of the monumental in their lifetimes or after their deaths: Gerard Manley Hopkins is an example. This last group is made of minor figures, one might say, and that is often the case. Yet canons can and do respond to the pressures of revisionary readings, and when that happens a minor writer can be declared major, like Frances Burney, whose novels now enjoy a higher place in English literary history than ever before. Monumentality, as I am using the word, has traditionally functioned within a patriarchal culture and required a popularity (though not necessarily one with a popular base), as my examples suggest. But it also needs something else. A monument is a rallying point for a community; it must be the focus of a large and usually diffuse cultural will, the centre of a network of imaginary relationships and real desires.

Like most monuments, Johnson is usually regarded from a distance. One has to stand a good way off to take in the extent and weight of the work, to appreciate its gravity and achievement; while, for its part, the monument seems designed to be approached like that. Squarely built, it objectifies public virtues which we should admire and to which we should aspire. We look around it with the awe that is asked of us, always aware that this is a public property, a national heritage, an official face of British culture. Or, just as often, we glance dutifully at it and then look elsewhere. People visiting Lichfield, for instance, can view the brooding memorial statue in Market Place but are likely to spend more time in the nearby Johnson Birthplace Museum. They move with visible relief from the grand to the tiny, from the public to the private. Inside the museum one can see Johnson's knife and fork, his tea-pot and punch bowl, even his bib-holder and walking stick; and the curious can inspect his armchair from Bolt Court, perhaps hoping to find a trace of fur from Hodge, the fine cat that Boswell immortalised in the *Life*. If an identification with Johnson is to take place it is more likely to be inside than outside. And if it has just happened, even very slightly, one might select something on the way out from the wide range of Johnson badges and teaspoons, Johnson pens and pencils, not to mention the collection of postcards and posters.

A similar situation can beset the person approaching that other monument, the *Works*. New and old versions can always be found in libraries, and even in a few second-hand and specialist bookshops. Even here, though, there is much that has been built around the monument, not least of all biography and criticism, some of which attracts by its own lights. Then there are sumptuous or rare editions of texts to admire and linger over, paperbacks presenting Johnson's views – or purported views – on everything and nothing, and of course those tantalising if not always reliable compendia, the *Johnsonian Miscellanies* and the *Johnsoniana*, offering diary entries and anecdotes, right down to wise or feisty remarks utterly detached from their original Johnsonian contexts, if they ever had them in the first place ('Whoever thinks of going to bed before twelve o'clock ... is a scoundrel').[18] There is an air of the excessive and a whiff of the eccentric. By and large, the monument itself is left to be admired and caressed by the overlapping communities of the academy and the Johnson societies, and most people with a mind to take home a book will settle for an apparently less imposing volume, a copy of *Rasselas*, say, or a modern omnibus collection like John Wain's *Johnson on Johnson*.[19]

More often than not, though, people look for a guide to the monument, usually a biography of Johnson, and usually the best known, *The Life of Samuel Johnson, LL.D.* For it is Boswell who is taken, time and again, to offer a natural and inevitable introduction to Johnson. More than anyone else, Boswell liked to see himself as the special recipient of everything to do with the man. It would be wrong to say that he truly finds himself only as he crosses Johnson's path; for Boswell is always Mr James Boswell of Auchinleck, a proud Scottish baron of ancient family, and it is in the web of family relations and political responsibilities, both acutely real and romantically imagined, that he lives and moves. Even so, Boswell chooses to become not merely Johnsonian but *Johnsonianissimus*; he is not content to have read and benefited from his mentor's writings and example, he longs to have '*Johnsonised* the land' (*Life*, I, 13). When seen clearly, Boswell's project is nothing less than the monumentalisation of Johnson's name. But this act has an inevitable side effect: to present Samuel Johnson as he wishes, as a living man in conversation with himself and others, he must also create and maintain another literary figure, one James Boswell, Esq. As biographer, Boswell gives us a certain 'Dr Johnson', a powerful and seductive character who derives as much from Boswell's mastery of realism as from reality. That folk who know little or nothing of the *Rambler* or 'The Vanity of Human Wishes' still visit Gough Square in London and Market Place in Lichfield testifies to the success with which Boswell has Johnsonised the land. But of a piece with this success is the fact that, like it or not, he has Boswellised Johnson.

'A marble monument might be erected for the answer; but who would think of building one for the question?'[20] So asks Edmond Jabès, a writer as distant from Johnson in stance and style as one could readily imagine, and yet his remark helps to bring his apparent anti-type into sharper focus. Johnson is commonly regarded as someone with ready and Bullish answers to all manner of questions. Some of Boswell's images of his friend stick in the popular imagination so firmly that nothing can dislodge them. There is the story – perhaps apocryphal – of Boswell trying to defend Lady Diana Beauclerk, who had been divorced and remarried. 'Seduced, perhaps, by the charms of the lady in question, I thus attempted to palliate what I was sensible could not be justified; for, when I had finished my harangue, my venerable friend gave me a proper check: "My dear Sir, never accustom your mind to mingle virtue and vice. The woman's a whore, and there's an end on't"' (*Life*, II, 247). And there is the even better-known story of Johnson answering Boswell on the truth of Bishop Berkeley's theory of the non-existence of matter. 'I observed, that though we are satisfied his doctrine is not true, it is impossible to refute it. I never shall forget the alacrity with which Johnson answered, striking his foot with mighty force against a large stone, till he rebounded from it, "I refute it *thus*"' (*Life*, I, 471). The longer we stay with the *Works*, though, the more often Johnson appears as a thinker of the question than as someone with a quick answer.

Not that he is shy of delivering judgements in his writings, but in the

best work they are offered only after he has taken responsibility for a
question. In practice that often means uncovering a question behind the
question, showing the issue to be moral before it is anything else. And
when an answer is given it tends not to be in the spirit of a full and
complete solution. At their most compelling, Johnson's views of conduct
and writing are the results of thinking through a matter, of working at it
from the ground up. True, this thinking takes place within the broad
frameworks of Anglican Christianity and monarchism, but he does not
use these as abstract systems to generate neat solutions. Neatness and
uniformity are not features of his moral thinking, even in the *Rambler*, so
often mistaken as a storehouse of settled Johnsonian morality, even
moralism. His aphorisms are knots of thinking and as often as not they
are partly unravelled by the essays in which they occur.[21] What one
actually finds there is an interlacing of first- and second-order moral
judgements, the latter frequently mitigating the former. The *Rambler*
teems with examples of follies that call out for moral censure but it is also
informed by a nagging second-order concern, 'Since life itself is uncertain, nothing which has life for its basis, can boast much stability' (Yale,
v, 204). His two papers on prostitution, 171 and 172, for example, are not
short apologues or treatises on the subject. It never becomes a 'subject'.
We read the story of a prostitute, Misella, told from her perspective; and
her imagined response to her situation, banishment to a colony, seems to
her the only feasible way of escaping perpetual misery, living, as she
does, amidst people 'crowded together, mad with intemperance, ghastly
with famine, nauseous with filth, and noisesome with disease'. Prostitution is condemned as a social evil while Misella herself is treated with
compassion.[22]

There is no uninterrupted border between Johnson the moralist and
Johnson the literary critic. Yet there is certainly a common image of him
as a magisterial even tyrannical critic, delivering unreasonably harsh
judgement on Milton's 'Lycidas', Swift's *Gulliver's Travels* or Gray's odes.
He can be unreasonable, he can be one-sided, he can confuse art and
reality. (That said – and it can weigh heavily on some passages – he is
one of those very rare critics whose views, even when rejected, are none
the less taken as touchstones for later criticism.) In principle, though,
Johnson maintains the importance of the writer's powers of invention
over the critic's rules and regulations. 'It ought to be the first endeavour
of a writer to distinguish nature from custom, or that which is established because it is right, from that which is right only because it is
established; that he may neither violate essential principles by a desire of

novelty, nor debar himself from the attainment of beauties within his view by a needless fear of breaking rules which no literary dictactor had authority to enact' (Yale, v, 60). The monumentalisation of Johnson has tended to hide this aspect of him from sight. To think of anyone as a monument, even for a second or two, is to realise that a doubling has taken place. A monument tells us that an individual has been made into more than himself, made sublime or into a spectacle. Once that is realised there begins a slow and usually incomplete process of de-monumentalisation: a quest for the individual, the idiom, the question. At the very least, it is a search for what he wrote and for the overlaid contexts in which that writing was done: how he embodied them, cut through them, contended with them, or acceded to them.

The monumentalisation of Johnson takes many forms. Boswell's biographies are no doubt a large part of it, along with all the others, but the funereal process touches the works as well as the person. Take the *Dictionary* for example. Christopher Smart commended it to the world as 'a work I look upon with equal pleasure and amazement, as I do upon St Paul's cathedral'. That image of the monumental persists through generation after generation, from John Walker's praise of the work as 'the monument of English philology erected by Johnson' to W. K. Wimsatt's view of the *Dictionary* as a 'public monument' and a 'monumental English Dictionary'.[23] Before going any further there is a difficulty that needs to be eliminated, namely a possible confusion of first- and second-order concerns. Someone can offer a sane account of insanity, or a sober report on drunkenness; and in the same way people can rightly acclaim as monumental a work that views the monumental with suspicion. This is the case generally with Johnson, I think, and the *Dictionary* bears it out as well as any of his other works. The Preface tells a story of overcoming a temptation to fix English, to make it a language of stone. It begins with the lexicographer at the start of his labours gazing at the chaos of the English language – 'I found our speech copious without order, and energetick without rules' (para. 4) – and in due time we learn that 'Those who have been persuaded to think well of my design, require that it should fix our language, and put a stop to those alterations which time and chance have hitherto been suffered to make in it without opposition' (para. 84).

This desire to set the language had been in the air for several generations. How could there be English classics when the language was in such disarray? The question niggled Edmund Waller in his lyric 'Of English Verse':

Poets that lasting marble seek,
Must carve in Latin, or in Greek;
We write in sand, our language grows,
And like the tide, our work o'erflows.[24]

The response to this o'erflowing took two related forms. Notables from the mid-seventeenth century on had mooted the idea of an English academy, roughly modelled on the Accademie della Crusca or the Académie Française. The basic tune is set in Sprat's *History of the Royal Society* (1667), though Matthew Prior hits upon more memorable phrases in his celebration of William's reign, *Carmen Seculare* (1699). Perhaps one of the glories of the king's future years will be an academy:

Some that with Care true Eloquence shall teach,
And to just Idioms fix our doubtful Speech:
That from our Writers distant Realms may know,
    The Thanks We to our Monarch owe;
And Schools profess our Tongue through ev'ry Land,
That has invok'd His Aid, or blest his Hand.[25]

One aspect of this wish to 'fix our doubtful speech' was a deeply felt need for a dictionary of the English language. Addison and Pope had collected materials, and with their work at hand Ambrose Philips went so far as to publish proposals for a dictionary in two folios, but in the end he made nothing of it.[26]

More forceful than Philips's outline was Jonathan Swift's *A Proposal for Correcting, Improving and Ascertaining the English Tongue* (1712), cast as a letter to Robert, Earl of Oxford. Like others before him, Swift suggests that a society be formed to establish and supervise proper linguistic usage. 'But what I have most at Heart, is, that some Method should be thought on for *Ascertaining* and *Fixing* our Language for ever, after such Alterations are made in it as shall be thought requisite. For I am of Opinion, that it is better a Language should not be wholly perfect, than that it should be perpetually changing...'[27] There is a sense in which Johnson's *Dictionary* comes as an unwelcome answer to Swift's proposal, unwelcome not because it is superfluous (English dictionaries published between 1712 and 1755, like Bailey's and Chambers's, could not compare with his in scope or strength), but because it partly fulfils the need for a standard that Swift outlined while strongly resisting a temptation to embalm the language.

Towards the end of the Preface, Johnson slights Swift's *Proposal* as a 'petty treatise' (para. 88). All the same, it is worthwhile to examine in more detail how Swift and Johnson vary over language. That Swift's proposal was a factional work, one that would perhaps raise him in the eyes of Harley, and that in any case he believed language and government to be interlaced, has been noticed before.[28] For Swift, linguistic changes can be traced to political causes: Latin started to degenerate when Rome became a tyranny, and English has fallen into decline since the Glorious Revolution. Yet Swift's main quarry is not the political absolutism of the past so much as contemporary political and religious dissent. Language is under threat here and now, and so an academy is needed to regulate it. The political implication is clear: proper use occurs in a Tory tradition that is grounded in property, and not in the Whig alternative of money and trade. A language should be able to preserve great writing and great deeds. The case is first made for literature. 'What *Horace* says of *Words going off, and perishing like Leaves, and new ones coming in their Place*, is a Misfortune he laments, rather than a Thing he approves: But I cannot see why this should be absolutely necessary, or if it were, what would have become of his *Monumentum aere perennius*' (*Proposal*, 16). And then Swift applies the Horatian boast to regnal history:

Your Lordship must allow, that such a Work as this, brought to Perfection, would much contribute to the Glory of Her Majesty's Reign; which ought to be recorded in Words more durable than Brass, and such as our Posterity may read a thousand Years hence, with Pleasure as well as Admiration. I have always disapproved that false Compliment to Princes: That the most lasting Monument they can have, is the Hearts of their Subjects. It is indeed their greatest present Felicity to reign in their Subjects Hearts; but these are too perishable to preserve their Memories, which can only be done by the Pens of able and faithful Historians. (17)

A monumental history, of letters or deeds, can be recorded only in stone. No writer will trust a medium that itself has no chance of survival: 'This is like employing an excellent Statuary to work upon mouldering Stone' (*Proposal*, 18).

That Johnson at first thought, like Swift, that the language can and should be fixed is evident in *The Plan of a Dictionary of the English Language* (1747) and the Preface itself.[29] 'With this consequence I will confess that I flattered myself for a while; but now begin to fear that I have indulged expectation which neither reason nor experience can justify' (para. 84). To determine a language once and for all is a vain wish:

When we see men grow old and die at a certain time one after another, from century to century, we laugh at the elixir that promises to prolong life to a thousand years; and with equal justice may the lexicographer be derided, who being able to produce no example of a nation that has preserved their words and phrases from mutability, shall imagine that his dictionary can embalm his language, and secure it from corruption and decay, that it is in his power to change sublunary nature, or clear the world at once from folly, vanity, and affectation. (para. 84)

This is in no sense a case against establishing proper use. Negatively, it is one of Johnson's duties as lexicographer to proscribe 'improprieties and absurdities' in orthography (para. 6). And positively, he prefers to draw his illustrative quotations from 'masters of elegance or models of stile', and when he does not it is for a very good reason, since 'in what pages, eminent for purity, can terms of manufacture or agriculture be found?' (para. 59). His original intention, before he realised just how much material he had gathered, was that the quotations do more than illustrate meaning but be in themselves an 'accumulation of elegance and wisdom' (para. 57).[30] The intention of establishing a fund of propriety still informs the whole work, truncated though it is. One reason why Johnson sought to build up that fund is because he half agrees with the slighted author of the *Proposal*. He finds, as Swift does, that the Elizabethan age shows English at its apex, for in those days 'a speech might be formed adequate to all the purposes of use and elegance' (para. 62). And he is Swiftian also in seeing 'in constancy and stability a general and lasting advantage' (para. 16) and even in wishing, in the very teeth of what his labours have taught him, that words 'might be less apt to decay, and that signs might be permanent, like the things which they denote' (para. 17).

Inevitable and melancholy as linguistic change is, English people must none the less resist the imposition of an academy to arrest it. In the paragraph immediately after the reference to Swift's *Proposal* we hear Johnson hope that 'if an academy should be established for the cultivation of our stile . . . the spirit of *English* liberty will hinder or destroy' it (para. 90). It is a view to which he held firm, right up to his lives of Roscommon and Swift.[31] Johnson is as zealous as Swift for the proper use of language, but his lights lead him far from the Dean. Swift's politics of language add up to a radical conservativism; his enemy is change in whatever shape or form it comes. Johnson implicitly agrees with him that 'tongues, like governments, have a natural tendency to degeneration' (para. 91), but his politics of language is a linguistic nationalism. The very publication of the *Dictionary* is a sufficient sign that no academy is needed, for he has already done much of what continental academies are required to do. The language does not need to be regulated from within its national boundaries; it is those limits themselves that need to be exposed and patrolled. The guilty ones are those translators 'whose idleness and ignorance, if it be suffered to proceed, will reduce us to babble a dialect of *France*' (para. 90), and the lesson is finally political: 'we have long preserved our constitution, let us make some struggles for our language' (para. 91).

Although Johnson trusts that his *Dictionary* will 'add celebrity to *Bacon*, to *Hooker*, to *Milton*, and to *Boyle*' (para. 92), this hope stems more from motives of national pride than from a monumental conception of history and writing. Where Swift wishes to see the English language as a hard stone, Johnson conceives it as a complex organism, both living and dying. The *Proposal* argues that while new words can be introduced old words should never be abandoned. Yet Johnson is reconciled to the fact that words die: 'But what makes a word obsolete, more than general agreement to forbear it? and how shall it be continued, when it conveys an offensive idea, or recalled again into the mouths of mankind, when it has once by disuse become unfamiliar, and by unfamiliarity unpleasing' (para. 88). In the same spirit, he realises that he cannot define all verbal forms because 'it must be remembered, that while our language is yet living, and variable by the caprice of every one that speaks it, these words are hourly shifting their relations, and can no more be ascertained in a dictionary, than a grove, in the agitation of a storm, can be accurately delineated from its picture in the water' (para. 46). In its conception of language, and of the *Dictionary*'s task, the image is as far from the monumental as one can get. What makes us choose a word like 'monumental' when talking about the *Dictionary* is not Johnson's conception of language and learning but his extraordinary labours in compiling it and the myths of a national hero that surround and partly conceal them.

I return to my opening story. Before anything else, it needs to be stressed that it is not related in a neutral or steady space. Although the visits to Poets' Corner and Temple-bar are told in Johnson's voice, they resonate in Boswell's *Life* and form part of his project. Compared with other stories about Johnson, this anecdote is not especially well-known. Many people know the tale of Johnson being tricked into dining with John Wilkes at Dilly's, or the one about his late night frisk through the streets of London with Beauclerk and Langton; and almost everyone can recognise, if not repeat exactly, those quips that make up his popular image. The story of Johnson visiting Poets' Corner is not one of these – and yet it underpins all the others. For if Johnson had not desired literary fame and achieved a fair degree of it in life, none of those other stories would have been recorded.

Or made up, I have to add, since Johnson like all celebrities is often the subject of anecdotes that have little or no historical basis. Not all his *dicta philosophi* are authentic, nor are all the tales told about him. It is a sign of his monumentality. And it is a problem for anyone concerned to establish the historical facts about his life and opinions. Yet for those intrigued by narratives about Johnson not even historical truths can supply the bottom line. Take my opening story for instance. Even if it were Johnson reported word for word, once included by Boswell it is affected by the whole of his composition; it takes on new tasks, and we notice motifs and themes that have been in operation long before reaching this point. Thus, when placed in the *Life*, the story acts out a strange logic of 'already–not yet' that it catches from its surroundings. There has to be a sense in which the visit to Poets' Corner takes place in something that is already 'the Age of Johnson' but by the same token the story tells us that this age has not yet come except in desire.[32]

Whose desire? Well, Johnson's as we have seen, if the story has any basis in history. But there are other desires at work, his admirers', editors' and biographers' – most notably Boswell's. Perhaps no one lives more fully or more securely in 'the Age of Johnson' than the narrator of the *Life*. I will talk about this epoch in the next chapter and suggest why it needs those prim quotation marks around it. That age is not wholly Boswell's construction, but he has done more than anyone else to place his friend at the centre of an imaginary cultural unity, one that as the *Life*'s full title tells us, exhibits 'a view of literature and literary men in Great-Britain, for near half a century, during which he flourished'. For Boswell it is indeed an age of literary men. The women with whom he competed for Johnson's friendship and, later, for the right to transmit his memory to posterity, are seldom seen, and when they appear it is all too often to be criticised or slighted.

That said, let us return to the narrative space included, rather than excluded, by Boswell. I would like to mark several ways in which it is arranged.

The first polarity that organises Boswellian space is so general and so familiar that it can easily escape our attention. It is the distinction between life and death: Johnson's life and death, of course, but also

Boswell's life and Johnson's death, and Boswell's life and death. In any formulation it constitutes a major structural support of our opening story and, as I will argue, of the relationship between Johnson and Boswell. In the story to hand we see two living writers gazing first at dead poets and then at dead rebels. In Poets' Corner the monuments and the quotation from Ovid serve to mediate life and death, showing that even this distinction is far from absolute, that there is a life-in-death and a death-in-life. Literature offers a chance of surviving death, if at the cost of petrifying oneself in the midst of life. No such chance is possible for those who absolutely defy the State; the Jacobite Lords have no tombs, and when Goldsmith repeats the line from Ovid while facing their heads the altered context now presses us to recall the Roman poet's official disgrace for his *carmen et error* and his perpetual exile in Tomis on the Black Sea.

Overlaying this polarity is another much favoured by Boswell, one that is difficult to specify exactly because it functions in ideas and feelings, in the general cast of his mind, as much as in individual words and phrases. Perhaps the distinction between the proper and the improper best brings it into focus. Certainly it follows most of the senses that the adjective 'proper' had in the late eighteenth century. Johnson lists ten in his *Dictionary*: '1. peculiar; not belonging to more; not common; 2. Noting an individual; 3. One's own; 4. Natural; original; 5. Fit; accommodated; adapted; suitable; qualified; 6. Exact; accurate; just; 7. Not figurative; 8. It seems in *Shakespeare* to signify, mere; pure; 9. [*Propre*, Fr] Elegant, pretty; 10. Tall, lusty; handsome with bulk.' One of the main impulses of Boswell's biographical writing is to declare Johnson proper, an impulse that sometimes gains energy from the resistance it meets in his writings or his talk. So Boswell's Johnson is an individual, very much his own man (but his oddities are to be noted). He is natural, original (though also a cultural icon). He is eminently suited to his profession (yet gains little pleasure from writing). His talk and writing are exact (if not always just). He is an embodiment of common sense (albeit given to faction), and a man of imposing physical presence (but verging on monstrosity). Needless to say, Boswell's Johnson is not always everyone else's Johnson. Horace Walpole, that most unfriendly of contemporary witnesses, excepted, there is no one else who makes such high play about the man's supposed Jacobite sympathies.[33]

To return to the story. Not only do we see there the living meditating on the dead but also we respond to a system of value: while the nation's poets are hallowed by Church and State, the Jacobite Lords are publicly reviled. The comedy of the story derives from the faint possibility that the categories of poet and rebel, proper and improper, will not stay in place. Johnson's and Goldsmith's improper sympathy for James, as imagined here, could upset their literary ambitions, suddenly exchanging literary honour for political disgrace. As I have suggested, a strong impulse of Boswell's writing is to represent Johnson as proper, that is, as marked by a tendency to appropriate a certain image of himself, one that might well differ from his own self-understandings. This story is an instance. Gazing at the funeral sculpture, Johnson acts out a rapid process of exappropriation, no sooner imagining himself dead than being restored to life. There is no reference to his fear of death and divine judgement: that belongs to another thematics of which we hear a lot in the *Life*. Rather, he is depicted in a civic and secular sublime, experiencing the life-in-death of a monument and the death-in-life of monumentality.

Another division is again likely to pass by unnoticed simply because it has become so pervasive in modern biography. It is the distinction between private and public. One of the most outrageous aspects of the *Life*, both in its morality and its modernity, is Boswell's generous use of ana and anecdote. In the *Dictionary* Johnson defines 'ana' as 'loose thoughts, or casual hints, dropped by eminent men, and collected by their friends'. Collections of ana had been in Europe since the fifteenth century, though they passed from private to public circulation only in the seventeenth century with the *Scaligerana* (1666), the first of many in a genre that was to become popular in the eighteenth century, especially on the continent.[34] Far from increasing the reputation of their subjects, ana often brought them into disrepute, making them seem more dogmatic or vain than their writings suggested. Anecdotes can have much the same effect. Johnson defined the word as 'something yet unpublished; secret history'. To some extent, as he tells us, Boswell modelled his *Life* on William Mason's *Memoirs of Gray* (1775), which made extensive though discrete use of letters.[35] But in publishing ana and anecdotes Boswell goes further than this, exceeding propriety and making his work disjunctive with the style and stance of the age it delineates.

In the *Life* Boswell draws the distinction beween private and public in different ways and to different ends. Knowing that a space between them is crucial for his depiction of Johnson, he never wholly turns the private into the public. At times in the *Tour* and *Life*, though, he seemed to his contemporaries to do just that. A sense of how close to the bone he gets can be gained by Lord Monboddo's exclamation, 'Before I read his

Book I thought he was a Gentleman who had the misfortune to be mad;
I now think he is a mad man who has the misfortune not to be a
Gentleman'.[36] With hindsight we can tell that Boswell's favoured area is
between the private and the public, between his personal experience
and the impersonal structures of institutions. That Hanoverian Britain is
regulated by king and parliament, church and law, trade and school, is
something anyone interested in eighteenth-century culture knows well.
Yet what we encounter in Boswell is his lived experience of those codes,
his attempts to appropriate what must finally exist outside him: in social
interactions with court and parliament, with advocates and judges,
professors and writers. This is the realm of the everyday, the sphere
where society reproduces itself in the hum and buzz of ordinary exchanges: conversations, eating and drinking, gossip, playing games, cracking
jokes, writing letters, paying visits, going for walks, and so on. Much of
what we think we see in Boswell's biographical writing is this everyday
life, apparently an escape from all that is monumental and proper,
though, after a second look, often fuelled by his admiration for those he
believed to be great.

Indeed, this very tension between the everyday and the great orients
so much of Boswell's writing that it merits attention on its own account.
My opening story begins with the most quotidian of occasions, a walk
around London, but turns on the possibility of transcending the everyday, in a positive way (as with the dead of Poets' Corner) or in a negative
way (as with the Jacobite Lords), a chance that we know has been
realised even as we read the story: in Boswell's pages Goldsmith and
Johnson exist in the ordinary world while having already risen above it.
Even as the story is being related it is an everyday occurence, a
conversation over dinner, yet in Boswell's narrative it gains drama from
the possibility that the narrator will that evening receive a clear sign of
cultural acceptance by being admitted to the Club. To take it a step
further, reading the story ourselves takes place in the everyday, whether
at home or at work, while realising all the time that the text is very far
from the everyday, being one of those books to look out for, a recognised
classic of English literature.

Being inside and outside an 'Age of Johnson' is a game that Boswell
plays with consummate skill, frequently dividing himself into narrator
and character in order to do so. The passage in which Johnson tells his
story about visiting Poets' Corner is a case in point. Notice that the story
is told with no reference to Boswell. We see Johnson imaginatively
sending himself through history with no aid from anyone, although it

takes only a moment's reflection to recognise Boswell behind the story, placing it where he wishes in his narrative. It is instructive to see the tale in the larger frame of the *Life*, a long passage artfully worked up from notes taken on Friday, 30 April 1773. This episode consists mainly of dinner conversation, mostly in direct speech, about Goldsmith's ignorance, the merits and demerits of contemporary historians and the possible establishment of monuments in St Paul's. (Johnson argues against Pope being the first, because of his Catholicism, and prefers Milton instead. As it happens, it was Johnson who was first commemorated there.) It is amusing that a passage devoted to eminent persons is framed as it is. It begins with Boswell telling us that later in the evening there was to be a ballot for him to be admitted to the Literary Club, which consisted of many of the most noteworthy persons in England. And it ends with Boswell being elected, attending the Club's meeting, and repeating some conversation heard there. The whole passage is marked by a drama as to whether Boswell has sufficient weight to belong to the Club. It is not enough that Johnson be a monument, we need to be discreetly assured that Boswell is a reputable mason.

I am just returned from Westminster-abbey, the place of sepulture for the philosophers, heroes, and kings of England. What a gloom do monumental inscriptions and all the venerable remains of deceased merit inspire! Imagine a temple marked with the hand of antiquity, solemn as religious awe, adorned with all the magnificence of barbarous profusion, dim windows, fretted pillars, long colonades, and dark ceilings. Think then, what were my sensations at being introduced to such a scene. I stood in the midst of the temple, and threw my eyes round on the walls filled with the statues, the inscriptions, and the monuments of the dead.[37]

It is not Johnson who speaks but a Chinese visitor to London, Lien Chi Altangi, who is writing to Fum Hoam, first president of the Ceremonial Academy at Pekin, in China. His letter is published in the *Public Ledger* for Monday, 25 February 1760, as several others have been and as many more will be. They will be collected two years later and published as *The Citizen of the World*, which will be known in London by those who know these things to be the work of Oliver Goldsmith. It is pleasant to think that the experience of writing about Poets' Corner may have came from the day when Goldsmith and Johnson walked around London together. But the idea rests on charm, not fact. Certainly, though, when Johnson and Goldsmith gazed at the tombs and memorials in Poets' Corner that part of the Abbey had long been a site of national pride, having become a prime manifestation of the cult of British Worthies. More recently, it had become a site where a new sensibility of melancholy could be indulged. It can be sensed in James Hervey's *Meditations Among the Tombs* (1746), much read in the eighteenth century (and much derided by Johnson),[38] but an early number of the *Spectator* in 1711 offers a sharper taste of the new feeling. Joseph Addison observes, 'When I am in a serious Humour, I very often walk by myself in *Westminster* Abbey; where the Gloominess of the Place, and the Use to which it is applied, with the Solemnity of the Building, and the Condition of the People who lye in it, are apt to fill the Mind with a kind of Melancholy, or rather Thoughtfulness, that is not disagreeable'.[39]

From mid-century on, in letters, poems and sermons, this traditional Christian reflecting on vanity yields more and more to a romantic feel for melancholy.[40] Fifty years after Addison, in 1763, the young Boswell (who admired Hervey's meditations) also visited the Abbey and confided to his journal, 'I heard service with much devotion in this magnificent and venerable temple. I recalled the ideas of it which I had from *The Spectator*.' The year before he had also gone there and recorded that 'among the tombs [he] was solemn and happy'.[41] The Abbey was not a free house: in 1697 the entrance fee was 3d; in 1723 it was raised to 6d; and in 1799 to 9d.[42] Goldsmith's Chinese visitor to London complains about having to pay to see the monuments and is insensed by a request for a gratuity by the 'tomb-shewer' (as they were called). '*What more money! still more money!* Every gentleman gives something, sir. I'll give thee nothing, returned I; the guardians of the temple should pay you your wages, friend, and not permit you to squeeze thus from every spectator'.[43] Neither cultural nationalism nor romantic melancholy comes cheap.

The image of Johnson standing before the poets' tombs and memorials functions in the *Life* as an enabling condition. I have suggested that this condition is divided by its context, yet that is not all that can be said on the matter. For the context is not all of a piece, and the moment this becomes important is worth examining. This is of course when the author encounters his subject, when Boswell meets Johnson. It is the moment when Boswell divides himself into narrator and character, and – at the same time – it is the moment that separates Johnson as man and character. I want to look solely at a detail which is not recorded in the journal but which is elaborated in the *Life*. Boswell has been angling for an introduction to Johnson, but the meeting, when it comes, is accidental:

At last, on Monday the 16th of May, when I was sitting in Mr Davies' back parlour, after having drunk tea with him and Mrs Davies, Johnson unexpectedly came into the shop; and Mr Davies having perceived him through the glass-door in the room in which we were sitting, advancing towards us, – he announced his awful approach to me, somewhat in the manner of an actor in the part of Horatio, when he addresses Hamlet on the appearance of his father's ghost, 'Look, my Lord, it comes.' (*Life*, I, 391–92)

It is a startling introduction to the man from Lichfield (meaning 'field of the dead', as he had pointed out in his *Dictionary*). Although it is an unexpected visit, it is quickly removed from the everyday and framed as a drama by Tom Davies. Or, rather, it is made into *his* everyday, since he had been an actor. At any rate, Johnson is figured as returning from the dead: an image compounded from the distortion of the glass and his usual uncouth appearance. It is unlikely that Davies would have known of Boswell's fear of ghosts or of his difficult relationship with his father when he spontaneously cast him in the role of the dead man's son. However, the meeting sets a story in motion no less surely than in *Hamlet*, giving a chance the eerie feel of inevitability.

A sense of inevitability is not a sense of an ending, although an ending is always coiled up in inevitability, sometimes as a sting. It applies in different ways to Shakespeare and Boswell. Perhaps *Hamlet* could be read as a tragedy of unsuccessful mourning as well as a story about a phantom, a crypt that silently passes from parent to son, though I do not propose to do so here. Questions of mourning need to be separated from questions of haunting. In the same spirit, I do not want to suggest that Boswell's *Life* is simply a mourning of Johnson expressed in narrative form, the consequence of having learned of his death. The labour of mourning that is the *Life* began long before 17 December 1784, the day when Boswell heard of his friend's demise. It commenced much earlier, just over a year after Johnson had escorted him to Harwich and watched him put out to sea for Holland. The young Boswell had been flattered by his new friend's kind attention, but his love of distinguished men, alive or dead, was hardly quenched by it, and once in Europe he sought out the eminent. Throughout the August and September of 1764 he was in Berlin, scouting for an introduction to Frederick the Great, and having no success whatsoever. He left Berlin a little deflated. Then, on 30 September, he rode from Dessau to Wittenberg in Saxony where he visited the graves of Luther and Melanchthon. The dead are always ready to receive homage. His journal evokes the occasion and its significance:

I was in a true solemn humour, and a most curious and agreeable idea presented itself, which was to write to Mr Samuel Johnson from the tomb of Melanchthon. The woman who showed me the church was a good obliging body, and very readily furnished me with pen and ink. That my paper might literally rest upon the monument, I laid myself down and wrote in that posture. The good woman and some more simple beings gathered round and beheld me with wonder. I dare say they supposed me a little mad. Tombs have been always the favourite resort of gloomy, distracted mortals. I said nothing of hot-headed Luther. I only mentioned the mild Melanchthon, and that at his tomb I vowed to Mr Johnson an eternal attachment.[44]

And not just an eternal attachment. The letter goes on, 'It shall be my study to do what I can to render your life happy, and if you die before me, I shall endeavour to do honour to your memory.'[45] For months Boswell had set himself the aim of becoming *retenu*. But this is hardly *retenu*, and for fear of being chided by Johnson, the letter was not sent until 1777. Yet here is the first suggestion that he will write Johnson's life, the first time that the young man foresees the role for which he will be remembered. What ties Boswell to Johnson, then and for all time, is *The Life of Johnson*.

Almost all discussion of Boswell's connection with Johnson, even when Boswell is the focus, works with a distinction between Johnson's life and work. No one has stated this more clearly than Bertrand H. Bronson when he evoked the spectre of 'the double tradition of Dr Johnson', the interlacing of learned and popular traditions about our man, about what he wrote and how he lived.[46] I will be discussing this motif in a later chapter, but it touches on my present concerns. Bronson helped to formulate a tale that many Johnsonians love to tell in book after book, essay after essay. In the beginning Johnson was an author; then Boswell's wicked art turned him into a mere character; now modern criticism must bravely rescue him from that sad fate. There are many things to say about this distinction and the story it spawns, but one topic they occlude is the importance of Johnson's death to Boswell's project. When people today choose Boswell as a guide to Johnson, they pick up his biography little realising it is a sepulchre. His contemporaries knew better. 'I have lately perused with very peculiar pleasure your *Life of Dr Johnson*. That Work must be gratifying in a high degree to all who were particularly acquainted with its illustrious Subject. They will find your great Friend and Master as it were embalmed in your Narrative; and may daily live over those scenes which are long since past.'[47] Thus wrote the Reverend John Campbell to Boswell, but the notion of embalming Johnson had long since occurred to him, and he saw the *Life* as 'a monument', 'a pyramid' and even a 'mausoleum'.[48] Edmund Burke went further than Boswell could have dared hope in observing that the *Life* was 'a greater monument to Johnson's fame, than all his writings put together'.[49]

What has happened here? A strange shift has occurred. I began by thinking of Johnson and his *Works* as monuments, but now that role has been usurped by Boswell's *Life*. One can only wonder which monument tourists admire in London and Lichfield: Johnson the man, the writer or the character in Boswell. Doubtless the lines between them are sometimes broken; a breath of air can pass between even the tightest distinctions. But in any case we do not have a simple alternative between writing and living. Something else has appeared that touches both, the fact of death. When Boswell heard of Johnson's demise on 17 December 1784 the desolating news was followed in the very next mail by a request from Dilly his publisher for 'an octavo volume of 400 pages of his conversations ready by February'.[50] Yet Johnson's death was not merely an event in Boswell's life, a momentary feeling of 'just one large expanse of stupor', as he put it on receiving the news; it was, as he must have known, a precondition for his major literary work.[51] The point is quietly made, just before the *Life* begins, in four lines quoted from Shakespeare's *Henry VIII*:

> 'After my death I wish no other herald,
> 'No other speaker of my living actions,
> 'To keep mine honour from corruption,
> 'But such an honest chronicler as Griffith.'
>
> (*Life*, 1, 24)

The kind of honesty valued here demands a certain relationship with death. In order to speak after Johnson's demise, Boswell must faithfully record his words in life: before the moment of death yet in the knowledge of death. For Boswell, Johnson's death notionally occured in his twenties, the very time he thought of raising a monument to him.

In 1773, near the end of their Highland jaunt, Boswell was wandering with his friend in the groves of Auchinleck, his family home. There he told Johnson that, 'if I survived him, it was my intention to erect a monument to him here, among scenes which, in my mind, were all classical' (*Tour*, 380).[52] It was not to be; but all the same the young Boswell had progressed from writing to Johnson while lying on a tomb to erecting Johnson's own tomb, a crypt composed entirely of words.

'He has made a chasm, which not only nothing can fill up, but which nothing has a tendency to fill up. – Johnson is dead. – Let us go to the next best: – there is nobody; – no one can be said to put you in mind of Johnson.'[53] So lamented William ('Single-Speech') Hamilton to Boswell several years after their friend's demise in 1784. It is a noble statement, a powerful testimony to Johnson's sublimity and uniqueness. For all that, the image is a familiar one in eighteenth-century criticism. In 1752 for instance we find John Hill writing in the *Monthly Review*, 'After the days of MILTON there was a chasm; after the death of POPE there was another: none cared to appear in a situation where they must be seen with disadvantage; none dared to imitate what it was so difficult to equal'.[54] Johnson himself remained sceptical of this critical commonplace. Thinking of Cowley, he had written in the *Rambler*, 'It was, perhaps, ordained by providence, to hinder us from tyrannising over one another, that no individual should be of such importance, as to cause, by his retirement or death, any chasm in the world' (Yale, III, 34). Contradicted by Johnson, Hamilton will also be rebutted by Boswell who, if anyone, 'can be said to put you in mind of Johnson'. Not because he resembles his friend but because his biographies evoke him so vividly.

Death has a remarkable power, even in life: it slips between name and person then prises them apart. It makes endless duplicates of a name, and hands them out to anyone, friend or foe, who wants to use it. The proper name 'Samuel Johnson' was never one man's private property. In the first place, there were other people living who answered to that name. One was a librarian of St Martin's-in-the-Fields; another lived in Connecticut, corresponded with the lexicographer, and called his son 'Samuel' to boot; one wrote a book entitled *Hurlothrumbo*; while yet another worked in the Secretary's Office of the India House.[55] Stumbling across news of a Samuel Johnson's death gave Hester Thrale slight pause one day, then several years later gave her a fine story for the *Anecdotes*:

Knowing the state of Mr Johnson's nerves, and how easily they were affected, I forebore reading in a new Magazine one day, the death of a Samuel Johnson who expired that month; but my companion snatching up the book, saw it himself, and contrary to my expectation – 'Oh (said he)! I hope that Death will now be glutted with Sam. Johnsons, and let me alone for some time to come: I read of another namesake's departure last week.[56]

Namesakes aside, Johnson could never master his own name; and why would he want to, literary fame being his oldest and deepest ambition? His name circulated widely in his lifetime, being used in many contexts, spoken over a range of tones, from reverence to contempt. Used in magazines and pamphlets, spoken in coffee shops, bookshops and sitting rooms, the name 'Johnson' took on all sorts of meanings. By the 1760s it had started to signify everything from 'authority', 'classic' and 'English' to 'tyrant', 'bully' and 'pomposity'. It is the intensity invested in that name, and the conceptual and emotional ranges it covers, that makes Johnson's death a chasm.

Hamilton's idea that nothing has a tendency to fill that chasm, that Johnson was unique and irreplaceable, was widely echoed. Johnson was valued for his literature – his learning – and for the moral uses to which he put it. One of the many poems on his death regards his demise as a national calamity:

> Dead! dead's the MENTOR of this impious age!
> Who now with Infidels the war will wage?
> Or whom the bold presuming factions doom
> To dark oblivion and an early tomb! –
> Smile, smile, my weaving sisters, smile;
> Discord shall reign throughout this isle. – [57]

Yet, as I have suggested, no sooner does a chasm appear than people rush to fill it. The spectacle is comically described in an anonymous poem entitled *Johnson's Laurel: or, Contest of the Poets* (1785). Here one reads in workaday couplets how all England grieves the Doctor's exit; and as the poem limps on, it becomes evident what is at issue, each writer's secret longing to replace the man he mourns:

> But soon the bards (a hungry envious crew,
> Who hate each other, yet who flatter too)
> Too fiercely rag'd for hypocritic guile,
> To deck their angry visage with a smile.
> All bards GREAT Johnson's wreath (the laurel) claim;
> To touch it honour, and to wear it fame!
> A furious war with ardour now they wage,
> And fiercer far than hungry tygers rage;
> When a deep voice from Heav'n is heard to say,
> 'Whose mind is warm'd by Genius' brightest ray!
> 'Be his the wreath!' Each bard abides the test,
> For each, in wit, believes himself the best.[58]

All the notable versifiers of the day – Pratt, Whitehead, Cumberland, Stratford, Topham, Tickell, Colman, Sheridan and Pye – try their best, until, at the very end, the laurel is given to Hayley. It goes without saying that time has not supported his claim. Yet the chasm has been filled, in an unexpected manner, by Boswell.

The contestants for the laurel think that they can fill the space in literary history left by the great Cham and let the tradition continue in the same direction. After all, they might say, it is *Johnson*'s laurel we are fighting over, and we all wish to keep faith with his spirit. Yet literary history prefers to tell another story, that it is impossible both to fill the space and for the tradition to continue in exactly the same direction. We are now used to seeing literary history as a narrative of refractions and distortions, and we know that without Blake, Wordsworth and a host of lesser writers regarding Johnson as the dead hand of literature, he would not be quite the figure we encounter today. And we are used to poets slighting their forebears, taking them down a peg or two, or even attacking them indignantly. Because Boswell reveres Johnson, and never passes an opportunity to tell us, but also because he has nothing whatsover of the monumental in his character or style, we can sometimes miss the point that he too, in his own way, is claiming creative space at his mentor's expense. In the dedication of the *Life* to Sir Joshua Reynolds, Boswell promises to tell 'nothing but the truth' (even though it may not always be 'the whole truth': some proper names will be suppressed), but he exceeds his promise in the book's short title, doing more than he says he will do. Any reader of the biography knows that Boswell not only traces Johnson's life year by year, from imposing child to imposing adult, but also adds something extraneous, unpredictable, annoying and labile: himself.

The *Life* begins with an unstated question: how can one portray a man who, on any account, was extraordinary and who happened to be the finest biographer in the language? Any way one looks at the matter, Johnson exceeds what can be written of him. Except from one angle:

Had Dr Johnson written his own life, in conformity with the opinion which he has given, that every man's life may be best written by himself; had he employed in the preservation of his own history, that clearness of narration and elegance of language in which he has embalmed so many eminent persons, the world would probably have had the most perfect example of biography that was ever exhibited. (*Life*, 1, 25)

But of course he did no such thing, and Boswell will try to fill the lack. And to do so, he will try a new method of biography:

Instead of melting down my materials into one mass, and constantly speaking in my own person, by which I might have appeared to have more merit in the execution of the work, I have resolved to adopt and enlarge upon the excellent plan of Mr Mason, in his *Memoirs of Gray*. Whenever narrative is necessary to explain, connect, and supply, I furnish it to the best of my abilities; but in the chronological series of Johnson's life, which I trace as distinctly as I can, year by year, I produce, wherever it is in my power, *his own* minutes, letters, or conversation, being convinced that this mode is more lively, and will make my readers better acquainted with him, than even most of those who actually knew him ... (*Life*, I, 29, my emphasis)

The ostensible aim then is to exclude the narrator as much as possible, to limit him to the subordinate tasks of explaining, connecting and supplying. In this way, Johnson 'will be seen in this work more completely than any man who has ever yet lived' (*Life*, I, 30). Boswell will have done what Johnson failed to do. It is a claim both modest and extravagant, for the biographer will have stood in the background and allowed the dead Johnson to produce the life he would have written. Only in death can Johnson achieve what was within his reach, and only with the help of one who waited for that death, anticipated it and dedicated himself to it.

Boswell's account of his method is accurate within limits, but limitation was never his strong point. As narrator, he does 'explain, connect, and supply', though whether he restricts himself to what is minimally necessary is highly doubtful. Taking leave of his readers at the end of the *Life*, he almost apologises for having 'obtruded himself too much upon their attention', his excuse being 'the peculiar plan of his biographical undertaking' (*Life*, IV, 380). Leaving aside that verbal slip in which he glimpses himself as Johnson's undertaker, we have also to remember that being a narrator is just one of Boswell's roles in the book. Much of what he presents as Johnson's life consists of conversations with none other than James Boswell, Esq. And not just talk, but question and answer; and it is in this grid our image of Johnson often appears. If the great man played up to that image from time to time, he could also reject it in no uncertain terms. Even taking account of her distaste for Boswell, Hester Piozzi opens a window onto a scene we seldom notice in the *Life*: "I have been put so to the Question by Bozzy this morning", said Dr Johnson on one day, "that I am now panting for Breath". "What sort of Questions I wonder." "Why one question was, Pray, Sir, can you tell why an Apple is round and a Pear pointed?" Would not such Talk make a Man hang himself?' (*Life*, III, 519).[59] And every so often one wonders what kind of book Boswell has written. Is it *The Life of Samuel Johnson* or *My Life with*

Samuel Johnson? Sometimes one feels like checking the book's title page to make sure.

But no one ever does. For we realise that, while Boswell supplies what Johnson lacks, an account of himself, he does it in his own style: overabundant, excessive, even frivolous. Considered simply as a biography, the *Life* produces a surplus value, a commerce between biographer and subject, where good things are exchanged. But the *Life* is a book which can never be considered simply. For one thing, as we have seen, it lays claim to being Johnson's autobiography, the one he never wrote. And if we demur over that, and insist we still call it, even for form's sake, a biography, it is still laced with an autobiography – Boswell's – and it is often difficult to tell which story is the more beguiling. It is certainly true that, in selecting material from the journals for the *Life*, Boswell tended to play himself down rather than up; but this is a consideration of degree, not class. The Reverend Samuel Martin makes the point very cleanly when reflecting on Boswell's death. 'While his great Johnson is rever'd and painted', he says, 'His Boswell is more fully represented'; and in case we have missed the joke, he repeats it several lines later:

> The life of Johnson is a vast levee:
> Many we know, we love, we hear, we see;
> But, never in the crowd entirely lost,
> The introducer's introduc'd the most.[60]

Thinking of heavy drinking, Boswell one day exclaimed, 'It is wonderful what joy there is in excess' but, given his biographical method, he could just as well have had writing in mind.[61]

CHAPTER 2

'The Age of Johnson'

'No action in his life became him like the leaving it. His death makes a kind of era in literature. Piety and goodness will not easily find a more able defender, and it is delightful to see him set, as it were, his dying seal to the profession of his life, and to the truth of Christianity.'[1] So wrote Hannah More of her friend Samuel Johnson in 1785, and literary historians have generally agreed with her, even without knowing it, in calling his times 'the Age of Johnson'. For More, Johnson's death and the era whose limits it reveals are characterised by a religious faith strongly operating in both the private and the public spheres. 'Literature', here, is meant as Johnson defined it in the *Dictionary*, 'Learning; skill in letters', a sense derived from the Latin that was slowly fading from use even as she wrote. The power of invention that Johnson believed to be the heart of poetry, and that would soon become the hub of literature understood as creative or imaginative writing, is not the issue. Johnson is exemplary, she thinks, by dint of the moral and religious ends to which he put his learning; and the manner of his death brings his life and writings into complete harmony. To modern ears the loud echo of Cawdor's death from *Macbeth* may seem out of place ('Nothing in his life/Became him like the leaving it', I. iv. 7–8), but in the terms of the evangelical piety that More fervently embraced, every sinner waits under sentence of execution, and a sure sign of having made a true and lasting conversion in life is to 'set forth/A deep repentance' in the face of certain death and judgement.

Several days after Johnson's demise More had been assured in a letter that her friend had passed away without horror. It was welcome news, for many of his company had feared he would die badly. That fear weighed on Johnson's friends, to be sure, yet his death was a public as well as a private affair: how would he die, this Christian moralist who was so given to melancholy? As death approached, Sir John Hawkins

39

pressed Johnson to make a will, not only to distribute his property but also to make a profession of faith, since 'it would afford an illustrious example, and well become him, to make such an explicit declaration of his belief, as might obviate all suspicions that he was any other than a Christian'.[2] He must die properly. Johnson took the hint, bequeathing his name to orthodoxy and his soul to God. In their different ways both were immensely valuable properties. More suggests that Hawkins encouraged Johnson to make this profession to counter David Hume's 'impious declaration of his opinions' in his final moments, and the deaths of these two men, and their responses to death, informed the contemporary discourse on mortality.[3] In 1786 the Reverand William Agutter preached a sermon before the University of Oxford on the theme. One problem, as he saw it, was that while Johnson, a convinced Christian, was terrified by death, the sceptical Hume died in great tranquillity. 'Supposing then that the enemy of the gospel, the champion of infidelity, descended to the grave in peace, felt no remorse of conscience on the review of life, and expressed no apprehensions on the verge of the eternal life, what would this prove?' Very little it seems, for Hume's 'placid appearances resulted from the strength of his constitution, or the nature of his disease' while Johnson's anxiety was caused by 'a constitution enfeebled by frequent diseases, tainted by morbid melancholy, and bowed down by the pressure of age'.[4]

Not everyone was so dismissive of the visible signs of Johnson's death. Hannah More certainly was not, nor was a quite different friend, Hester Piozzi: 'I have many times made it my request to heaven that I might be spared the sight of his death', she wrote in the *Anecdotes*, 'and I was spared it!'[5] After the event, though, she can tell another story, in its own way no less pious than More's. 'And now what remains?' she asks at the end of her edition of Johnson's *Letters*. Nothing but 'to reflect, that by that death no part of Johnson perished which had power by form to recommend his real excellence; nothing that did not disgrace the soul which it contained'. All this slowly leads to an elaborate image. Her friend and mentor's soul is 'like some fine statue, the boast of Greece and Rome, plastered up into deformity, while casts are preparing from it to improve students, and diffuse the knowledge of its merit; but dazzling only with complete perfection, when the gross and awkward covering is removed'.[6] Death separates the true Johnson, his soul, from his body, revealing him to be a classical figure, not unlike John Bacon's monument to him in St Paul's Cathedral. His end does not make 'a kind of era in literature' so much as continue a classical tradition. The dead Johnson takes his rightful place alongside Socrates and Plato, Seneca and Cicero.

Did Johnson's death reveal a great Christian, a great classic, or both? For Arthur Murphy the question would have been beside the point. 'It may be said, the death of Dr Johnson kept the public mind in agitation beyond all former example. No literary character ever excited so much attention'.[7] Murphy was thinking of the thick crop of lives that had appeared in the 1780s – 'anecdotes, apophthegms, essays, and publications of every kind' – but what also captures his imagination is something quite different from what touched either More or Piozzi: the modern phenomenon of literary fame. In 'The Vanity of Human Wishes' Johnson had evoked 'the fever of renown', but in this satire the tyro's desire was to be known for scholarship and writing. Johnson had enjoyed that order of renown from the mid-1750s and even, like Pope, had achieved an air of monumentality. But he had also, like Rousseau and Sterne, become something of a celebrity. Like them, the notional basis for his fame was his writings and, again like them, it had been transfered onto his person.[8] As early as 1753, just before the *Dictionary*, Garrick taunted Johnson after his late night frisk through the streets of London with Beauclerk and Langton with 'You'll be in the Chronicle' (*Life*, 1, 251).

More revealing are a couple of glances of Johnson's fame that Frances Burney has preserved. The first is a private family story, of her father in 1760 secretly cutting a tuft of Johnson's hearth broom to send to one of the Rambler's distant admirers, a Mr Bewley, who thought the token 'more precious than pearls'.[9] The second glimpse is of a day in August 1778, and it has more public resonance. We hear Johnson talking of the different wits he had known, 'from Mrs Montagu, – down to Bet Flint!' ('a fine Character... She was *habitually* a slut & a Drunkard, & *occasionally* a Whore & a Thief') which drew Mrs Thrale to ask why he had never gone to see Mrs Rudd, the bewitching adventuress who was tried for forgery with the Perreau brothers but, unlike them, acquitted. 'Why, Madam, I believe I *should*, said he, if it was not for the *News papers*; but I am prevented many frolics that I should like very well, since I am become such a Theme for the papers'.[10] When Johnson died far more people wished to read about him than read or re-read what he had written. Boswell, already a celebrity himself, did not create that desire by his biographies; it was already in place. One of the things that distinguishes Boswell from the earlier biographers is that his writing at once embodies that desire while letting it remain desire. His unique vision often plays on Johnson at the threshold of private and public – at the Mitre Tavern, at St Clement Danes, walking down Fleet Street with a friend – as well as in the intimacy of private life itself. In this fashion readers were and are offered vignettes to savour of Johnson at home and opportunities to identify with him. Even without Boswell, Johnson had become famous as a character to an extent that did not happen for earlier literary lions like Ben Jonson, John Dryden and Joseph Addison. In this respect at least he is closer to the times of Sir Walter Scott and Charles Dickens.

A useful label like 'the Age of Johnson' can be used to support quite different conceptions of history. In one context it can bespeak a large claim about the unity of an entire national period, in another the smaller claim of the uniformity of the literature of the time. Even when dealing with literary history expressions like 'the Age of Shakespeare', 'the Age of Dryden', and so forth, can tend to flatten out the past, giving the impression that the eras are all formed by much the same conditions, whether internally (in a recognition of greatness), or externally (in a later period's fixing of a canon). There may be good reasons for positing a fuzzy set of years – the Renaissance, say – yet it hardly follows from this that history is composed of successive periods or that such divisions are historically useful. As the *Annales* school shows, writers separated by two or more centuries may share the same attitudes to life and death; and more generally different historical conventions tend to interfere with one another, for example, 'The Age of Johnson' and Romanticism.[11] And even if one ventures to divide the past completely into periods the reasons for marking different divisions might well vary considerably. What entices people to put Shakespeare at the centre of his times is not exactly the same as what sets Johnson on his pedestal. The bard may well have been 'a monument without a tomb', as Jonson wrote, but he was not a celebrity as Johnson was. In the poem from which I have just quoted, 'To the Memory of My Beloved, The Author, Mr William Shakespeare, And What He Hath Left Us', Jonson places his friend clearly apart from his contemporaries,

> For if I thought my judgement were of years
> I should commit thee surely with thy peers:
> And tell how far thou didst our Lyly outshine,
> Or sporting Kyd, or Marlowe's mighty line,

and insists that 'he was not of an age, but for all time!'[12] That sentiment may well complicate the expression 'the Age of Shakespeare' but no one given to labelling eras in this way could offer an alternative like 'the Age of Kyd' without its polemic edge being uppermost (and with people mildly testing its sharpness). That is not so with all periods. Tags like 'the Age of Dryden', 'the Age of Johnson' and 'the Pound Era' are all made in the teeth of viable alternatives.[13]

So when people use a description like 'The Age of Johnson' it is worth knowing their reasons for doing so. There is no shortage of examples – in history, as well as in literary history. 'The object of this work is to depict life of the period in English history which may legitimately be described as the Age of Johnson'. Thus writes A. S. Turberville in his preface to *Johnson's England* (1933).[14] He goes on to characterise the age as roughly 'the last fifty years of his lifetime', though no reason is offered why history should be carved up into periods and why Johnson should be accorded pre-eminence. In an earlier study he answers the latter, saying that Johnson 'in later life became a literary dictator, so that the age in which he lived is often known as the age of Johnson'.[15] But does literary culture have such caché as that casual 'so that' implies? Returning to *Johnson's England*, we see that the first essay is by G. M. Trevelyan and is entitled, suitably enough, 'The Age of Johnson'. Again, neither the question of periodisation nor the choice of man is explained and Johnson enters the essay in name only to be described as 'the most abnormally English creature God ever made' (6). What animates the period for Trevelyan are the nation's free institutions, and elsewhere he fleshes out the thought. The ministries of Walpole and the Pitts marked 'the heyday of unchallenged abuses in all forms of corporate life', he informs us. 'It is not, therefore, surprising that the greatness of England during the epoch that followed the Revolution is to be judged by her individual men ... The glory of the Eighteenth Century in Britain lay in the genius and energy of individuals acting freely in a free community.'[16] He then supplies a list of such individuals, amongst them Burke, Hume, Reynolds, Smith and, of course Johnson.

I will come back to the importance of institutions and individuality in making sense of Johnson. For the moment, though, let us see what people principally interested in literature rather than history have to say about the expression 'the Age of Johnson'. To begin with, there is James Engell introducing a collection of essays by various hands on English writing of the later eighteenth century. The book was published in 1984, 'the bicentennial of Johnson's death'. Engell starts by recalling the difficulty of choosing a title for such a collection. 'Neo-classicism' excludes the incipient Romanticism of the times, while 'Augustan' comes up short by a generation. Several 'Age of' formulations – Sensibility, Sentiment, Passion and Reason – are weighed and found wanting. And the word 'Enlightenment' appears too broad, stretching back as it does into the early decades of the century. When all these monoliths have been knocked down there is really only one choice remaining. The title must be 'The Age of Johnson' or (as he finally decides) *Johnson and His Age*. Why this? Because here,

> the man remains preeminent: a man of letters, whom Eliot ranks as a major poet and whom many consider the best of English critics; a moral philosopher imbued with practicality and humor; and one of the most entertaining and provoking conversationalists and essayists in any national literature... Individual aspects of Johnson's life and work (aspects that in other writers of his stature might not always attract our attention), his religious convictions and struggles, lexicography, travels and views of travel, political writing and journalism, poetic style, criticism, anecdotes – each of these has been the subject of several full length studies, not just in the recent surge of academic criticism and scholarship, but continually since the late eighteenth century. There are few literary or historical figures in whom we find such power, depth, and combination of mind. To paraphrase Johnson's remark on the source of happiness, 'multiplicity of agreeable consciousness', we find in him a multiplicity of powerful consciousness.[17]

And he goes on to quote William Hamilton whose sonorous eulogy on Johnson we have heard before, 'He has made a chasm, which not only nothing can fill up, but which nothing has a tendency to fill up.'

The emphasis falls first on Johnson 'the man' and then on his 'life and work'. In effect Engell asks us to balance the singularity of an extraordinary man against the interaction of many cultural, social and political forces. We are invited to see an individual transcending his immediate contexts and reaching out to us. Death, for him, is a passage that can be crossed by means of the power and variety of his consciousness. By virtue of Johnson's range and strength, as well as by the continuity of critical response they elicit, the later eighteenth century in Britain can be grasped as 'his age'. Paul J. Korshin adopts another view when prefacing a new annual, *The Age of Johnson*, also established to commemorate the bicentenary of the Doctor's death. 'We construe that age broadly', prospective contributors and readers are told, 'starting with the period that influenced Johnson and his intellectual growth and ending with the first decade or two of the nineteenth century, during which most of the members of his original circle died or ceased their literary activity.'[18] Here the individual is of less importance than the epoch that can be gathered around him. Although his life and writings may feature in the journal, it is his name which serves to organise a body of knowledge. In the preface to the first volume we hear that the annual 'is hospitable to many approaches to the literature, history and culture of Johnson and his age'. By the fifth volume, the editor has to concede that 'the impact of new literary methodologies on our offerings has been relatively minor'; the signal change has not come from critical theory, still kept at arm's length by most scholars of the eighteenth century, but from 'the upsurge of interest on women and gender studies', and we are assured that the annual 'will continue to stress perspectives of this kind'. Where 'the Age of Johnson' signifies to Engell a dominant character and his masterpieces, for Korshin the expression defines a period far longer than any lifetime, an age whose interest is marked partly by Johnson, partly by what he did not or could not comment on, and partly by contemporary institutional desires.

Should one say 'the Age of *Johnson*' with Engell or 'the *Age* of Johnson' with Korshin? How has the expression come about? And what effect does it have on reading Johnson? The easiest way back from here is to recognise that by the time Korshin published the first number of the annual, his title had been used several times before in other contexts. Of immediate interest is a collection of essays edited by Frederick W. Hilles, *The Age of Johnson* (1949): it was a *Festschrift* for Chauncey Brewster Tinker, and it takes us a little deeper into the history of the expression. It turns out that the title of the collection quotes the name of two subjects offered by the Yale English Department.[19] Tinker had inherited an undergraduate course entitled 'Dr Johnson and His Circle' from Charles G. Osgood who left Yale in 1905 for Princeton where he established a similar course. Under the revised title of 'The Age of Johnson' Tinker made the course into a highly regarded unit of the college's English curriculum, then offered a seminar of the same title in the Yale Graduate School. (Courses with the same name were later taught by Walter Jackson Bate at Harvard and James Clifford at Columbia.) Introducing Hilles's collection of essays, Wilmarth Sheldon Lewis evokes Tinker's graduate seminar:

Although I had not the privilege of taking the graduate 'Age of Johnson', various of its former members have told me what happened in it – Mr Tinker himself has told me. It was limited to about six students a year and was divided into two sections that met fortnightly. At these two-hour sessions each student read aloud a ten-minute paper – exactly ten minutes – on a subject that he had been given. The subjects were *almost anything dealing with the literary life of the eighteenth century* [my emphasis]. Frequently Mr Tinker gave a student a MS from his own library to edit or lent him a book that suggested a bibliographical problem.[20]

On the face of it, Lewis was an odd choice to introduce the collection. He was not known as a Johnsonian but as the editor of the Yale edition of Horace Walpole's correspondence and as a member of the advisory committee of the Yale editions of the private papers of James Boswell. But this is precisely what made him suitable. The accent of Tinker's graduate seminar fell on 'Age' rather than on 'Johnson', and that was a matter of historical honesty as well as pedagogic technique, for elsewhere he devotes part of an essay to debunking the view of Johnson as 'somehow the symbol and exponent of his age'.[21] The stress on 'Age' rather than 'Johnson' is maintained in the *Festschrift*. Of the thirty-six essays included only four mention Johnson in their titles, and just one centrally addresses him. That single essay is Katherine C. Balderston's 'Johnson's Vile Melancholy', an influential piece but one very much concerned with Johnson the man and not the writer. If this lack of sustained interest in Johnson's writing seems surprising given the collection's title it should not be given the man it honours. Tinker was first and foremost a Boswellian. It was Tinker who in *Young Boswell* (1922) and his *Letters of James Boswell* (1924), had excited interest in the biographer, and Tinker who, in 1927, was offered (and declined) the editorship of Boswell's private papers by the renowned collector Lieutenant-Colonel Ralph H. Isham.

Before pondering any further the relations between Boswell and 'the Age of Johnson', we need to look more closely at the assumptions at work in the expression. They uncoil the questions at issue more surely than can any amount of debate about whether the age should be known as Johnson's, Burke's, Hogarth's or Hume's. In the *Dictionary* Johnson defines one sense of 'age' as 'the time in which any particular man, or race of men, lived, or shall live; as, the *age* of heroes.' From biblical times onward people have had a sense of ages coming and going with rulers, catastrophic events like invasions, wars and natural disasters, and even big round dates on the calender. The idea of the eighteenth century marking the start of a new epoch was declared by the general Chorus at the end of Dryden's *The Secular Masque* of 1700, *''Tis well an Old Age is out /And time to begin a New.'*[22] Regarding history as divided into periods is a familiar way in which it can be rendered intelligible, redeemed from a mere flux of events with no order or significance beyond their occurrence.

No sooner is this admitted, though, than the concept 'history' itself begins to divide. Maurice Mandelbaum makes the point cleanly when observing that what marks the beginning of a new economic period does not necessarily coincide with an epoch inaugurated by scientific discoveries or changes in philosophical assumptions.[23] Unless this variety of temporal dislocation is kept in mind, historiography will fall into a monism that obliterates the independence required for genuine inquiry into the past. For this very reason Mandelbaum distinguishes general and specific histories. A general history will be oriented towards society, while a specific history will attune itself to culture. This distinction plainly needs considerable clarification before it can be of much help. For how can culture be separated from society? Only by rigidly defining the word 'culture' so that it designates 'whatever objects are created and used by individuals and whatever skills, beliefs, and forms of behavior they have acquired through their social inheritance' (12). As that last phrase suggests, the line between culture and society is not unbroken. None the less it is firmly drawn, for 'culture' 'does *not* include institutions, such as kinship systems or rules governing the distribution of property and the division of labor, which define the status of individuals within a society and regulate the organization of its life' (12). Thus we have general histories which look to the institutions of society, and specific histories which focus on culture. The general historian will speak of an epoch in terms of 'the reign of a ruler or a dynasty', 'the beginning and the end of some significant economic development within a society or group of societies' or 'the rise and decline of a nation or an alliance of nations' (165). Meanwhile a specific historian will be sensitive to 'a dominant style in literature or a style that is held to characterize various forms of art at the time' or 'the acceptance and subsequent rejection of a set of presuppositions in philosophy' or the 'development, and final acceptance of a series of epoch-making scientific discoveries' (165). In this way different sorts of historians can still talk intelligently of periods without subscribing to 'an overriding unity that embraces all aspects of social life' (22), presumably the national spirit that Turberville and Trevelyan invoke when discussing 'the Age of Johnson'.

So Mandelbaum's distinction provides a useful corrective to the vagaries of an earlier historiography. To call the whole later eighteenth century in Britain 'the Age of Johnson' is to bypass much of the culture and politics of the times and to ignore the varied surfaces of everyday lives in order to make a certain depth legible, a depth common (if only they knew it) to parliamentarians and prostitutes, Oxbridge Fellows and poor apprentices.[24] But the depth is illusory; it mediates an individual consciousness and intersecting strata of economic, social and political realities, and since no method will ever isolate it, let alone yield it up for examination, it can be moved more or less as circumstances dictate. Trevelyan talks of two pictures of eighteenth-century life that can be held in balance by the name of Johnson: one is 'the peculiar civilization of the period' and the other is 'the earlier stages of those fundamental economic and social changes known as the Industrial Revolution'.[25] One can object that in the times of Boulton and Watt it looks odd to choose Johnson of all people to stand for and illustrate the Industrial Revolution. But a sufficiently keen Johnsonian will always point to the great man's interest in economics, machinery and trade. That these interests were genuine is one thing, but that they can hold together the two pictures of eighteenth-century life is another. Surely Mandelbaum is right to stress the need for specific histories. And yet is he right also to discriminate between general and specific histories as he does?

Even if one agrees that culture and society can be partly separated, it remains difficult to imagine a culture having such an attenuated relationship with social institutions. That culture is transmitted by society is not in question for Mandelbaum; it is, as he says, 'acquired' by an individual through 'social inheritance'. Yet how can one explain on that basis how a writer like Johnson moved up through society by virtue of his culture, beginning as the son of an impoverished provincial bookseller and ending as a semi-permanent guest of the Thrales at Streatham?

It is also hard to see how one could talk of eighteenth-century literary culture without understanding that writers like Goldsmith and Johnson had to labour for the booksellers, and that the law concerning literary property reset the very idea of authorship. Literary culture may not be reducible to social categories, but by the same token it cannot be thought about without close reference to a society that precedes individual writers, even if its institutions are no more than differential and changing sets of relations. Johnson's writings, his literary skills, his beliefs, and his behaviour – all the elements that comprise his culture for Mandelbaum – are not simply or equally acquired by him through inheritance. They are imbricated with specific institutions of the time: the booksellers, the school, the courts, the parliament and the church. The *Dictionary* was a venture proposed and financed by a group of London booksellers, as was the *Lives of the Poets*, a work that George III had desired Johnson to undertake years before. The very title 'Dr

Johnson' comes from the LL.D. conferred on him by Trinity College, Dublin (1765) and the D.C.L. bestowed on him by the University of Oxford (1775); and an important aspect of his behaviour in later life, his freedom to talk rather than write, was made possible by the pension arranged for him.

Were this kind of analysis to be persued over a wide range of cases it would become increasingly difficult to see why Mandelbaum's general history is not itself a cluster of specific histories. That economics, nationhood and politics deeply involve one another does not need elaborate justification, but it does not follow from this that culture is not often caught up in the circle they describe. On Mandelbaum's model, literary history would be a process of hollowing out history in favour of literature, making literature itself a palid ahistorical category. What could literary history here be other than the study of the history of styles? Yet even a moment's thought about the expression 'the Age of' shows that it must do more than isolate a style, even if understood fairly broadly; it gathers together a period, an individual, and – more stealthily – a nation. 'The Age of Johnson' does not cross the channel, even though Johnson visited Paris. (And yet there is a certain 'Age of Rousseau' in Britain, partly because of significant English influences on him and partly because of his influences on British writers.) Culture can do some of the work set for general history, even though it may not get the credit for doing so. One reason why culture must be treated like this is because Mandelbaum wishes to shore up one of his favourite theses, the objectivity of general history. And that thesis can best be protected if literature and everything that goes along with the word – fiction, narrative, rhetoric, style, taste – are kept at arm's length from economics, nationhood and politics.

I do not want to engage at any length with the large questions in the philosophy of history that are now beginning to raise their heads. And yet this last consideration raises a couple of difficulties that need to be acknowledged in passing. In the first place, there is the question of what happens if we think only of specific histories. Do they need to be referred to a general history or, failing that, at least a general notion of history? Certainly if the assumption of an essence of history (or of a species of history deemed essential to history) is discharged, the word and concept 'history' still remain in a network of other words and concepts. In a sense nothing has changed for the practising historian yet something has become more clear, the view that historiography depends on the possibility of repetition and traces.[26] The concept 'history' does not necessarily assume an essence, although the Socratic move to find a common idea in different kinds of history is seldom slow in being made. This brings us to the brink of the second question. Would a monopoly of specific histories remove objectivity from the horizon of historiography? For Mandelbaum general histories lay claim to objectivity because they can exclude nothing in principle, while a specific history can and should exclude what does not concern it. There may be occasions when Johnson usefully enters a general history like J. Steven Watson's *The Reign of George III*, though a literary history like Edmund Gosse's *A History of Eighteenth Century Literature* would exclude or marginalise most of what is discussed there while making far more of Fielding and Richardson, Collins and Gray. More than that, each literary historian works with a tacit notion of 'literature', perhaps one that has not been fully spelled out, that cannot in theory be reconciled with alternate notions. It is not a matter of literary taste but a question of what genres at a particular time and place will count as literature. A literary historian writing about 1920 may include Hume's *History*, Junius's *Letters* and Warburton's *Divine Legation*, while another writing forty years later may not. It is unreasonable then to demand objectivity in literary history, Mandelbaum thinks, but not in general history. For there, even when dealing with works leaning on different grounds, we can still expect a 'reconciliation of their differences' (163) and, if that is not forthcoming, we must reject either or both accounts. This is the meaning of historical objectivity for Mandelbaum.

It is logically possible, however, that any number of accounts may be capable of being reconciled and that none of them depicts an event as it happened. General history is characterised by being unable to exclude anything that brings about change in the society under consideration. Yet this history must be a narrative; it must not knowingly neglect relevant information but it has to shape what information it has. And this evidence, even if it comes from impeccable first-hand witnesses, will itself be perceived in one way rather than another and patterned in the telling, even to oneself. The example of an important disagreement over the Tories' relation to the Jacobites after George I acceded to the throne might help to make this clear. Eveline Cruickshanks uses a wealth of English, French and Scottish manuscripts to relate a new and surprising story about eighteenth-century political life. 'It was the proscription which turned the Tory party into a Jacobite one', she says.[27] Cast into the political doldrums after 1715, the Tories aligned themselves with the Stuart cause in order to survive. 'English Tories were Jacobites in the

sense that their leaders, answering for the party, wanted a restoration of
the Stuarts in the person of Charles Edward, hoping he would conform
to the established church, but they had said again and again that only
regular troops could bring it about.'[28] Linda Colley also takes a fresh
look at the Tories, but her focus is on their organisation after the
proscription; and she comes up with a quite different view of them. To
be sure, Tories did incline toward the Stuart cause at particularly
difficult times – in 1715, of course, but also in 1720 with the Whig reunion
and in 1742 with the defection of the Patriot Whigs – yet these are
exceptions. Colley sums up, with Cruickshanks's story in mind, 'Jacobitism, in short, was not the tory *raison d'être* but one political option
amongst many, to be considered if and when it became viable.'[29]

Are these two stories about the Tories and the Jacobites irrecon-
cilable? Not at all, says Paul Kléber Monod: since Jacobite politics did
not feature in parliamentary politics one would hardly expect it to
appear as an important factor in Colley's study.[30] At a general level,
then, it would seem that there is no reason why the two stories could not
be intelligently combined. Over the interval from 1715 to 1745, the Tory
leadership would be covertly leagued with the Stuart cause, while of
course never declaring their ideology or their tactics in the Parliament.
It does not follow, though, that even the most careful synthesis of
Cruickshanks and Colley – even one that judiciously includes the
different insights of Jonathan Clark and Donald Greene[31] – would yield
a complete and coherent view of political life in Britain during the
eighteenth century, or even objectively present one particular event.
The two styles of shaping evidence may not account for other areas
which turn out to be relevant, and the two sets of assumptions about
historical method may not mesh as nicely as one would hope.

That said, any reader of a narrative, manuscript or a later reconstruc-
tion, is entitled to enquire about this shaping of evidence. Three prelimi-
nary questons may be posed: Who is speaking? To whom? Why? Let us
restrict ourselves to the historian. When he or she answers these questions an image of the historian begins to form. It is an image that bears
traces of other images, the person's ideology often showing through
more clearly than a personality. Issues of class, gender and race will
become apparent in the selection and arrangement of material, as will
the kind of historical vision – comic, ironic, nostalgic, romantic or tragic
– that sustains and organises the whole. But even the most finely-tuned
theory of ideology will not account satisfactorily for all important
influences on the historian. Considerations as woolly as 'attitude to

other people', 'cast of mind' and 'motivation' will impinge – and all that well before reaching for the vocabulary of psychoanalysis. None of these should be overlooked; they affect how a historian will exercise the principle of charity, for example, and in some circumstances that can be at least as helpful as an identikit of his or her ideology.

To maintain that information about a social institution exists by way of narrative, ideology and the rest is not thereby to dismiss objectivity in favour of subjectivity. The suggestion, rather, is that an historical 'fact' is always relative to its contexts of production and reception. Sometimes this is trivially the case, as in the ordinary sentence 'George III acceded to the throne in 1760', for it would take a fanatical anti-Hanoverian to argue that the coronation was invalid, or a desperate sceptic to doubt the date on which the ceremony took place. Sometimes interpretation mimics the voice of fact, as in the opposed sentences 'Prince Charles landed at Moidart in Scotland on 15 July 1745' and 'The Pretender landed at Moidart in Scotland on 15 July 1745', yet even when this act is noted and erased (leaving the bare statement 'Charles Edward Stuart landed in Scotland in 1745') it may well remain in the historian's mind and silently arrange other material.[32] Objectivity, as I am using the word, is not to be understood as the avoidance of conflict in accounts sharing commensurable assumptions. It is a horizon, not a state of affairs. For the writer, it is experienced as a potentially endless process of correcting (and not just re-touching) a story about the past with the help of fresh evidence that will itself stand in need of correction.

One thing that Mandelbaum teaches us about periodisation, even though it does not appear on the surface of his argument, is that different ways of dividing up the past imply not only varying historiographies but also competing claims to authority. This is most readily seen in church history, the touchstone being Augustine's *The City of God*. Once cyclical theories of history are rejected on the theological ground that Christ dies once and for all, history becomes both linear and the history of meaning. The world has seven ages, Augustine says, and we can distinguish them by decoding God's design in each. For later ecclesiastics this schema, once suitably refined, stands in dire need of value distinctions. Thus eastern and western Catholics will disagree whether Constantine's conversion divides two epochs, while Catholics and Protestants differ over what kind of division is marked by the Reformation. This theology of history can be, and often is, diluted and rendered implicit. Leopold von Ranke, for instance, sought to establish history as an autonomous discipline, and yet he none the less affirms that each period 'was immediate to God'.[33] It is not far from the more overt theological view of his contemporary Philip Schaff that 'every period of the church and of theology has its particular problem to solve'.[34] This move is best seen in the early years of the history of ideas where a cultural or intellectual history was projected as a series of periods animated by an overarching idea of development, each being marked by a 'climate of opinion', collective unconscious, spirit, or whatever. Can one still preserve the notion of an age while dissolving all grounds for redemption or development? Jacob Burckhardt proposes that chronological time is not homogeneous, that distinct epochs express human activities in terms of a harmonious whole; while Michel Foucault maintains that a period meets an epistemic limit without any crossover from earlier times, its principles of order and reason being wholly immanent.[35]

Johnson's views on the topic best come into focus when he discusses Shakespeare. He says little here that points to a theology of history, and is typically sceptical about timeless grounds for human enterprises. Yet, just as characteristically, he does not allow that view to limit the scope of moral perception. In the Preface to his edition of Shakespeare (1765) he indicates how questions of judgement need to be taken in tandem with a certain historical relativity. 'Every man's performances, to be rightly estimated, must be compared with the state of the age in which he lived, and with his own particular opportunities.' Historical relativity need not imply critical relativism, however, as he immediately makes plain: 'though to the reader a book be not worse or better for the circumstances of the authour, yet as there is always a silent reference of human works to human abilities … curiousity is always busy to discover the instruments, as well as to survey the workmanship, to know how much is to be ascribed to original powers, and how much to casual and adventitious help' (Yale, VII, 81). And an important aspect of what makes a book 'worse or better' is its morality, specifically the conduct it sanctions. One of Shakespeare's faults is that 'he carries his persons indifferently through right and wrong, and at the close dismisses them without further care, and leaves their examples to operate by chance'. There is no point appealing to moral relativism, 'this fault the barbarity of his age cannot extenuate; for it is always a writer's duty to make the world better, and justice is a virtue independent of time or place' (Yale, VII, 71).

To weigh Shakespeare's merits against 'the state of the age in which he lived' is a fair way from conceiving a period as 'the Age of Shakespeare'. The first thinks of literature in history; the second, of literary history – and, in doing so, places us in the nineteenth or twentieth century. This needs a word of explanation. In the first decades of the nineteenth century people experienced a strong sense of living in a distinct period themselves. In 1831, for example, John Stuart Mill begins a series of five articles in the *Examiner* by reflecting on the title he has given them. 'The "Spirit of the Age" is in some measure a novel expression. I do not believe that it is to be met with in any work exceeding fifty years in antiquity.'[36] At the time he writes, however, it is a dominant idea, one 'essentially belonging to an age of change'. Where does this idea come from? It was in the air, like all important social ideas, but it was also on paper. William Hazlitt had published portraits of older contemporaries in the *New Monthly Magazine* under the title of 'Spirits of the Age', though when he collected them in 1825 he chose a stronger title, *The Spirit of the Age; or, Contemporary Portraits*, perhaps thinking or half-thinking of David Hume's use of the expression in his 1754 essay 'Of Refinement in the Arts' or more likely of a book he knew fairly well, Ernst Moritz Arndt's *Der Geist der Zeit* (1805).[37] Certainly Hazlitt was a step or two closer to a mood of German philosophical speculation than to a Scottish scepticism when he exclaimed in a central passage, 'Mr Wordsworth's genius is a pure emanation of the Spirit of the Age.'[38] Hazlitt went no further than this, but if he had wanted to baptise the period two possibilities were open to him. He could have called the times 'the Age of Revolution', since, after all, it was the spirit of the French Revolution he found in Wordsworth's early poetry or, equally, he could have hit upon 'the Age of Wordsworth'.

But he did not. In the eighteenth century and beyond history was frequently seen in terms of the rise of property and trade. One might divide the past into an age of hunters, followed by an age of pasturage then, once 'ideas of property begin to take root', one of agriculture, crowned by one of commerce; and this might be put to distinct literary ends, as Hugh Blair did when arguing for the virtues of Ossian.[39] But viewing history through the lens of property is a fair way from regarding it by way of proper names. Literary historians began to think of sublime individuals who somehow embody their ages only later, following examples first set by social history and the history of philosophy. Beginning with Voltaire, modern historians had started to view an entire epoch through the life of one illustrious man. *The Age of Louis XIV* (1751) began by dividing history into four ages: the Greek, the Roman, the Renaissance, and that of Louis XIV. Voltaire announces his bold aim of depicting 'for posterity, not the actions of a single man, but the spirit of men in the most enlightened age the world has ever seen', and his original intention was to conclude with a full history of the arts (it was reduced to two chapters, followed by several more on ecclesiastical affairs).[40] As long as history was the medium of narration and discussion it would be difficult to move conclusively to cultural history: Church and State would always call the writer back to their affairs. To end with cultural history, it seems, one must also start with it, maintaining all the while that it offers a unique mode of understanding. And that requires a new kind of thinking about history or, rather, histories.

This new thinking has many strands, one or two of which run through Hazlitt and Mill. With the benefit of hindsight we can pick up another with Giambattista Vico arguing in the *New Science* (1725), against the current of his times, for the independence and value of historical understanding, as well as for a cycle of historical epochs. Bypassed for almost a century, these ideas came into their own only with the rise of Romanticism. Now they can be seen to run parallel with J. G. Herder's case against universal criteria to judge all human actions. There are general laws, he thought, but they cannot be deduced from metaphysical grounds; rather, they must be induced from experience of the world. The practical lesson Herder taught historians is that context rules supreme: each age has a unique character, a sense of its own time, that is formed by circumstance and the *Volksgeist*. Or, in the philosopher's own words, 'every thing earthly and human is governed by time and place, as every particular nation is by it's [*sic*] character, uninfluenced by which it can do nothing'.[41] I quote from Herder's *Outlines of a Philosophy of the History of Man* which appeared over the years 1784–91 (the interval, as it happens, from Johnson's death to Boswell's *Life*). An English translation was published in 1800. Another strand of speculative thought in this area took far longer to find a sympathetic hearing in England.[42] I mean Hegel's doctrine that history develops in specific epochs through heroes actualising the *Zeitgeist*. Let the philosopher speak in his own words: 'Such individuals had no consciousness of the general Idea they were unfolding, while prosecuting those aims of theirs; on the contrary, they were practical, political men. But at the same time they were thinking men, who had an insight into the requirements of the time – *what was ripe for development*. This was the very Truth for their age, for their world...'[43] Such is Hegel's general thesis about world-historical individuals. A version of the same line is run in his *Aesthetics*, and it was that course of lectures that first attracted attention in Britain in 1842.[44] Talking of epic poetry Hegel observes, 'Although an epic does express the affairs of an entire nation, it is only individuals who can write poetry, a nation collectively cannot. The spirit of an age or a nation is indeed the underlying efficient cause, but the effect, an actual work of art, is only produced when this cause is concentrated into the individual genius of a single poet; he then brings to our minds and particularizes this universal spirit, and all that it contains, as his own vision and his own work.'[45]

Hegelianism started to take root in England much later in the Victorian era, and with the benefit of hindsight it might seem merely to confirm and support earlier growths, some of which had developed from Coleridge and his interest in German metaphysics. Yet the originality of the British Hegelians should not be played down: T. H. Green developed the ethical and political dimensions of continental idealism in a distinctive way, while F. H. Bradley reset Hegel on a quite new logical foundation. In sections of the civil service, in adult education, as well as in the corridors of Cambridge and Oxford, strains of Hegel's thought were profoundly influential in the last thirty years of the nineteenth century.[46] But at first they met with considerable native resistance, Mill's reaction being fairly typical. In a throwaway line in a now largely forgotten tome he suggested that the German philosopher 'has fairly earned the honour which will probably be awarded to him by posterity, of having logically extinguished transcendental metaphysics by a series of *reductiones ad absurdissimum*'.[47]

As it turns out, it was Fichte rather than Hegel whose name was crucially cited in British literary circles, not his theory of the five ages of history in his *Die Gründzüge des gegenwärtigen Zeitalters* (1806) but his observations on the nature of the scholar of 1805. And the person citing Fichte was not a philosopher but a literary and cultural critic, Thomas Carlyle, who had been familiar with the German's writings for well over a decade:

Fichte, in conformity with the Transcendental Philosophy, of which he was a distinguished teacher, declares first, That all things which we see of work with in this Earth, especially we ourselves and all persons, are as a kind of vesture or sensuous Appearance; that under all there lies, as the essence of them, what he calls the 'Divine Idea of the World'; this is the Reality which 'lies at the bottom of all Appearance'. To the mass of men no such Divine Idea is recognisable in the world; they live merely, says Fichte, among the superficialities, practicalities and shews of the world, not dreaming that there is anything divine under them. But the Man of Letters is sent hither specially that he may discern for himself, and make manifest to us, this same Divine Idea: in every new generation it will manifest itself in a new dialect; and he is there for the purpose of doing that.[48]

That could be from *Sator Resartus* or one or two of the *Essays*, but in fact it is from Carlyle's 1840 lecture series *On Heroes, Hero Worship, and the Heroic in History*, a passionate argument for the great man theory of history. His case has two main aspects which quickly run into one another, the nature of history and the nature of heroism. It is easier to begin with the first. In his 'On History' (1830) Carlyle proclaimed that 'Social Life is the aggregate of all the individual men's Lives who constitute society; History is the essence of innumerable biographies', though this democratic spirit is eliminated ten years later when we are told that 'the History of the world is but the Biography of great men.'[49] This great man or hero responds intuitively and powerfully to the unseen 'dynamical' needs of a society and not to its surface 'mechanical' needs; he sees 'truly, what the time wanted', receives the admiration of those about him who express it by an unfeigned loyalty. 'Hero' is taken broadly to encompass gods, prophets, poets, priests, political rulers, and – men of letters. Carlyle offers three examples of this last group, the first of whom is Samuel Johnson.

'The concept of the author is as good as unknown in our age', writes Fichte in 1805, and Carlyle in turn stresses that the hero as man of letters is a new phenomenon, barely a hundred years old. For Fichte, there is a sense in which the author does not even have a life of his own. 'The idea itself must speak, not the author', he declares. 'His will, his individuality, his peculiar method and art, all must disappear from his page, so that only the method and art of his idea may live the highest life that it can attain in his language and in his time.'[50] For Carlyle, the man of letters is more to be noted for how he acts in death than in life. 'He, with his copy-rights and copy-wrongs, in his squalid garret, in his rusty coat; ruling (for this is what he does), from his grave, after death, whole nations and generations who would, or would not, give him bread while living, – is a rather curious spectacle! Few shapes of Heroism can be more unexpected' (133). This is so for all writers, including the 'heroic bringers of the light' like Goethe, but the three on whom he will meditate were seekers of the light; they could not 'unfold themselves into clearness, or victorious interpretation of that "Divine Idea"'. So in discussing Johnson and the others Carlyle has a melancholy task, 'It is rather the *Tombs* of three Literary Heroes that I have to shew you. There

are the monumental heaps, under which three spiritual giants lie buried'
(136–37).

Carlyle's Johnson endures as a man rather than a writer. 'I have
always considered him to be, by nature, one of our great English souls. A
strong and noble man; so much left undeveloped in him to the last: in a
kindlier element what might he not have been, – Poet, Priest, sovereign
Ruler! . . . The world might have had more of profitable *work* out of him,
or less; but his *effort* against the world's work could never have been a
light one' (*Essays*, 153). In the last paragraph devoted to Johnson we hear
of his writings, 'now as it were disowned by the younger generation',
which are marked by a 'wondrous buckram style, – the best he could get
to then; a measured grandiloquence, stepping or rather stalking along in
a very solemn way, grown obsolete now' (157). In short, Johnson is a
monument like his *Dictionary*: 'There is in it a kind of architectural
nobleness; it stands there like a great solid square-built edifice, finished,
symmetrically complete: you judge that a true Builder did it' (157). Since
Johnson's life is so exemplary, one might think that Carlyle will turn to
praise Boswell for his biographies which portray it. But no, the *Life* is not
mentioned. It is Boswell the man rather than the author who attracts
Carlyle's attention:

One word, in spite of our haste, must be granted to poor Bozzy. He passes for a
mean, inflated, gluttonous creature; and was so in many senses. Yet the fact of
his reverence for Johnson will ever remain noteworthy. The foolish conceited
Scotch Laird, the most conceited man of his time, approaching in such
awestruck attitude the great dusty irascible Pedagogue in his mean garret there:
it is a genuine reverence for Excellence; a *worship* for Heroes, at a time when
neither Heroes nor worship were summised to exist. (157)

It is sometimes said that Carlyle naturalises transcendental philosophy.
This might be true in some respects but certainly not in all. Where
Fichte argues that the spirit abides in the author's writings, not his life,
Carlyle in his lectures on heroes maintains the exact opposite – and to
such an extent that it is hard to see how he *knows* that people have been
worshipped as heroes.

'It is the proper ambition of the heroes in literature to enlarge the
boundaries of knowledge by discovering and conquering new regions of
the intellectual world' (Yale, iv, 362). This is not Carlyle but Johnson: to
some extent they both see authors as heroes, though Johnson was far less
taken with military heroes than the Victorian sage.[51] 'They who have
attentively considered the history of mankind, know that every age has

its peculiar character' (Yale, II, 456).[52] Again, this is not Carlyle but Johnson, writing the *Adventurer* for 11 December 1753, and here Johnson's conception of his times is very different from his Victorian admirer's. 'The present age, if we consider chiefly the state of our own country, may be stiled with great propriety the Age of Authors; for, perhaps, there never was a time, in which men of all degrees of ability, of every kind of education, of every profession and employment, were posting with ardour so general to the press.'[53] In that age Johnson's own writing was mostly anonymous, and it could only be a later time marked by Romantic individualism or the Victorian cult of the hero, that could choose a description of his times that is centred on his name. More often than not, though, 'the Age of Johnson' alludes to the man rather than his writings and to the age rather than either. Let us trace this more closely.

Certainly the influence of Macaulay and Carlyle did not go unchecked in the Victorian era. A writer for the *Quarterly Review* in 1885 took both to task for their views of Johnson and it is here, incidentally, that we find the expression 'Samuel Johnson and his Age' for what may well have been the first time. The great Cham is more significant now than when he died, we are told, even though his literary output was modest and does not have a wide readership. Why then is he important? 'The truth is that Johnson is interesting chiefly because he unites in himself so much that was great, but yet diverse, in his own age.'[54] The thought that the eighteenth century was a significant age but with an undistinguished literature, in the new Romantic sense of the word, was a commonplace by the time the anonymous reviewer made his remarks. Commonplaces are always overdetermined, and numerous threads are tied together in this one, not least of all several to be found already interlaced in Matthew Arnold's influential inaugural lecture as Professor of Poetry at Oxford. 'On the Modern Element in Literature' was delivered in 1857 though published only in 1869. In his most authoritative manner Arnold speaks of the intellectual deliverance that marks certain epochs as modern. For this to occur there must be 'the presence of a significant spectacle to contemplate' and 'the desire to find the true point of view from which to contemplate this spectacle'.[55] Arnold's interest in this lecture was classical literature, and his concern was to defend its study. The Greek and Roman classics are not of mere antiquarian interest; they speak to modern epochs like our own. Yet his distinctions lend themselves to general use, even if their precise terms are questionable. He talks of 'a significant, a highly-developed, a culminating epoch, on the one hand'

and 'a comprehensive, a commensurate, an adequate literature on the other' (6); and it follows that there can be periods that are greater than their literature and other periods whose literature is greater than the age. This seems to offer Victorians a way of resolving their complex feelings toward the eighteenth century, especially its latter half. One could say that it was an epoch whose greatness exceeds its literature – it was an impressive spectacle – and then stop there. Or one could go further and say that the true point of view from which that spectacle could be contemplated was not in its poetry, novels or drama, which look thin and pale compared with what went before and has come after, but in a lesser literary form, Boswell's *Life*.

Literary historians from the end of the nineteenth century through to the first decades of the twentieth century tended to adopt one or the other of these views. They all accepted that literary history occured in epochs. In the closing years of the nineteenth century George Bell and Sons began publishing a series of 'Handbooks of English Literture' under the general editorship of J. W. Hales, each study consecrated to a particular age of literary history. In 1900 Thomas Seccombe's *The Age of Johnson* appeared in that series. He starts his first chapter by reflecting on the title he has been assigned. 'Dr Johnson is more readily accepted as a literary figurehead than any English author, and when we speak of "the Age of Johnson" the expression is less an arbitrary chronological convention than an admission that in the popular imagination Johnson's figure dominates the literary group in which he was a unit.'[56] After some apt remarks on his man's contemporaries he goes on to say that 'Johnson was thus in a very partial sense only the literary representative of his age; but he was, as we shall perceive, greater as a man than as an author, and as a man he was to a rare extent typical of a common English ideal.'[57]

So powerful is the need to call those times 'the Age of Johnson' but so deep is the divide felt between man and author that Seccombe finds himself skirting a paradox: 'If a man were restricted to the writings of a single author of the Age of Johnson, he would show both wisdom and taste in naming those of Henry Fielding.'[58] The basis of Johnson's appeal, it seems, is a popular rather than a learned tradition, one that squares with a national ideal. Hardly alone in his judgement, Seccombe is the voice of the Johnson Club, founded on 13 December 1884, whose 'Brethren' published two collections of papers. The first of these gatherings begins with Augustine Birrell's influential 'The Transmission of Dr Johnson's Personality' where it is steadily maintained

that 'to transmit personality is the secret of literature'. That much is
very familiar to readers of Carlyle's 1841 lecture on the hero as poet.
To this Victorian commonplace Birrill adds another, that 'Johnson's
personality has been transmitted to us chiefly by a record of his *talk*'.[59]
To be Johnsonian, it seems, is to receive and approve his personality,
and the best way to do that is to read Boswell, not Johnson. And if one
has missed that point while reading Birrill's essay or the papers that
follow it, it is underlined in the concluding verses by Lionel Johnson,
'At the "Cheshire Cheese"':

> With the best of goodwill, but rough numbers, I raise
> To our excellent selves a song-offering of praise:
> Away with mock modesty! We are the men
> Who love to live now as the *Doctor* lived then.
> For his writings ... 'tis true that not all of us read them:
> But we walk in his ways, and his precepts, we heed them.[60]

The verses ask our indulgence on the ground of sincerity, 'the best of
goodwill', and it is sincerity that becomes one of the central criteria of
the two collections of papers.

Seccombe and his fellow brethren are followed by the early literary
historians of the twentieth century. In *Dr Johnson and his Circle* (1913) John
Bailey notes that Johnson has become 'the embodiment of the essential
features of the English character' and that 'in Johnson we see our own
magnified and glorified selves'. In short, Johnson is 'a national institution'.[61] Notions of embodiment and representation persist over the
years. George Saintsbury in his influential *The Peace of the Augustans* (1916)
tells us that 'Johnson is not only by common consent one of the most
striking figures of the eighteenth century, but he is, from a certain side
and in a certain sense, *the* eighteenth century...'[62] Bernard Groom
prolongs the emphasis: 'the "age of Johnson", in fact, was one of
remarkable achievement', he writes in 1929, 'but the use of his name
must be understood as a tribute to his greatness as a man, not as the
token of superior literary genius. In many ways Johnson was no more
than a representative man, an embodiment of eighteenth-century and
of English common sense.'[63] And so it goes on, right down to the present
day with Pat Rogers writing of Johnson that 'no one has a higher
visibility in mid-Hanoverian culture, and no one embodies so fully the
temper of his time.'[64]

For all these writers it would seem that Johnson 'embodies' or
'represents' a national spirit in a way that presumably cannot be done –

or seen to be done – by Burke, Gibbon, Goldsmith, Hume, Richardson, Sterne or Walpole. It should be noted right away that the great man theory of history does not have to merge with a cultural nationalism. Isaac D'Israeli in his *The Literary Character, Illustrated by the History of Men of Genius* (1818) certainly extols 'the founders of National Literature and Art... The master-spirits who create an epoch' while distinguishing sharply between 'the genius of the individual' and 'the genius of society'. Indeed, for him there is more that binds together isolated geniuses than that ties each one to his or her culture. 'There is a singleness and unity in the pursuits of genius, though all ages, which produces a sort of consanguinity in the characters of authors. Men of genius, in their different classes, living at distinct periods, or in remote countries, seem to be the same persons with another name'.[65] Carlyle would accept only a part of this; and, as the century wore on, the notion of embodiment began to take on a life of its own apparently without reference to great men and their deeds. It is most readily seen in J. R. Green's *A Short History of the English People* (1874), very popular in its day. 'The aim of the following work is defined by its title', we are told in the preface; 'it is a history, not of English Kings or English Conquests, but of the English People'.[66] And we are straightaway told what this will mean in practice, 'I have devoted more space to Chaucer than to Cressy.' The intention is to strike a balance between individual and community, and from time to time that will mean seeing social history refracted through cultural history. The revolt of the Lollards, the battles of Crécy and Poitiers, represent a 'new gladness of a great people', but where are we to find it? Not in source documents, for it 'utters itself in the verse of Geoffrey Chaucer' (I, 417). Trevelyan himself points to 'the golden age' of Green and a number of other Victorian historians – Froude, Lecky, Morley, Motley, Stephen, Symonds and Spencer Walpole – who have followed Carlyle and Macaulay in carrying on 'the tradition that history was related to literature'. With the labours of these people, 'the foundations of a broad, national culture, based upon knowledge of our history and pride in England's past, seemed to be securely laid.'[67] It is in terms of this national culture that Johnson can be seen as embodying or representing his age.

It is worth while to spend a moment or two thinking about these metaphors that are used almost interchangeably. To say that Johnson embodies his age is to suggest that he gives a concrete character or form to it, if not in his written *corpus* or even his physical body then in his life. More, it is to assume a gulf between discourse and the social body:

spoken or written, the words of Johnson become in effect the privileged site where the eighteenth century is produced for another time.[68] This shifts our attention toward the verb 'to represent'. There is more at stake here because the verb has a larger number of relevant senses, some of which are more misleading than others. If we range Johnson alongside other writers what becomes clear is how much he differed from contemporaries in matters of substance and style; and if we focus exclusively on the man's life – accenting his psychological struggles or his social mobility through literature – it is either too general or too specific to be of much use in thinking about the later eighteenth century. There is a curious logic in expressions like 'the Age of Johnson', for even though they isolate an individual and draw attention to his singularity they can do so only because he marks the times by memorably repeating something felt to be there. So Johnson, valued for being himself, is divided. He becomes a sign, indicating not just himself but something else. He does this only under the sign of death, in the pages of the biographies about him, especially Boswell's. There not only is Johnson brought into presence but also a highly skewed vision of his times. How this occurs is something I will turn to in the following chapter, but there is a matter that needs attention now.

The claim that Johnson represents his age relies on another claim that passes by without drawing attention to itself, namely that literature is a true and proper medium in which that kind of representation can occur. According to this assumption, literature is capable of suspending an epoch, of revealing its reality without reference to material institutions like Church and State. In reading an age's literature we experience directly its people's hopes and fears, their pleasures and pains. To object that the other arts do exactly the same, that one can get as good a grasp of the times by viewing Hogarth's paintings or listening to Handel's music is right but mistaken. The claim that literature enables us to understand an epoch and to render it present to us can be used equally well for music or painting, but literature has quietly taken primacy partly because of its links to literacy and partly because, as Arnold and Herder both stressed, the various projects of culture work more perfectly through language and literature than the other arts. One does not need to read Johnson for this to happen, any more than one has to read Shakespeare for it to happen; it is enough that they are ensconced as national literary figures. Indeed, as we have seen, literary historians have tended to stress that Johnson the man is more significant than Johnson the author. This move can be made with any writer, even one whose literary genius is not in doubt and about whom we know very little. For instance, here is Dryden in a famous passage in *An Essay of Dramatic Poesie*. Shakespeare, he writes,

was the man who of all Modern, and perhaps Ancient Poets, had the largest and the most comprehensive soul... If I would compare him [Jonson] with *Shakespeare*, I must acknowledge him [Jonson] as the more correct Poet, but Shakespeare the greater wit. *Shakespeare* was the *Homer*, or Father of our Dramatic poets; *Johnson* was the *Virgil*, the pattern of elaborate writing; I admire him, but I love *Shakespeare*.[69]

'I love *Shakespeare*': and there can be little doubt it is the man that Dryden has in mind. The case of Johnson is a little different since he is a biographical subject, perhaps the most familiar in the language. Yet precisely by being distanced from his writing Johnson can stand for eighteenth-century British culture as a whole and not just its literature. People can speak of 'Capability' Brown, Chippendale, Gainsborough, Handel, Hogarth, Kent and John Wesley as all living in the age of Johnson.[70] So Johnson becomes the bass voice of the epoch, the voice, as Walter Raleigh put it, of 'a kind of Chairman to humanity, whose business it is to cry "Order, Order", an embodiment of corporate tradition and the settled wisdom of the ages'.[71]

Few writers can elicit this class of rhetoric, for good or ill. Goethe is one. Where the idea of a *Goethezeit* can be sharply criticised for imposing a false unity on a period divided by the French Revolution and by Germany's later cultural and political changes, 'the Age of Johnson' can be placed between two ruptures, both of which were resisted in Britain: the Jacobites of 1745 and the Jacobins of half a century later. More than that, it is because it comes just before a time of tremendous social unrest and cultural change and because its years can be seen, under the distorting lens of ideology, as relatively stable and unified, that it is an 'age' at all. W. J. Dawson argues that the epoch was divided in Johnson. 'Two periods met in him', he suggests, 'he was the last man of the one and the first of the other; the last great English author who wrote dedications to wealthy patrons, and the first to cast himself boldly on public appreciation for support'.[72] It is too neat – surely Pope called on the public in just that way through subscriptions to his Homer – yet the general point can still be taken. The *Goethezeit* can be questioned, further, for implying that Goethe served as standard model for the literary activity of his generation.[73] And much the same case can be made with respect to Johnson. In the final analysis, the 'Age of Johnson', like the *Goethezeit*, is an imaginary social space, a world where characters perform and not the changing and chancy historical world where people live and die.

Let us pause for a moment. It has become clear that the transmission of Samuel Johnson is a complex affair, though to get a sense of its origins and destinations we have to realise that the name 'Samuel Johnson' occurs not just in one register but in at least three.

First of all, the name refers to someone whose writings impinge on other readers and writers; it figures in the discourses of literature. The plural – discourse*s* – is needed for several reasons. One need not go past Johnson's criticism to trace a semantic shift from 'literature', meaning secular learning in any number of genres, to 'literature' meaning imaginative writing in poetry, prose fiction and the drama. For those who inherit and naturalise the second sense of the word, the Romantics and post-Romantics, much of Johnson's own writing no longer counts as literature. His versions of Juvenal's satires and the elegy for Dr Robert Levett do not suffice for him to be remembered as a poet (and when T. S. Eliot crowns him a major poet solely on the basis of 'The Vanity of Human Wishes' we see Eliot's anti-Romanticism collapse into special pleading). *Irene* cannot support claims for Johnson as a dramatist, nor *Rasselas* as a novelist. Therefore (and we have to imagine the word said by a literary historian, not a logician) Johnson enters posterity primarily as a critic and moralist, a designation that brings the *Lives of the Poets*, some of the periodical papers, and the edition of Shakespeare to the fore while leaving everything else out of focus or out of ken.

In the early years of the century Johnson becomes a significant factor in the academic discourses of literature. His name had extensive organisational power in the institutional rise of literary criticism in general and in eighteenth-century studies in particular.[74] This is more apparent in the United States than in Great Britain, partly because of the nature of the North American curriculum and partly because of a greater professionalisation of studies on that side of the Atlantic.[75] On the east coast of the United States, at Columbia, Harvard, Princeton and Yale, the eighteenth century was approached as the 'Age of Johnson'. This professional concern with Johnson goes hand in glove with amateur interests. The various Johnson Societies of the world to which many scholars belong and contribute is an obvious example, though not the only one. Chauncy B. Tinker was a collector of Johnsoniana as well as a university professor, and some of his students became key benefactors and collectors themselves, not the least of them being Edwin J. Beinecke

Sr and Paul Mellon. It was Mellon who established the Old Dominion Foundation which, in 1949, enabled Yale to purchase the Boswell papers and deposit them in the Beinecke Library. R. B. Adam of Buffalo, followed by his son, built up a fine library of Johnson and Boswell, while collectors of eighteenth-century materials like Arthur Houghton, Donald and Mary Hyde, and Ralph Isham, made possible the prestigious Yale editions of Boswell and Johnson.

Although this first entry of 'Samuel Johnson' might seem the obvious one to make, his reception history tells another story, that Johnson the character or personality is to be preferred. That this is a view that begins before Boswell, although the successes of his *Tour* and *Life* contribute to it, is richly supported by Macaulay and Carlyle, and it becomes a loose orthodoxy, even in academia and even in eighteenth-century studies, until well after the Second World War. Boswell's *Life* has so often been taken as the natural and inevitable guide to Johnson that it will take more than a vigorous demythologising to change that state of affairs. To think of Johnson primarily, even crucially, as a character is not simply an historical mistake that can be corrected and set right: readers from all spheres make powerful transferences onto Boswell's Johnson, they respond to the charismatic authority that Boswell and others felt, and here more than elsewhere rational argument cannot make as much headway as one might like to think it can.

The expression 'charismatic authority' is not Freud's, as my context might imply, but Max Weber's. He distinguishes it from two other domains of authority: that based on rational grounds (an appeal to legality), and that based on traditional grounds (an appeal to past practice). Charismatic authority, by contrast, rests 'on devotion to the specific and exceptional sanctity, heroism or exemplary character of an individual person, and of the normative patterns or order revealed or ordained by him'.[76] To be sure, Johnson could never be a pure case of such authority, if only because he wholeheartedly accepted the rights of Crown and Mitre. That said, there is no doubt that his charisma affected a number of his contemporaries, especially the so-called 'Johnson circle'. It was experienced in different ways and to different extents: Boswell's devotion was doubtless not the same as Burke's. A similar regard for Johnson can be found in a number of Johnson Societies. To take an extreme example, in 1988 the Bishop of Oxford who was then serving as President of the Johnson Society (Lichfield) entitled his presidential address 'Johnson – A Church of England Saint?' and concluded by offering a draft of a commemoration service for Johnson. The collect gives the flavour of the whole:

Almighty God, in whose hands are all the powers of man and by the inspiration of whose Spirit thy servant Samuel Johnson gave ardour to virtue and confidence to truth, direct, we beseech thee, our desires and fortify our purposes, that being enlightened with the knowledge of thy will, we may be invigorated with resolution to obey it through Jesus Christ our Lord. Amen.[77]

It can come as no surprise after hearing of Johnson as a Church of England saint that his name is associated with a cultural nationalism. This too works in several ways, the most familiar of which is surely Boswell's repeated description of Johnson as 'a true-born Englishman'.[78] This John Bull figure has prejudices that extend 'not only against foreign countries, but against Ireland and Scotland' (*Life*, I, 129–30). Boswell's anxieties about being a North Briton aside, 'England' for Johnson cannot be satisfactorily defined geographically; it is crosshatched with social and religious values. I have already touched on this when discussing the *Dictionary*, and it is no less apparent in his *Lives of the Poets*, commonly regarded these days as having helped to establish a national literature, if not a national canon. As that hesitation indicates, caution is needed here – and an example should indicate why. In a recent study John Lucas argues that Johnson's last work 'collaborates with and endorses the notion of cultural nationality that Dryden virtually inaugurated', which sounds plausible enough, although it skips past works like William Camden's *Britannia* (1610) and Michael Drayton's *Polyolbion* (1612–22). Lucas goes on to deduce that Johnson's *Lives* 'therefore has to leave out of account, or downgrade, writers who implicitly or explicitly contest that notion. Milton is more or less anathematised, Bunyan – the author of some very remarkable poems – ignored.'[79] True enough, the monarchist Johnson rides hard over Milton's republican politics, yet *Paradise Lost* is commended as the second finest epic ever written, hardly an anathematising for a poet whose book is ranked above the *Odyssey* and the *Aeneid*. It is true also that Johnson would scarcely have sympathised with Bunyan's non-conformism, yet *Pilgrim's Progress* was amongst his favouite reading, and the poets to be introduced in the *Lives* were determined almost entirely by the booksellers for reasons to do with maintaining copyright and competitive edge rather than generating national feeling or forming a canon.[80]

The Johnson who is made to collude with a cultural nationality is not only the author of the *Lives* but also a semi-legendary figure whose name carries more weight than all his works. This figure appears most forcefully in Victorian and Edwardian England and more explicitly in the context of Johnson societies than in the academy. Thus Lord Rosebery, addressing the Johnson Society at Lichfield in 1909, roundly declares of

Johnson, 'He was John Bull himself. He exalted the character, of which he may be regarded as its sublime type, but he embodied the spirit'.[81] And when the nation is under threat that character can be shaped to distinct rhetorical ends. For example, here is Sir W. Ryland Dent Adkins proposing the toast of 'The Immortal Memory of Dr Samuel Johnson' at the 1916 Birthday Celebration at Lichfield:

> Whatever else Samuel Johnson was, he was one of the most typical Englishmen who ever lived. He was one of those Englishmen who were not only marked illustrations of the characteristics of the race, but he, as it were, hugged those characteristics. He would almost rather have the foibles of an Englishman than the merits of another country, and in this gigantic war in which the whole future of our race throughout the world was involved they [*sic*] were thrown back upon the notion of race and nationality. Therefore they were specially attracted, or should be, to a man who was the quintessence of the English characteristics.[82]

'Johnson' has become a proper name charged and re-charged with ideology, one that circulates without reference to his written works and that caricatures even Boswell's Johnson. Certainly, though, the *Life* has been used to patriotic ends. A vivid instance can be found in the London *Times* for 17 December 1943, an anniversary of Johnson's death. It is announced there that the King and Queen's annual Christmas gift to 'British prisoners of war and interned persons in Europe' will be the Clarendon edition of the *Life of Johnson*. 'One hundred and twelve sets were sent off by the Indoor Recreation Section of the Joint War Organization from June onwards, so that each camp in Germany should have the royal gift set in its library by Christmas.'[83] It was a suitable choice partly because the *Life* can be enjoyed piecemeal but chiefly because it covertly explains to the interned why they have been fighting for England and why they are now suffering for it. Their sacrifice is for the country that produced a man like Johnson, a man who can be identified with the language they speak and who, as John Bailey had put it a generation before, was 'the most national of our men of letters' and who had 'a sort of central sanity ... about him which Englishmen like to think of as peculiarly English'.[84] It was ideologically appropriate that the gift be the *Life* and not an older edition of Johnson's *Works*. For Johnson saw all too clearly how a solider was forced to live in times of war, and English soldiers may well have found themselves reading from 'Thoughts on the Late Transactions Respecting Falkland's Islands' (1771):

The life of a modern soldier is ill represented by heroick fiction. War has means of destruction more formidable than the cannon and the sword. Of the thousands and ten thousands that perished in our late contests with France and Spain, a very small part ever felt the stroke of an enemy; the rest languished in tents and ships, amidst damps and putrefaction; pale, torpid, spiritless, and helpless; gasping and groaning, unpitied among men made obdurate by long continuance of hopeless misery; and were at least whelmed in pits, or heaved into the ocean, without notice and without remembrance ... (Yale, X, 370–71)

The King and Queen could not have allowed those words to come into the hands of English soldiers. It was politically preferable, in every sense, that prisoners of war be exposed to Johnson the man rather than that dangerous fellow Johnson the writer.

CHAPTER 3

Property lines

Let us return to Carlyle for a moment. The hero as man of letters is a new phenomenon, he says, a man who rules from his grave. Why new? He tells us in the very first phrase of the passage I quoted in the last chapter, 'He, with his copy-rights...' The man of letters is not someone who simply interprets the 'Divine Idea', he has a secular legal existence as well. Two codes are at work here, and if we go back to 1759 we can see them cross one another in a manner that was to seem natural for later generations: 'let not great examples, or authorities, browbeat thy reason into too great a diffidence of thyself: Thyself so reverence, as to prefer the native growth of thy own mind to the richest import from abroad; such borrowed riches make us poor.' This is Edward Young in his *Conjectures on Original Composition,* and his message is plain: the true genius looks within for inspiration. No sooner are we directed inside ourselves, though, than we find ourselves returned to the market place. 'The man who thus reverences himself, will soon find the world's reverence to follow his own. His works will stand distinguished; his the sole property of them; which property alone can confer the noble title of an *author*; that is, of one who (to speak accurately) *thinks,* and *composes*; while other invaders of the press, how voluminous, and learned soever, (with due respect be it spoken) only *read,* and *write.*'[1] Originality comes from within, it is proper to a writer, and is his property.

Young's theme that originality is found in inwardness belongs to a historical sequence that goes back at least as far as the Pseudo-Longinus in the first century whose treatise on the sublime had been revived to increasing acclaim in the seventeenth century. What intrigues in the remarks I have quoted from Young is the introduction of the word 'property' in the context of aesthetic theory. Its value in the *Conjectures* is uncertain. With hindsight we can see Young speculating on originality at a moment between personal experience and act of law, with his sombre long poem *The Complaint; or Night Thoughts* (1742–45) behind him and with legal questions of intellectual property to be answered finally only after his death. As we have seen, those questions had come to the fore in 1709 when an act was passed, 'An Act for the Encouragement of Learning', known as the Statute of Anne, which brought both relief and worry to the London booksellers. There was relief because, with the lapsing of the Licensing Act in 1694, there had been a ruinous free-for-all with Irish and Scottish booksellers. And there was concern because the statute perplexed the common law understanding of copyright. The statute limited the copyright of books, until then mostly owned outright by the powerful London booksellers, to twenty-one years for works already published and to fourteen years for works that appeared after 1 April 1710. To the anxious London booksellers it looked as though provincial booksellers would be able to publish titles whose copyright had expired. And it also looked as though authors would be able to own the copyright of their works.

In practice, however, the London booksellers steadily maintained that copyright had not really changed; it was still at heart a matter of common law: a book was like any other property, owned in perpetuity, not a special sort of property that could change hands after a number of years had passed. The booksellers tried, predictably, to have perpetual copyright affirmed by statute in 1724, when the first term of fourteen years was up, and in 1731, when the first term of twenty-one years had run its course. They met with no success until, in 1769, when hearing the case of *Millar* v. *Taylor*, the Court of the King's Bench declared in favour of perpetual copyright. The matter seemed settled. Then, two years later, an Edinburgh bookseller by name of Alexander Donaldson invaded the property of a London bookseller, Thomas Becket. The consequence was the case of *Donaldson* v. *Becket* which was heard by the House of Lords in 1774: the earlier decision of the King's Bench was overturned and it was finally ruled that literary property was a statutory and not a common law right. In one sense nothing had changed; there was no new law. Yet in another sense a new balance in the literary world had been struck. From now on booksellers outside London could publish the works of poets whose copyright had expired: cheap editions of individual works and selections of the English poets could be prepared for the press. And from now on authors were legal owners, their property being none other than their works. Johnson's famous letter to Lord Chesterfield of 7 February 1755 is a familiar index of the decline of patronage (though one that must be read alongside the dedications to patrons that he continued to write for friends).[2] The Lords' decision can stand as another emblem of that same decline.

The Lords' decision ran with the grain of John Locke's influential theory of property as outlined in his second treatise on government. 'Property', for Locke, designates the rights to one's person as well as one's land and goods, and in that sense the individual's right to property precedes any claims of the State. With this in mind, the heart of Locke's theory can be found in one memorable sentence about the man of property: 'Whatsoever, then, he removes out of the State that Nature hath provided, and left it in, he hath mixed his *Labour* with it, and joyned to it something that is his own, and thereby makes it his *Property*.'[3] So wrote Locke in 1690, and at a pinch one could construe the Lords' ruling in 1774 to imply that the author's act of writing was a mixing of labour with natural genius. The Statute of Anne had already made moves in that direction. Now that the Statute had been confirmed, writers could begin to enjoy some of the pleasures of possessive individualism that Locke had bequeathed to all in theory.[4] No longer could there be a family business like that of Jacob Tonson and son which largely owned the property rights to Addison, Congreve, Dryden, Milton, Shakespeare, Spenser, not to mention several others.

With the Lords' ruling, writers did not all become rich but they all became authors.[5] This may look like the law catching up with philosophical insight, but that would put the matter oddly. Aesthetics is not necessarily done in a philosophical vocabulary or in the quiet of a study. It can be done in legal argument, and done well. From the perspective of contemporary literary theory, it was in the cases of *Millar* v. *Taylor* and *Donaldson* v. *Becket* rather than in the volumes of Lord Kames and Joseph Priestly, that the question of textual borders was most rigorously posed and the values of signatures most finely determined.[6] Even if English literary theory often adduces another genealogy for itself, citing Coleridge as father rather than Blackstone, there is no doubt that modern thinking about literature has been traversed by questions of relating originality and alienation, insides and outsides, the rights of the individual and those of the public: in short, questions of the law of the proper and the proper of the law.[7]

That said, the Lords' decision concurred with a growing sense of the value of originality in writing. A new discourse was in the air. As it happened, Young's *Conjectures* was to have greater influence later on the continent, where a philosopher like Fichte was more comfortable with metaphors like 'native growth' than were the more empirically minded literary men of Britain. But the treatise was not the first or only place where the idea of originality was urged on the public. Young had already raised it in his essay 'On Lyric Poetry' (1728), and in any case it would be more accurate to say that he ordered and intensified a number of ideas currently circulating in England and France than to suggest he proposed an original theory of originality. When Johnson heard Young read from the *Conjectures* at Samuel Richardson's house he was surprised, he said years later, 'to find Young receive as novelties, what he thought very common maxims' (*Tour*, 269). Originality had long been in the air, and Johnson had long prized it. A popular image of Johnson is of someone standing indomitably at the antipodes of Romanticism, fearing that an unrestrained imagination will bring madness in tow. This image is accurate if 'imagination' be glossed as 'fancy', but even so Johnson always judges poetry first and foremost by its power of invention. This power gives authors 'a stronger right of property than that by occupancy', he said in conversation the year before *Donaldson* v. *Becket*, 'a metaphysical right, a right, as it were, of creation, which should from its nature be perpetual'. And yet, Johnson added, an author should not be entitled to remove a work from the public sphere, the very place where it can benefit 'the interests of learning' (*Life*, II, 259).[8] So for Johnson the metaphysical gives way on this point to the social.

Originality in poetry was not the Lords' interest in any shape or form, yet after their judgement in 1774 the notion that what is valuable in a work is its originality is indirectly strengthened. Of social curiosity already for his genius, the author now had rights to the labour of that genius and could raise himself more surely in society. The writer's internal property, an animating genius, is projected onto a social grid where it can be recognised as a legal right. This alteration in the status of writers is easily documented, and should be viewed against an interest in composition that steadily grew over eighteenth century. One index is Aaron Hill's posthumous opera, *The Muses in Mourning*, most likely dating from the 1730s, where the Genius of England declares to the Muses:

> – All England writes;
> Learn'd, and unlearn'd, each sex, all ages, write!
> Untaught, unask'd, unprais'd, unread, they write.[9]

In 1753, thinking of the increasing number of books pouring from the presses, Johnson had styled his times 'the Age of Authors', and in 1774, responding directly to the new ruling on intellectual property, the

Monthly Review had declared it to be the 'Golden Age of Authors'.[10] The magazine's adjective was apt for more than one reason. There were more writers, they enjoyed new privileges, there had been a tremendous rise in both population and literacy over recent decades, and the print revolution had been making the production and dissemination of books and pamphlets more economically feasible.[11] But since authors had proven themselves to be of increasing interest their lives were also becoming objects of public attention.

The old distinction between public and private was slowly being adjusted as far as writers were concerned. The change in the copyright law was helping to redraw the borderlines, as was the growing phenomenon of literary fame; and, inevitably, so was the fact that authors were themselves becoming the subjects of biographies. The last things that could be alienated from writers, their lives and personalities, were becoming valuable property. And it was not always their property. As a group, authors were beginning to feel the force of Addison's remark in the *Freeholder* that Johnson had mischievously quoted to illustrate the word 'biographer' in his *Dictionary*: 'Our Grubstreet *biographers* watch for the death of a great man, like so many undertakers, on purpose to make a penny of him'. And indeed 'characters', lives, memoirs and portraits – everything that is today subsumed under the heading of life-writing – had been immensely popular for well over a hundred years, though until the mid to late eighteenth century literary figures had been marginal as subjects. More energy had been devoted to criminal lives.[12] One has to look closely, but over the seventeenth century one can make out a growing interest in keeping track of writers amongst other notables. Some literary names can be found in weighty historical compilations like Thomas Fuller's *History of the Worthies of England* (1662), Edward Phillips's *Theatrum Poetarum Anglicanorum* (1675) and Anthony Wood's *Athenae Oxonienses* (1691), even if they preserve no more than the skeletons of people and do so as part of a national memorialisation of celebrated names.

Somewhat different in tone and style from these tomes or tombs is Thomas Sprat's 'An Account of the Life and Writings of Mr Abraham Cowley Written to Mr M. Clifford'. Prefixed to the 1668 edition of the poet's *Works*, the essay sketches Cowley's virtues while studiously avoiding all intimate details that could be gleaned from his personal correspondence. In his private letters to friends, Sprat says, Cowley 'always express'd the Native tenderness, and Innocent gayety of his Mind. I think, Sir, you, and I have the greatest Collection of this sort.

But I know you agree with me, that nothing of this Nature should be published...'[13] Old-fashioned readers a century or so later might momentarily feel they should agree as well, but if truth be told it was intimate details of club and family life, of friendships and solitudes, that tended to capture their imaginations. William Mason's *Memoirs of Gray* (1775) set a fresh example for biographers by being little more than an arrangement of the poet's letters. 'How it is liked, I do not yet know', wrote Horace Walpole to Mason on the book's publication, 'Were I to judge from my own feelings, I should say there never was so entertaining or interesting a work: that it is the most perfect model of biography; and must make Tacitus, and Agricola too, detest you.'[14] Startling as Mason's style of biography seemed to be at the time it did not break all the proprieties at once, for letters were silently edited to keep private details from public view. If the people who might dip into Mason to overhear Gray going about his daily life were at all drawn to the life-writing of the previous century they would bypass works like Sprat's account of Cowley and linger instead over a work like Izaak Walton's *Lives* (1670). For here was a book which, while leaning toward encomium, sympathetically shows aspects of the everyday life of writers the stature of John Donne and George Herbert. It was amongst Johnson's favourite reading, and in the *Rambler* he gives us an idea why: 'more knowledge may be gained of a man's real character, by a short conversation with one of his servants, than from a formal and studied narrative, begun with his pedigree, and ended with his funeral' (Yale, III, 322).

To pass from Walton to Johnson is to leap over a vast amount of life-writing, though not much about authors, the bulk of which can be found in the first attempts at English literary history and the biographical encyclopedias that continued to appear and even to improve.[15] With its fuller entries, Thomas Birch's *Biographia Brittanica* (1747–66) was of use to Johnson while meditating his *Lives*, and at one time he had been asked to take on a new edition of it. And yet in 1777, when writing on Cowley for the first of those *Lives*, Johnson got no further than his opening sentence before complaining of 'the penury of English biography', by which he meant the paucity of lives of authors. And Sprat's 'Account' is now mostly remembered because it is named as an exception to this general state of neglect. The complaint about literary biography had not suddenly occured to Johnson in old age. His current work was composing prefaces 'Biographical and Critical, to each Author' for *The Works of the English Poets*, a huge anthology financed by a syndicate of London booksellers. It was a consequence of the new law on literary property. The London booksellers needed to secure their property in the English poets, especially those of the Restoration, against an invasion from Martin's, a firm of Edinburgh booksellers whose works were being sold in London by Bell. How to compete with a cheap northern edition? By producing a more attractive and more accurate text, for one thing, and by getting the most authorative critic of the day, Samuel Johnson, to write prefaces, for another.

Johnson's interest in literary biography had different and far deeper roots than this particular publishing project. In the case of his own writing there were those early lives of Browne and Sydenham, not to mention his passionate *Life of Richard Savage*. More generally, though, he had felt the need to make a case for literary biography when writing the *Idler*:

It is commonly supposed that the uniformity of a studious life affords no matter for narration; but the truth is, that of the most studious life a great part passes without study. An author partakes of the common condition of humanity; he is born and married like another man; he has hopes and fears, expectations and disappointments, griefs and joys, and friends and enemies, like a courtier or statesman; nor can I conceive why his affairs should not excite curiosity as much as the whisper of a drawing room, or the factions of a camp. (Yale, II, 312)

The emphasis is on 'curiosity', and Johnson goes on to talk of the 'very amusing scenes' that lives of authors could provide. What captivates and instructs is how a single life, whether of an author or a soldier, crosses 'the common condition of humanity'; and what must be preserved are (as he says elsewhere) 'those minute particularities which discriminate every man from all others'.[16] In his longest and most memorable lives, those of Savage, Dryden and Pope, there is a respectful attention to the uniqueness of each man, and an unfeigned interest in the individual as he goes about ordinary life. Yet the works of his day that focus most self-consciously on 'minute particularities' are neither Johnson's lives nor Mason's *Memoirs* but Boswell's *Corsica*, *Tour* and *Life*, and they attend not only to the heroic individual but have the effect of representing individuality as a prime value.[17] These are powerfully original works, narratives that marked a change in the art of biography.

Boswell took pains over his titles, both in their content and presentation. If one looks at the corrected proof of the *Tour*'s title page, one sees a handwritten note by his friend, the great Shakespearean editor Edmond Malone, pointing out that the page looks as though it were from a book of the previous century. It was changed accordingly.[18] The expanded title focuses almost exclusively on Johnson; and the book contains, we are told, 'Some Poetical Pieces by Dr Johnson, relative to the TOUR, and never before published; A Series of his Conversation, Literary Anecdotes, and Opinions of Men and Books', and then, in a careful phrasing that was summarily approved by George III during an interview at court, 'With an Authentick Account of The Distresses and Escape of the GRANDSON of KING JAMES II in the Year 1746'.[19] It is instructive to compare that with the title of the *Life*, which I give in its original layout:

THE

L   I   F   E

OF

SAMUEL JOHNSON, LL.D.

COMPREHENDING

AN ACCOUNT OF HIS STUDIES
AND NUMEROUS WORKS,

IN CHRONOLOGICAL ORDER;

A SERIES OF HIS EPISTOLARY CORRESPONDENCE

AND CONVERSATIONS WITH MANY EMINENT PERSONS;

AND

VARIOUS ORIGINAL PIECES OF HIS COMPOSITION,

NEVER BEFORE PUBLISHED:

THE WHOLE EXHIBITING A VIEW OF LITERATURE AND
LITERARY MEN IN GREAT-BRITAIN, FOR NEAR
HALF A CENTURY, DURING WHICH HE
FLOURISHED.

From the outset it is made plain that the *Life* is not only a biography of an impressive man but also an account of the 'half a century, during which he flourished'. Boswell was not the first to see his friend as an immensely valuable piece of cultural property. In 1764 David Erskine Baker began a piece on Johnson, then very much alive, by evoking 'This excellent Writer, who is no less the Glory of the present Age and Nation, than he will be the Admiration of all succeeding ones...'[20] And of course there was the flurry of lives of Johnson that appeared before the *Tour* and *Life*. But Boswell was the first writer whose works about Johnson would bear persistent repetition. More than that, they came to be more popular than his friend's writings themselves and to become a privileged site of discussion about the eminent lexicographer and moralist and whatever it was he 'embodied' or 'represented'. It is an edition of the *Life*, remember, and not of Johnson's *Works* that brought forth Carlyle's and the first of Macaulay's two stirring essays on 'Dr Johnson'. Markedly different editions of the *Life* and the *Tour* appeared throughout the nineteenth century, as did numerous reprints, both the expensive and the cheap. There is then a plain material sense in which each text is plural, and this sense bears upon the questions at hand. If Carlyle's and Macaulay's essays helped to popularise a certain 'Age of Johnson', it was also promoted by varying editorial practices, as I shall try to show.

The expression 'Age of Johnson' nowhere appears in the *Life*, yet it none the less structures it in two quite different ways, depending on whether we take 'Johnson' as subject or object. In the first place, as we read the *Life* we follow the subject year by year from imposing child to imposing adult. No reader can possibly forget Johnson's age; both the year and his years of age are carried along the top of the outer margins. And so we read of Sam aged three, between three and eight, then between eight and ten, ten and sixteen – all quickly passing before us from 1709 until 1763 when Boswell finally meets his subject and the narrative slows down to a more human pace. 'In following so very eminent a man from his cradle to his grave, every minute particular, which can throw light on the progress of his mind, is interesting. That he was remarkable, even in his earliest years, may easily be supposed...' (*Life*, 1, 38).

In his childhood and youth Boswell's Johnson is more remarkable than he is minutely described. Almost from birth he is 'Johnsonian' in Boswell's sense of the word: at three he is that 'infant Hercules of toryism' while at about ten he is already that 'king of men' (*Life*, 1, 38, 47). These are memorable instances 'of what has been often observed, that the boy is the man in miniature: and that the distinuishing characteristicks of each individual are the same, through the whole course of life' (*Life*, 1, 47). If these emphases are very much Boswell's own, they are also Johnsonian at least in their desire to uncover early signs of later genius.[21] For Boswell, Johnson is already an individual, and he goes to some lengths to show that this unique self survives largely on its own credit which it was later to make good. Johnson's father, Michael, is introduced as being 'of obscure extraction', the story of the three-year-old poet composing an epitaph on the death of a duck is renounced – Johnson has genius enough without calling upon sentimental apocrypha for support – and the narrator is careful to report that Queen Anne's touching of the infant to cure his scrofula was 'without any effect' (*Life*, I, 34, 40, 43). All that the child inherits is 'a vile melancholy' (*Life*, I, 35). Not only is Johnson an individual but he has the makings of a Romantic individual.

Boswell will sometimes talk up a Romantic side of Johnson – his fear of death, his solitude, his preying imagination, the disparity between his mind and body, the discord between himself and his times – just as in his journals and letters he will often style himself a Romantic. He too is an original, he tells himself, though it would be closer to the mark to say he is a transitional figure, oscillating like many others of his day between the limits of 'Classic' and 'Romantic'. Certainly he is not Romantic in his emphasis on extensive empirical detail in his biographies; by and large, Romantic biographers were to follow Johnsonian portraiture rather than Boswellian exactitude.[22] Nor is Boswell enough of a Romantic individual to exclude those who leave traces in his work. While the *Life* is signed 'James Boswell' it includes much that comes from other pens. As the original manuscript of the *Life* shows, Boswell's creativity is expressed in redaction as much as in original composition. In the advertisement to the first edition we are given the image of 'the grateful tribes of ancient nations, of which every individual was eager to throw a stone upon the grave of a departed Hero, and thus to share in the pious office of erecting an honourable monument to his memory' (*Life*, I, 5). The Boswell who stretched himself out on Melanchthon's grave and promised there to honour Johnson's memory is now the chief architect of his tomb. The image suggests that people generally helped Boswell. And so they did, with stones and – unfortunately – with odd bits and pieces of stucco as well. Edmond Malone in particular encouraged Boswell to keep working, solicited material for him, helped him revise his manuscript, and advised him about printing the *Life*.[23] But not all who knew the dead man contributed. There were those, like Hawkins and Piozzi, who published rival lives (and in due course met with Boswell's rebukes in the *Life*) and there were those who simply would not succumb to his charm.

A passage from a letter by Frances Burney to her sister in late 1790, when the *Life* was imminent, suggests that Boswell was not always regarded as a proper channel for transmitting Johnson's memory. At the time Burney was a lady-in-waiting for the Queen, and Boswell caught her at the gate of St George's Chapel, and asked for her help. 'My help?', she asked.

'Yes, Madam; you must give me some of your choice little notes of the Doctor's; we have seen him long enough upon stilts; I want to show him in a new light. Grave Sam, and great Sam, and solemn Sam, and learned Sam, – all these he has appeared over and over. Now I want to entwine a wreath of the Graces across his brow; I want to show him as gay Sam, agreeable Sam, pleasant Sam; so you must help me with some of his beautiful billets to yourself.'

I evaded this by declaring I had not any stores at hand. He proposed a thousand curious expedients to get at them, but I was invincible...

He then told me his *Life of Dr. Johnson* was nearly printed, and took a proof-sheet out of his pocket to show me; with crowds passing and repassing, knowing me well, and staring well at him; for we were now at the iron rails of the Queen's Lodge.

I stopped; I could not ask him in: I saw he expected it, and was reduced to apologize, and tell him I must attend the Queen immediately.

He uttered again stronger and stronger exhortations for my retreat, accompanied by expressions which I was obliged to check in their bud. But finding he had no chance for entering, he stopped me again at the gate, and said he would read me a part of his work.

There was no refusing this; and he began with a letter of Dr. Johnson's to himself. He read it in strong imitation of the Doctor's manner, very well and not caricature. But Mrs Schwellenberg was at her window, a crowd was gathering to stand round the rails, and the King and Queen and Royal Family now approached from the Terrace. I made a rather quick apology and, with a step as quick as my now weakened limbs have left in my power, I hurried to my apartment.

You may suppose I had inquiries enough, from all around, of 'who was the gentleman I was talking to at the rails?' And an injunction rather frank not to admit him beyond those limits.[24]

It is a story of public and private borders, and for once Boswell was unable to cross either. Burney's Johnson – more often playful and affectionate than anyone else's – is not entombed in the public monument, nor does Burney's experience of life at home and court fold readily into Boswell's sense of the age.

That age is fundamentally literary, social and masculine; and while Boswell's Johnson is indeed a shared character, now and then speaking from places where the biographer could not be present, he still appears only within horizons that Boswell could countenance. At a certain stage we have to ask whether we keep Boswell and the teeming yet incomplete world he projects or we search out a fuller world where he is one amongst others. A bold answer to this question was provided by J. W. Croker in his first edition of the *Life* in 1831. Let us take a moment to look over his preface and see what he was trying to do. He begins by saying that the *Life* is itself a mixed genre, combining 'the four most entertaining classes of writing – biography, memoirs, familiar letters, and that assemblage of literary anecdotes which the French have taught us to distinguish by the termination *Ana*'.[25] If part of the *Life*'s pleasure is its formal mix, another part is social, and Croker evokes the 'delight which we feel at being introduced, as it were, into that distinguished society of which Dr Johnson formed the centre, and of which his biographer is the historian' (vi). Given this, adding to the mix and telling us more about that society should by rights give higher pleasure. And that is exactly what Croker tries to do, not just by adding notes to Boswell's already heavily annotated text but by making radical interpolations of 'numerous other authentic works connected with the biography of Johnson' (viii), which amounts to ten different kinds of material: some private papers and correspondence by Johnson, all of Boswell's *Tour*, and all sorts of contemporary memoirs by other hands.

Where some reviewers were to regard these additions by other hands as wreaking violence on Boswell's text, Croker saw himself as merely completing it. 'Notwithstanding the diligence and minuteness with which Mr Boswell detailed *what he saw* of Dr Johnson's life, his work left large chasms' (xi–xii). Not only does Johnson's death leave a chasm in history, as William Hamilton thought, it also leaves chasms in the *Life*, the very text that tries to fill it. But Croker follows the spirit of Boswell's biographical method. 'Mr Boswell endeavoured, indeed, to fill up these chasms as well as he could with Johnson's *letters* to his absent friends; but much the largest, and, for this purpose, the most valuable part of his correspondence was out of his reach...', namely that sent to Hester Thrale (xii). And if the experiment fails at least no permanent harm will have been done. 'The additions are carefully discriminated, and hardly a syllable of Mr Boswell's text or of the notes in Mr Malone's editions have been omitted. So that the worst that can happen is that all the present editor has contributed may, if the reader so pleases, be rejected as *surplusage*' (xxiii). And so it gradually was, not least of all because of Macaulay's notice of Croker's edition, surely one of the most hostile reviews ever published. With the second edition four years later most of the additions were removed, although the *Tour* remained interpolated into the *Life* until Percy Fitzgerald's edition of 1874.

That Croker's editorial principles are now regarded with scholarly horror and that they were eventually replaced altogether should not blind us to the general acceptance of his edition by most readers of the time or to a deep continuity that joins Croker and Hill. Under their guidance, the *Life* is formally a site of intertextual adventure and thematically a window onto an imagined 'Age of Johnson'. In fact precisely because of its interpolations Croker's 1831 edition gives us a kaleidoscopic, if sometimes chaotic, view of the later eighteenth century as it slowly revolves around the still point of Johnson. The conclusion of his preface is especially interesting in this regard. Had Boswell not written the *Life*,

his name could never have become – as it is likely to be – as far spread and as lasting as the English language; and 'the world had wanted' a work to which it refers as a manual of amusement, a repository of wit, wisdom and morals, and a lively and faithful history of the manners and literature of England, during a period hardly second in brilliancy, and superior in importance, even to the Augustan age of Anne. (xxx)

What is striking here is that Johnson is not even mentioned; it is his *age* that has been faithfully transmitted by Boswell, and the *Life* itself has passed from being regarded as a biography to being a 'manual' and a 'repository' before it is a 'history'.

Strangely enough, words like 'manual' and 'repository' seem less in keeping with Croker's first edition of the *Life* and *Tour* than G. B. Hill's of 1887, over half a century later. Croker adds many notes, granted, but his edition's claim to notoriety is its narrative interpolations, while Hill adds by an extensive system of footnotes which often include parallel passages. In their utterly different ways each makes a *Life* composed of many voices, more than were in the editions of the text that appeared in Boswell's lifetime or those undertaken by Edmond Malone. Hill's edition is usually and rightly seen as breaking with earlier editorial styles. It parts company with Croker's 1831 edition of course, which is severely taken to task in the preface, but just as confidently it also strikes out in a different direction from Fitzgerald's 1874 edition which is an affirmation of the text as a free-standing, artistic whole. With its web of notes, Hill's edition is to be consulted rather than read for pleasure and he candidly advises people to read the text for the first time 'in one of the *Pre-Crokerian* editions' (*Life*, I, xlii) – those by Malone, Chalmers and Walesby – thereby quietly bypassing Fitzgerald's work which prides itself on being the most readable to date and on not making the mistake of 'converting notes into text and *vice versa*'.[26] For Hill the line separating text and note is far more fluid. Not only is Boswell's narrative to be thoroughly illustrated in the new edition, but also, he announces, Johnson's conversation will receive the same full treatment. 'I have sought to follow him wherever a remark of his required illustration, and have read through many a book that I might trace to its source a reference or an allusion' (*Life*, I, xxxv). As one of Hill's contemporaries, Austin Dobson, observed of the edition, there are two ways of illustrating remarks, 'the moderate and the immoderate':

> By the one nothing but such reference or elucidation as explains the text is admissible; by the other anything that can possibly be connected with it is drawn into its train, and the motley notes tread upon each other's heels much as, in the fairy tale, the three girls, the parson, and the sexton follow the fellow with the golden goose. To the latter of these methods rather than the former Dr Birkbeck Hill 'seriously inclines', and almost any portion of his book would serve to supply a case in point.[27]

And Dobson inevitably concludes that the edition 'unquestionably errs on the side of excess'.

Excess is also a dominant theme of Fitzgerald's remarks on both Croker's and Hill's volumes. In his proposal for a new edition of the *Life*, he observes how earlier editors, beginning with Malone, have failed to respect the distinction between text and commentary by adding letters, rearranging the narrative and supplying unnecessary notes. 'Mr Boswell was in his way an artist', Fitzgerald claims – and the point is essential if he is to maintain a stress on the integrity of the text he is editing – though he goes on wildly to mistake the nature of Boswell's art in observing that 'nothing is more remarkable in his great book than the tact, the self-denial, the power of selection, and the rejection of all that is surplusage' (*Life of Johnson*: xvi–xvii). 'Are we still talking of James Boswell?' one might well ask while reading this. For what is ignored here is the Shandeyesque quality of the work, its interlacing of biography and autobiography, its flaunting of surplus in the face of an avowed mimesis. In any event, Fitzgerald's edition of Boswell will break sharply with the overloading so characteristic of Croker's edition, and the great biographer's 'work – text, notes, and alterations – will now, for the first time, be given complete, distinct, and *fenced off*, as it were, from all notes and illustrations supplied from other sources' (xix; my emphasis). A strict editorial policy is required, or else 'the tide of commentary will rise higher and higher, until at last will fairly submerge, or at least inundate, the text', and that policy is set by posing a chastening question, 'Is the particular allusion or passage sufficiently intelligible as regards the purpose for which it was introduced, viz., to illuminate not so much Johnson's life as Mr Boswell's view of that life?' (xix). Where Croker's edition of the *Life* presents an intertextual, heteroglossial extravaganza and a mosaic of an age, Fitzgerald's edition proposes a Romantic work of art and one man's steady vision of a hero. It is no wonder that the edition is dedicated to Carlyle.

Nor is it a wonder that when Hill's editions of the *Life*, *Tour* and the *Johnsonian Miscellanies* appeared some fourteen years later Fitzgerald quickly published a fiery booklet of strictures on them. Far more fiercely than Dobson, Fitzgerald castigates Hill for his 'profuse notes, which literally whelm and submerge poor Boswell'. What is worse than this, he goes on to say, these notes 'are on every conceivable subject, lack relevancy, of course, and in many instances are founded upon a complete misconception of the text'. In short, they are 'skimble-skamble' and no more than 'eccentric enquiries'.[28] Is this a question of Fitzgerald exercising aggression against a latecomer editor who has usurped his position? The question of property is raised right at the beginning with Fitzgerald objecting to Hill's talk of '*My* book' and '*My* proof sheets' when the rightful owner is Boswell (2), and matters of propriety are raised also – some of Hill's pleasantries and exclamations are felt to be out of place; but the most critical energy is devoted to showing exactly how and when Hill oversteps the limits of proper editorial practice. Fitzgerald cites a straightforward line of Boswell's, 'On the 26th of April, I went to Bath' (*Life*, III, 45), and then asks, 'What *could* be added, unless a full account of Bath, Prince Bladud, Miss Burney, etc?' Boswell's simple half sentence becomes an opportunity for Hill's notes once more to supplant the text it is meant to illumine. That feared tide of commentary is rising higher and higher. 'Dr B. Hill fancies he has "discovered" that all the Abbey bells were set ringing to welcome Boswell, and this purely gratuitous assumption requires forty lines to develop. Goldsmith, it seems, had declared in 1762 that a stranger was always thus welcomed. It does not matter that this was ten years before, and that Boswell himself makes no mention of the salute. "Humphrey Clinker" is then quoted with the same view. But are such speculations "editing"?' (Fitzgerald, *Critical Examination*, 13–14).

Or, in other words, what kind of connection should there be between text and note? For Fitzgerald the editor should not obtrude in any way; there should be no judgements delivered from the bottom of the page, moral, political or religious. Even if one excludes such value-laden comments from consideration, there are others that seem merely frivolous. We can best see what is astir by looking at one of the notes under review. This one has the advantage of having been mentioned by both Dobson and Fitzgerald. It concerns Johnson's and Reynolds's visit to Devonshire in 1762:

They left London on Aug. 16 and returned to it on Sept. 26. Leslie and Taylor's *Reynolds*, i. 214. Northcote records of this visit: – 'I remember when Mr Reynolds was pointed out to me at a public meeting, where a great crowd was assembled, I got as near to him as I could from the pressure of the people, to touch the skirt of his coat, which I did with great satisfaction to my mind.' Northcote's *Reynolds*, i. 116. In like manner Reynolds, when a youth, had in a great crowd touched the hand of Pope. *Ib*. p. 19. Pope, when a boy of eleven, 'persuaded some friends to take him to the coffee-house which Dryden frequented.' Johnson's *Pope*, 13. Who touched old Northcote's hand? Has the apostolic succession been continued? – Since writing these lines I have read with pleasure the following passage in Mr Ruskin's *Praeterita*, chapter i. p. 16: – 'When at three and a half I was taken to have my portrait painted by Mr Northcote, I had not been ten minutes alone with him before I asked him why there were holes in his carpet.' Dryden, Pope, Reynolds, Northcote, Ruskin, so runs the chain of genius, with only one weak link in it. (*Life*, 1, 377, n. 1)

For Fitzgerald this is 'another of the editor's odd dreams' (*Critical Examination*, 26), and since Ruskin did not actually touch Northcote he chides Hill with the remark 'there are two "weak links" in the chain'. The otherwise reserved Dobson is far more generous, saying, 'This is an excellent specimen of the concatenated process at the best' (147).

An odd dream and an excellent specimen! Fitzgerald and Dobson cross at such a sharp angle here that several important motifs might not be noticed.

There is the topic, first of all, of originality. For Fitzgerald, Boswell's narrative is original in two senses; it is the product of a creative mind and it is primary with respect to the activity of editing. (The question of Boswell's originality *vis à vis* Johnson drops out.) It follows from this that commentary, by definition a belated activity, must regard itself as strictly functional. The editor's task is to preserve the eternal flame of the artwork and on no account to distract from it with lights of his own.[29] In their very different ways, Croker and Hill retrace Boswell's text looking for gaps that need to be filled and, in doing so, find opportunities to display their creativity as editors. And their desires, whether conscious or unconscious, are satisfied. Croker's labours 'have obtained even more recognition than even he himself could have hoped for' ('preface', xi) while Hill's preface 'is mainly about the editor himself' (Fitzgerald, *Critical Examinations* 1).

Once the borderline between primary and secondary is transgressed by an editor questions of property come into view. Thinking of Malone and Croker amongst others, Fitzgerald describes 'the fallacy that has misled so many editors', namely, 'that they believe themselves called on to supply *a* life of Johnson, *not Mr Boswell's "Life of Johnson"* – a fallacy founded on an inartistic appreciation of the nature of a written "life", which consists of the selection of particular materials, the rejection of others, and the extraction of an orderly purpose, harmony, or theory by a single mind' (xx). Croker metaphysically invades Boswell's property by granting his contemporaries rights there; Hill maintains the empirical borderline, keeping his notes outside and beneath the text, yet writes so much by way of commentary that the printed page is divided between Boswell and himself.

Also at issue is the status of the singular, whether it be a detail or an individual. On Fitzgerald's understanding, it is the editor's task to keep details related to the whole of which they are a part. A note which draws undue attention to a detail will inevitably impair the unity (and hence the artistic value) of the work; and the situation is only exacerbated by multiplying voices, as Croker does, or by increasing associative links, as Hill does. For Fitzgerald it is ultimately a question whether the *Life* is to be regarded as art or a resource, whether Johnson is to be approached as an individual living in the eighteenth century or as an example of the age. What is overlooked here is the possibility that the *Life* is art but does not cohere into this kind of unity. In that case there will be details that resist being subsumed into a whole. And what is rightly implied is that once we regard Johnson as an example (of his age, Englishness, or whatever) he is no longer singular.

These motifs bear upon the relations between Johnson as author and as personality, and between Johnson as subject and Boswell as biographer, as well as more narrowly on the relations between text and edition. They have concerned us already and will continue to do so. For the moment we will stay with that narrow focus. Before anything else, it must be noticed that in the movement from Croker to Hill *surplusage* has not been rejected but re-situated. The *Life* has changed from edition to edition, from a forcibly mixed narrative to a restored text overflowing with commentary. In his preface Hill often underlines the amount of work he has done on this project, even in sickness. Why does he choose Boswell's text for such an exhaustive and exhausting exercise in scholarship? For much the same reason as Croker. Not because Boswell tells the story of a remarkable life, as one might think, but because it opens a window onto a glorious age. 'Had it been merely the biography of a great man of letters that I was illustrating, such anxious care would scarcely have been needful. But Boswell's *Life of Johnson*, as its author with just pride boasts on its title page, "exhibits a view of literature and literary men in Great Britain, for near half a century, during which Johnson flourished"' (*Life*, I, xxxiv).

For Hill, the England of George III recommends itself as a more stable and far less vexed community than his own. 'Those troublesome doubts, doubts of all kinds, which since the great upheaval of the French Revolution have harassed mankind, had scarcely begun to ruffle the waters of their life. Even Johnson's troubled mind enjoyed vast levels of repose' (*Life*, I, xxxi–ii). One difficulty in interpreting this remark is that the French Revolution was not a single or simple event but a process ranging from constitutional reform to revolutionary government and it is not immediately clear which aspects of it so worry Hill. The complaint does not seem to centre simply on the violence of the Revolution; after all, the Gordon Riots of 1780 were far worse than anything seen across the channel until that time, so much so that a contemporary French witness, Sébastien Mercier, claimed that such anomie could not occur in a city as well-policed as Paris.[30] Nor, I think, is Hill ignoring the poverty and appalling cruelties that Hogarth recorded, or the moral licentiousness that led George III to call the period of his reign 'the wickedest age'. What principally shocks him is not the storming of the Bastille (where in fact there was remarkably little loss of life) but the affirmative symbol of radical change that it quickly became over Europe and beyond. Following the history of his day, he doubtless credits Diderot, Rousseau and Voltaire with having more moment in precipitating the Revolution than is now generally thought they had. The 'doubts of all kinds' that agitate him might involve intellectual aspects of the project of enlightenment and almost certainly the spread of atheism but, more generally, they are likely to converge on the disruption of the entire social order from within, the upsetting of what Defoe had called 'the Great Law of Subordination' and, of a piece with that, the setting of natural rights against the longstanding claims made in the name of property. At any rate, the period in England just before the Revolution becomes for him a golden age, not just for authors but for society at large. To edit *The Life of Johnson* in his chosen manner, then, is not simply a disinterested labour in the name of aesthetic value; it has a political motivation, one that is felt throughout even though Hill's notes focus on literary rather than political life.

Let us move an inch or two closer to notice a detail that might otherwise slip away. '*Merely* the biography of a great man': Hill's words would need to be repeated slowly to be taken in. In writing them, he devalues Johnson in favour of his age and prizes his edition for preserving that age for later generations. Fitzgerald denies that Hill's books – the *Life*, *Tour* and the *Johnsonian Miscellanies* – are editions at all, they are 'simply "encyclopedias of anecdotes"' though doubtless entertaining ones (*Critical Examination*, 86). That great Boswellian, Frederick A. Pottle, takes up the idea but regards it more positively, defending Hill's 'mass of notes' on the ground that 'it is a biographical encyclopedia, and in an encyclopedia one expects to find material for which he has no immediate use'.[31] Fair enough; but it is one thing to compile an encyclopedia and another to use a book as one. Without making too much of the analogy, it might be more suggestive to say that Hill's mass of references, cross-references and appendices detailing everyone mentioned by Boswell and everything pondered by Johnson has turned the *Life* into an annotated scripture for eighteenth-century literary scholars. Certainly Hill's notes tend to be associative, and the commentary serves to extend the text into an open network of historical and literary relations. Perhaps no book has been so extensively Grangerised.[32] Unlike Croker, Hill preserves the integrity of Boswell's text, but like Croker his work yields to an intertextuality that has an air of the excessive. The *Life* has become a sacred text not because its hero can offer a secular salvation by teaching us to avoid cant (as others will claim in effect) but because the age viewed there has a special value for him; it is a golden age, a world with which he has an imaginary relationship.

When L. F. Powell came to revise the text his attitude was not that of someone editing an encyclopedia. 'I need hardly say that I have regarded Boswell's text as sacred and have not tampered with it in any way' (*Life*, I, vii). A process of sacralisation has already occured; a book has been received as literature, deemed to be a classic. Now approached as a sacred text, the *Life* cannot tolerate any split between its letter and meaning, and regardless of the universal human appeal that people claim for it and its hero, it must remain profoundly embedded in English and surrounded by notes that make it at once readable and unreadable. It is a national monument. Of what, though? Seen from one angle it is 'Dr Johnson' and from another 'the Age of Johnson'.

Dividing history into periods is one way of rendering the apparently meaningless flux of time intelligible. And in much the same way, positing a relatively stable self as hero can order an enormous amount of disparate experience. *The Life of Samuel Johnson* is not unique as a biography in searching for and using either means of unifying phenomena. Nor is it unique in using a heroic individual to organise an age. The book's singularity consists, rather, in what has proven to be its extraordinary ability to clap subject to writer, Johnson to Boswell, so that people tend to approach Johnson and his times by way of Boswell's presentation of them. In no sense, though, does Boswell regard Johnson as simply embodying his age (spiritually, for example, his guide, philosopher and friend runs counter to his times); for Boswell, the epoch is Johnson's because he towers intellectually and morally over his contemporaries. In this he differs from those cultural historians who have used the notion of an 'Age of Johnson' to orient their work. For them the later eighteenth century in Britain is a community of essence, blessedly untouched by revolutionary fervour; it is a highly stratified community, no doubt, yet one in which men and women, rich and poor, share a common humanity which is best symbolised by that lone struggling individual, Samuel Johnson. And it is a relatively short step from here, in ideological terms, to the larger and more diffuse claim that Johnson stands for a peculiarly English character and – taking another, even shakier step – that he symbolises a universal human aspiration to authentic selfhood.

There is another way of looking at the whole issue, however. Could it be that Boswell and others have misconstrued things, that the truth of the situation is that the *age* is proper to Johnson, that it is the one and only time in which he could have succeeded as he did? That at least is the judgement of Henry Francis Cary, and he expresses it at the end of his life of Johnson, the first, as it happens, of his *Lives of English Poets* (1846). Why is Johnson to be remembered?

It was the chance of Johnson to fall upon an age that rated his great abilities at their full value. His laboriousness had the appearance of something stupendous, when there were many literary but few very learned men. His vigour of intellect imposed upon the multitude an opinion of his wisdom, from the solemn air and oracular tone in which he uniformly addressed them. He would have been of less consequence in the days of Elizabeth or of Cromwell.[33]

It is not so much a negative reassessment of Johnson as a slighting of the times in which he lived – a familiar gesture of early nineteenth-century literary historians. And however much Cary may chide Johnson, it is glaringly obvious that the Doctor is still too close to him and of rather too much consequence in his mind. After all, the devaluing occurs in a volume that is, as the title goes on to admit, *Designed as a Continuation of Johnson's 'Lives'*.

Taken literally, Cary's notion of Johnson chancing to fall upon his age would lead to a strange metaphysics of man. Yet the idea of the sage's fame being largely accidental finds support from other quarters. 'If it were not for Boswell the ordinary man would never have heard of Johnson at all, and there would be no admiration society in Lichfield', writes C. E. Vulliamy, more or less repeating Macaulay's sentiments in his review of Croker.[34] The thought may even be found expressed in reverse so that chance seems like fate, as happens at the end of James Clifford's biography, *Young Samuel Johnson*. There we are asked to imagine Johnson's astonishment on learning in 1749 that 'a Scottish boy of eight in far-off Edinburgh was preparing to assist him towards immortality'. The boy himself would have been surprised to know his future. 'Jamie Boswell, conning his lessons in his father's house in Parliament Close, was also on his way towards lasting fame. Two life lines were slowly converging towards that historic meeting in Tom Davies's back parlour.'[35] Charming as it is, Clifford's image works by eliding the proposition that the young Boswell is preparing himself for later life with the proposition that he is preparing himself in order to write *The Life of Samuel Johnson*. A conjunct is added to an undistributed term, thereby generating what logicians call a fallacy of the accident. And as we shall see, accidents tend to feature when people think about the unlikely relationship of Johnson and Boswell.

One can easily overstress that the meeting between famous subject and great biographer-to-be was accidental. To be sure, in the *Life* the encounter is presented as a stroke of good fortune: 'when I was sitting in Mr Davies's back-parlour, after having drunk tea with him and Mrs Davies, Johnson unexpectedly came into the shop' (*Life*, 1, 319).[36] Unexpected it may have been at that moment, but literary London being a small society and Boswell being an eager young lioniser it was only a matter of time before it occured. As Boswell himself says before telling us about the meeting, he had been scheming to be presented to Johnson since 1760, three years before that celebrated evening in Tom Davies's back-parlour. First he talked of it with Samuel Derrick (who died before it could be arranged) and then with Thomas Sheridan (who dashed Boswell's hopes by falling out with Johnson). At any rate, the meeting between Boswell and Johnson was an accident in a perfectly ordinary sense of the word that is still in use in English today. This sense has been around since Aristotle, it claimed a place in the *Dictionary*, and it bears upon the topic under discussion.

Aristotle distinguishes two senses of 'accident': that which belongs to something but which is not required for adequate definition, and that which truly applies to something but which is neither necessarily nor usually the case.[37] It is the second sense that is pertinent here, one that Johnson defines as 'the property or quality of any being, which may be separated from it, at least in thought'. It follows from the definition that it is always possible to conceive an accidental occurence not happening, and that is exactly what Donald Greene does with the renowned event in Tom Davies's back-parlour, even to the point of imaginatively re-writing history. I want to bring Greene into the discussion for a while partly because he represents an influential critical movement to reclaim Johnson as a writer and partly because in doing so he draws the firmest property lines between Johnson and Boswell. Since the late nineteenth century there has been a reaction by scholars against Macaulay's and Carlyle's emphasis on Johnson the man rather than the writer, although the Victorian sentiment persists to the present day. 'Boswell's Johnson is more continuously and perfectly Johnson than Johnson ever was himself, but it is still the essence of Johnson, not something else.'[38] So remarked a Johnsonian biographer, Joseph Wood Krutch, on North American radio in 1942. No one more than Greene argues as forcefully and persistently against the view that the 'essence of Johnson' is found in Boswell and for the view that Johnson should be approached as a writer.[39]

Greene pictures Johnson coming into Davies's shop when Boswell is in the back-parlour having been drinking tea, Boswell asking to be introduced, and then, after a brief exchange between bookseller and lexicographer, the young visitor being ruefully told by his host, '*He said that, even had he the time, he already numbers too many Scotsmen among his acquaintance, and that life affords more fruitful sources of delight and instruction than to meet another one.*' Boswell manfully takes the rebuff, leaves, and '*Soon afterwards he had the luck to be presented to the great David Hume, who good-naturedly permitted Boswell to attach himself to him and assiduously record the minutiae of his habits and conversation. The eventual result was that greatest of biographies, Boswell's* Life of Hume, *with its unforgettable picture of the amusing eccentricities and dry wit of the aging philosopher*'.[40] It is a pleasant piece of whimsy, even if one happens to know that Boswell had met Hume in 1758, several years before he encountered Johnson in Davies' shop.[41] But why should a lapse of historical fact impair literary pleasure?

This is the very question, as it happens, that Greene persistently attributes to his scholarly opponents, those who argue for Boswell's *Life* as a supreme biography, one that forever unites Boswell and Johnson, making the two what he factitiously calls 'the Immortal Package Deal' (199). A list of these opponents would of course feature Macaulay and include later editors and biographers associated with Boswell, people like Frank Brady, Frederick Pottle, Geoffrey Scott, Chauncy Brewster Tinker and Marshall Waingrow. From time to time, sometimes by dint of their cardinal scholarly interest and sometimes in a polemic vein, these people come to be called 'Boswellians', despite their admiration for Johnson. This group is sometimes imagined to be in tension with another group, inevitably called 'Johnsonians', a number of whom argue for their man's worth irrespective of his biographer (which, for some, shades into the stronger line of 'Johnson without Boswell'); and here one would list Harold Bloom, James Clifford, F. R. Leavis and Sir Walter Raleigh amongst others.[42] Standing firmly in this counter-tradition, Greene poses a question that no Boswellian can ignore, 'What would have happened if The Meeting had never taken place?' (199) and, from this counterfactual, he develops a compound case that is elaborated though not fundamentally changed over a number of essays.[43]

Let us separate the charges. First of all, Greene maintains that Boswell had little direct influence on Johnson's writing: the sole (and admittedly egregious) exception being his *Journey to the Western Islands*. Second, he proposes that, if the meeting had not occured, 'we should know almost as much about the *essential* parts of his life as we get from Boswell' [my emphasis], since Hawkins, Murphy and Hester Thrale would have recorded 'a fair amount of his conversation and written their admirable books about him' (199); and besides Boswell is not infrequently guilty of colourings, distortions and inaccuracies in his treatment of Johnson. Third, it is suggested that Boswell's writing, especially the *Life*, has hindered our appreciation of Johnson by focusing attention on accidental matters, how the great Cham looked, talked, dressed, ate, and so forth. 'What most of us do *not* know, or care enough about, is the important thing – how his fine mind worked when it addressed itself seriously to a serious matter – that is, when he wrote' (200). And fourth, it is urged that the *Life* is not a biography at all: 'as a diary – a record, essentially, of *Boswell* – the *Life* is a work of art, a minor masterpiece. As a biography – a serious attempt to set down in coherent order the significant facts of a person's life and to make such sense of them as the writer's lights afford – Sir John Hawkins's *Life of Johnson . . .* comes closer to the ideal' (201).

There is no pain in conceding Greene's first point; it does not contribute notably to his estimation of Boswell in general or to his sense of the *Life* in particular, nor would it be contested by even the most ardent Boswellian. Let us turn then to the second and third statements. These urge that the link between Johnson and Boswell is a relation between essence and accident, that Johnson could well have not met Boswell and remained essentially the same. More than that, what has followed from the meeting has been deliterious for all but Boswell whose living and posthumous reputation has increased at the expense of his subject's. Johnson's true destiny, Greene hints, was to be remembered as an author; however, he has been recast as a character, and a slightly ridiculous one at that. Under the influence of Boswell people have attended more closely than they and we should to inconsiderable aspects of Johnson in his conversations with Boswell (which, it is implied, turn mostly on the biographer's preoccupations), and his appearance and manners in society. So not only is Boswell an accident with respect to Johnson but also the Johnson represented in the *Life* and *Tour* is a character composed more often by accidents than by substance.

Before going any further we should put to one side a couple of matters that are likely to muddy the waters. Greene is by no means hostile to a distinction between life and work being used with respect to Johnson. On the contrary, he is in favour of an historically accurate life of the man being written but thinks it should be oriented by a full and detailed knowledge of all his writings rather than by reports, especially hearsay and elaborated reports, of his appearance and conversation. Nor is Greene arguing specifically against the use of detail in the *Life* and *Tour*. His point is that some of these details are incorrect, either through error or through doctoring the facts, and more generally that Boswell often chooses to accent the wrong kind of detail – accidental features of Johnson's character and person – which have no pressing connection with his consciousness. Fitzgerald's strictures on Hill's Johnsonian editions come to mind, for once again the complaint is that there is insufficient strength of connection between the primary and the secondary. By rights, Greene thinks, Johnson should remain himself, a thinker and writer, and not be divided, contaminated or sent astray by what Boswell chooses to write about him. Since Johnson has not been allowed to remain himself, he must be restored to himself so far as possible. Hence the importance of Sir John Hawkins's biography in the eighteenth century and James Clifford's in the twentieth as preferable models to the *Life*, and hence also the rationale for Greene's own writing.

As set up by Greene, the debate with the Boswellians repeats the old division of truth versus art, this time in its empiricist rather than idealist register. Biography differs from 'imaginative literature', we are told, because biography has 'a different end, which is most simply stated by the use of a somewhat old-fashioned term, the discovery of the truth'. Nothing is said about a relationship between 'imaginative literature' and truth. The truth, it would seem, answers to ostensive reference and so associates itself with history, not literature. And, as Greene goes on to say, this truth is to be understood in terms of completeness and continuity of representation, and to be established by following the canons of historical scholarship which rest, finally, on tests of empirical verification. In addition, objectivity should not be compromised, Greene says, by the pressing need to discriminate between grades of importance in the raw material that has been gathered, or indeed by the biographer's pre-judgements of the subject. Once these principles are accepted, the *Life* is open to two different sorts of attack.[44] The first is analytic, for it follows from Greene's axioms that the *Life* cannot be both true and art. 'If Boswell is reproducing the authentic Johnson, then whatever artistry his figure displays must redound to the credit of Johnson, not Boswell. Conversely, if the figure that appears in the *Life* is an artistic creation of Boswell, then he is *ipso facto* not the Johnson who was born in Lichfield in 1709 and whose bones lie buried in Westminster Abbey.'[45] The argument fails to persuade precisely because of the great gulf fixed by definition between art and truth. Boswell may well be 'reproducing the authentic Johnson', but in doing so we would expect him to be selecting material, framing it dramatically, on the look-out for telling detail, useful variety, and so on. In other words, he will not be imagining the events in the sense of willingly deviating from lived experience but will none the less be writing with art. If distortions of historical truth occur in the process of selection that is another issue, and Greene is on firmer ground when he draws attention to these moments. This brings us to the second argument, which follows from his notion of truth. It has two prongs: the *Life* fails to offer an account of its subject which is complete and continuous (yet judiciously selected), and its details are not always narrowly verified.

The most attractive alternative to this argument has been made by Ralph Rader whose essay was pressed into service by Frederick Pottle in a spirited reply to the remarks by Greene I have been quoting. On this rival account Boswell is not offering a life of Johnson so much as a character of the man, and so the issue turns on the rightness of a dominant image of Johnson's character rather than the book's chronological completeness and exactitude. That there is such a dominant image in the *Life* is surely right: as one reads its pages for however many days it takes history seems suspended by and for this image, and more than any other single thing it is this sense of suspension which communicates an 'Age of Johnson'. For Greene, though, Rader and Pottle offer a defence of the *Life* as art not biography; and quite clearly it is the status of 'biography' that prevents the discussion from getting far. Where Pottle conceives biography in generic terms, Greene uses scientific criteria; and so where the Boswellian can think in terms of a history of biography, the Johnsonian cannot: until the proper criteria are established, it could be no more than a history of failures, some of which are more interesting or serious than others. Greene talks of the present day being the 'golden age' of biography, though from his criteria it is hard to see how it could be anything other than the one and only age of biography. Of course, the criteria which would make us reject the *Life* as biography would also make us withhold the word from Johnson's *Lives*. And one would not have to look far to find modern sets of criteria by which Johnson's criticism, translation and travel writing can be shown to be inadequate guides to English poetry, Juvenal and the Hebrides. But there will always be people who will trust the forces and lustres of a literary work rather than the new criteria.

Like most commentators on the *Life*, Greene is troubled by the gaps in the narrative. Unlike Boswell's editors, however, his response is not to fill them up by interpolations or footnotes; and, unlike at least one younger critic, he has no wish to read the work as a discontinuous narrative.[46] In fact Greene finds more gaps in the text than people have noted, those places where the *Life* differs in what it reports of Johnson's conversation from what is recorded in the original journal entry. Greene's solution to this problem of the chasm is to cut the text along the edges left by the gaps, thereby eliminating the narrative connections and the lists of acontextual Johnsoniana that give the book the misleading semblance of continuity, and so preserving only Johnson's table talk. For the Boswellian the *Life* would undergo a forced change in genre, from biography to *Tischreden*, while Greene would say, on the contrary, that the cut would mark the book's main generic trait very exactly. Where Croker, Hill and Powell add material to preserve the

Life, Greene argues for radical surgery in order to preserve Johnson intact.

If it is a 'dire heresy', as Greene says, to declare that the *Life* is no biography, then it is 'a direr one', as he cheerfully admits, to recommend this textual violence.[47] This is not an isolated use by Greene of a theological term, nor is it an entirely innocent use. In a recent essay, 'The *Logia* of Samuel Johnson and the Quest for the Historical Johnson', he steadily applies the vocabulary of form criticism to the *Life*. Ronald Knox had done something like this before in a spoof explaining the *Life*'s variety by playing on the Wellhausen hypothesis (that Genesis is a redaction of several earlier documents). But Greene shifts the ground from the Old to the New Testament. And so the *Life* becomes 'the gospel according to Boswell', playing no doubt on Augustine Birrill's 'The Gospel According to Dr Johnson', and we hear of the flourishing 'Boswellian fundamentalism' that has survived the old view that the journalist had total recall, 'a miraculous gift, not far removed from divine inspiration'.[48] Where Hill and Powell effectively sacralise the *Life*, Greene desacralises it. Had he had world enough and time it would be possible for him to add notes on the *Logia* and on what Boswell omits to a new scholarly edition of the *Life* (if it is already three volumes, why not four or five?). And in any case it would be possible for him to leave the *Life* alone and silently compete with it as biography by adding his volume on Johnson's later years to the two volumes that Clifford has given us.[49] But he prefers another course: to cut the *Life* and effectively replace it for scholarly use with the new three-volume biography.

We have been pondering Greene's question 'What would have happened if The Meeting had never taken place?', and now we need to consider another question that follows from it, though it was formulated a number of years later. It is this: 'what useful function does the *Life* now serve for the serious student of Johnson?'[50] Greene's answer is, as one might expect, that it has little use. But before flatly agreeing or disagreeing with him there are a couple of assumptions that need to be brought to light. The first is that for Greene the *Life* (and by extension all Boswell's writing and all Boswellian scholarship and criticism) can at best serve Johnsonians. While Greene rightly rejects Macaulay's Johnson he none the less keeps his Boswell, maintaining in effect that the *Life* is no more than an 'accidental masterpiece' (as Clifford accurately describes Macaulay's notion of it).[51] The accident, for Greene, however, is one that does not indicate the substance in any significant way. And this leads us to the second assumption. Who is the 'serious student of

Johnson'? Why, the one who cares about 'the important thing', how Johnson's mind worked 'when it addressed itself seriously to a serious matter – that is, when he wrote'.

This can be taken in at least three ways. First of all, there is a claim of value, that Johnson when he wrote really *seriously* on *serious* matters produced extraordinary works like 'The Vanity of Human Wishes', the *Life of Savage*, the *Rambler* and *Rasselas*, and that these amply merit and repay the sustained attention of later generations. Then there is a methodological sense, and the aim here is to set Johnson's writing above his conversation when trying to interpret that writing. Relevant here are not simply Johnson's notable publications but everything he wrote at a given time, right down to the last scribbled letter and quick review. For example, when interpreting the early poem 'London' (1738) we should not appeal to the famous quip, 'when a man is tired of London, he is tired of life; for there is in London all that life can afford' because it is possible that Boswell worked it up years later from the less resonant 'You find no man wishes to leave it'. The journal entry dates from 1777 and the fuller version from 1791. It is unlikely that the journal entry, written almost forty years after the poem, could be of much exegetical help; but even if it were felt to be, its significance would have to be evaluated in the context of Johnson's regular trips to the Midlands where, as it happens, it was uttered.[52] Now one might say that the line as quoted in the *Life* is accurate, and that Boswell only remembered it fully all those years later, or that it is an instance of Boswell's art triumphing over the literal truth. In terms of a reading of 'London' it little matters, since there are far more pressing contexts to be used when encountering that poem or any other Johnsonian text. In this case it would be unwise to venture an opinion before consulting Johnson's estimation of the Walpole administration as gathered from *Marmor Norfolciense* (1739), *A Complete Vindication of the Licensers of the Stage* (1739) and even the 'Debates in the Senate of Lilliput' (1741–44).

I do not doubt that Greene is right to prize Johnson's writing in the first sense: it is valuable material. And he is right in principle also to stress the second sense, that Johnson's writing is to be prized over his conversation when interpreting his texts.[53] Yet one must add the proviso that these writings pose various hermeneutical difficulties, not least of all because they remark different generic codes and have different signatures. There can be no straightforward passage from text to opinion. Is there a third sense? Indeed there is, although it makes itself felt more in a shadow than in a clear, hard light. We can call it ontological, for the claim is that the essential Johnson, the individual who matters to us, is Johnson the author. And Greene implies that in making this claim he is speaking in the name of Johnson by quoting from, of all places, his conversation: 'Mrs Cotterel having one day asked Dr Johnson to introduce her to a celebrated writer, "Dearest Madam", said he, "you had better let it alone; the best part of every author is in general to be found in his book, I assure you"' (*Life*, I, 450 n. I).[54] Now Greene does not hail Johnson solely as author, holding up those works signed by him externally or internally, and disregarding his life as having no permanent value. No, there are empirical accidents that should appear in a biography but their significance is to be fixed by reference to Johnson as author, the most trustworthy evidence of his consciousness at its most settled. The corpus of Johnson's writings is to be used by way of regulating the accidents that compose his life, and in this manner a certain 'Samuel Johnson' is declared true and proper to the exclusion of other possible contenders. Some accidents will indicate his substance as an historical individual, and others – often those that Boswell fixes on – will not; and only if one eliminates the latter can one prevent 'Samuel Johnson' from losing his self-identity, from dividing into a writer on the one hand and a personality on the other and so generating what Bertrand Bronson aptly called 'the double tradition of Dr Johnson'.

The salient point for Greene is to look at how Johnson's 'fine mind worked when it addressed itself seriously to a serious matter – that is, when he wrote'. It is an image of Johnson appropriating a self as he writes, reducing all accidents. Yet surely there are prominent aspects of his life that are not affected by writing or by being serious. After all, was Johnson always serious when he wrote? There is a tradition he was. Hannah More records some of his dying words to Sir John Hawkins, 'Oh! Sir, said he, I have *written* piously, it is true; but I have *lived* too much like other men.'[55] The approach of death can throw a shadow over past events that seemed morally defensible or excusable at the time, and so the distinction is perhaps not as clear cut as it sounds. And yet, if Hawkins is to be trusted, a biography that looks to Johnson's writings to economise his life will run the risk of being a pious mystification. We know from Boswell and others that Johnson wrote in solitude and that when he was in company he often talked for victory, and simply knowing this inclines one to trust his writing more than his conversation. The point is reinforced by Johnson's remark in *Adventurer* 85 that in talk one will be tempted to use rhetoric rather than dialectic, and 'thus the severity of reason is relaxed' (Yale, II, 416). That Boswell's Johnson succumbs to this temptation invites parody, as in the Reverend Simon Olivebranch's hilarious account of Johnson arguing that 'a rope-dancer concenters in himself all the cardinal virtues'.[56] All the same it is hard to sustain a sense of Johnson's essential value as author rather than conversationalist, for contemporary testimonies blur sharp distinctions between his speech and writing.

Sir Joshua Reynolds can be counted a reliable witness here, especially because in these notes written after his friend's death he stresses he is offering a portrait of the man and not a panegyric. 'It has been frequently observed that he was a singular instance of a man who had so much distinguished himself by his writings that his conversation not only supported his character as an author, which is very rarely seen, but what is still rarer, in the opinion of many was superior.'[57] This oral power came about, Reynolds says, 'in consequence of *accidental* circumstances attending his life' (67, my emphasis). Not only is Johnson's conversation at least as valuable to his contemporaries as his writings but also it structures some of his professedly serious moments. For Reynolds goes on to say that 'he would sometimes risk an opinion expressed in the strongest terms [on a book in] which [he] had read only a few lines. When afterwards he was forced to read it with greater attention in order to give an account of it as a critic, he thought it right to adhere to his first *accidental* opinion and to use all his skill in vindicating that opinion, which was not difficult for him to do' (71–72, my emphasis).

The weight of contemporary evidence makes it hard to credit Johnson as author at the expense of Johnson as talker. One of the quietly attractive features of the *Life* is that it shows Johnson's consciousness to be essentially open to accidents of all kinds. If Greene's aim is to put Boswell into greater perspective in Johnson's life, then that can and should be done. Boswellians have long been aware of their man's self-dramatisings. But if Greene's wish is to minimise Johnson's accidents then the danger is that Johnson might well slip from focus as a living individual who was not always in earnest, even when writing. Perhaps there were times when he was 'writing for victory'.[58] It is possible and frequently desirable to have a Johnson without Boswell, for there we see a writer of wisdom literature whose full interest and value have yet to be recognised. At the same time, though, it is possible to have a Boswell without Johnson, and there we see a remarkable diarist whose arts of self-construction and portraiture are still to be fully appreciated. Like many another biographer and critic, Greene assumes it is viable and useful to judge between Boswell and Johnson. But that cannot be done without misvaluing either or both; for neither comes close to the other as writer or character, and there is no third term – not even Greene's scrubbed and polished sense of 'biography' – that can serve as a bench mark without introducing anachronism. Yet once the assumption is discharged, we can begin to see Johnson and Boswell as independent universes: differently composed, in dissimilar configurations, ultimately heading in contrary directions but, even as we watch, still luminously passing through one another at their edges, apparently for ever.

CHAPTER 4

Subordination and exchange

There have always been people who have felt uneasy about Boswell's biographical writing, even while admiring its freshness and vivacity. Sometimes this unease centres on the image of Boswell erasing himself in order to present Johnson. Here, they say, is admiration taken to a dangerous extreme: if Boswell becomes *Johnsonianissimus* he is, in a plain and important sense, failing to be himself. Sometimes, however, the unease comes from the reverse side of this image. The complaint here is that Boswell does not erase himself sufficiently when writing about his friend and mentor. This objection is usually made by people who style themselves as Johnsonians, and we have already heard the tenor of their concern: the *Life* not only appropriates Johnson, transforming a fa-voured author into a mere character, but also misappropriates him. The *Life*, they say, is too partial and too skewed to be regarded as authoritat-ive biography, and they suggest that we seek out a Johnson without Boswell. Usually the intention is to restore Johnson as an author so that we may appreciate his writing and be challenged by his ideas. On occasion, though, there is another intention: to replace the *Life* with a more comprehensive biography, one that does justice to the early years, corrects falsifications, and that offers perspectives on the later years that Boswell was unable or unwilling to give.[1]

The Johnsonians' case against Boswell centres on the *Life*, then, and runs out of steam or into trouble when it comes up against the earlier *Journal of a Tour to the Hebrides*. It is difficult to maintain that, in this book at least, Boswell has not offered a vivid and full account of part of Johnson's life: a short stretch, to be sure, but a fascinating and intense one all the same. Johnson read the journal in manuscript, approved the image of him it presented, and declared it publishable, were the subject of interest to others. And because Johnson wrote a fine reflection on his journey to Scotland, one to which Boswell directs us at the start of his book, there is far less cause to blame the shorter work for deflecting attention from Johnson as author. The argument that the success of the *Life* has distracted people from reading the *Rambler* or the *Lives*, does not work with the *Journal* which has usually been read alongside the *Journey to the Western Islands* and even, from time to time, been bound with it to make a single volume.

So the case for reading Johnson without Boswell is weakest when confronted with the visit to Scotland. Does it follow, though, that the tour provides good reason to read Boswell and Johnson together? The best answer would be a cautious yes. For it remains unclear how this reading is to occur. One could manage it by taking *A Journey to the Western Islands* as the primary text and using Boswell's *Tour* to illuminate Johnson's reflections on Scotland in particular and his thinking in general. Such would be the strategy of a Johnsonian, committed in advance to the significance of the man and his writings. A Boswellian, however, may well choose otherwise, and regard the relationship with Johnson as an important but not all-important facet of Boswell's quest for self-understanding. And here Johnson would be given high standing in a company that includes Auckinleck, Burke, Hume, Kames and Paoli. In this chapter and the one following it, I would like to try a different reading of the *Journey* and the *Tour*, one organised around the principal motifs of both works. To formalise things a little, I will call these motifs 'subordination' and 'exchange', ordinary words and common enough in the late eighteenth century, yet they are of thematic and structural importance when reading Boswell and Johnson. Where to start? Nowhere better than the beginning of the ramble, in a moment that Johnson does not mention but that contains much that will concern him and his friend in the weeks ahead.

On Monday 16 August 1773, two days after Johnson's arrival in Edinburgh, Boswell took him to visit the Parliament House. In the *Tour* we see the two friends inspect the Advocates' Library and the *Laigh* underneath the Parliament where the records of Scotland are kept. Boswell is pleased, he tells us, to observe 'Dr Samuel Johnson rolling about in this old magazine of antiquities', and doubtless he finds the 'numerous circle ... attending upon him' equally heart-warming. The scene combines two of Boswell's most fertile interests, national pride and Johnsonian greatness, and there is inevitably a struggle between them. Which will frame which? Or will both frame him? Boswell begins by taking nationhood as his text: 'I here began to indulge *old Scottish* sentiments, and to express a warm regret, that, by our Union with

England, we were no more; – our independent kingdom was lost.' Then Johnson interrupts:

Johnson. 'Sir, never talk of your independency, who could let your Queen remain twenty years in captivity, and then be put to death, without even a pretence of justice, without your ever attempting to rescue her; and such a Queen too! as every man of any gallantry of spirit would have sacrificed his life for.' – Worthy *Mr James Kerr, Keeper of the Records*. 'Half our nation was bribed by English money.' *Johnson*. 'Sir, that is no defence: that makes you worse.' Good *Mr Brown, Keeper of the Advocates Library*. 'We had better say nothing about it'. – *Boswell*. 'You would have been glad, however, to have had us last war, sir, to fight your battles!' – *Johnson*. 'We should have had you for the same price, though there had been no Union, as we might have had Swiss, or other troops. No, no, I shall agree to a separation. You have only to *go home*.' – Just as he had said this, I, to divert the subject, shewed him the signed assurances of the three successive Kings of the Hanover family, to maintain the Presbyterian establishment in Scotland. – 'We'll give you that (said he) into the bargain.' (*Tour*, 40–41)

The passage is vintage Boswell in its dramatic handling of dialogue, its economy of gesture and its realism. In a short conversation we hear Johnson pass from talk of 'gallantry of spirit' and 'sacrifice' to making pointed remarks about buying troops and striking bargains. The power of money and the status of signatures will interest us in this chapter and the next respectively. Let us begin, though, with the theme of subordination, and examine it before it passes into the theme of exchange. Boswell says that subordination was Johnson's 'favourite subject' (*Life*, II, 13) and it was surely one of his own, one he often introduces into conversation or, as here, keeps in play once it has been raised, however faintly or obliquely, by someone else. Often enough the topic serves to unite Boswell and Johnson since both are in their different ways true believers in grounds and hierarchies. But Boswell's version of subordination is not always Johnson's, even though he may give one to imagine that it is. In the *Rambler* Johnson memorably evokes 'the pyramid of subordination' (Yale, v, 9), and the *Dictionary* follows the lead of this image. 'Subordination' is defined generally as, first, 'the state of being inferior to another' and, second, 'a series regularly descending'. The illustrative quotation from Dryden for the first sense indicates the word's true – social and political – weight for Johnson: 'Nor can a council national decide, / But with *subordination* to her guide'. The belief that society is arranged by degrees from king to pauper and that this order is for the good was a commonplace of the times. Swift and Pope,

Fielding and Smollett, Burke and Goldsmith, all subscribed to it to varying extents and with varying degrees of warmth. And so did Johnson, though not in all respects and not without serious reservations. It is one thing to argue for subordination as a general social principle, as Johnson certainly does: in a society with very little law enforcement subordination was an important factor in the regulation of conduct.[2] But it is quite another thing to affirm subordination as a political principle, as the Jacobites did.

Subordination as a particular political principle enters the conversation, spinning, in the allusion to Mary Stuart, better known as Mary Queen of Scots. Doubtless Johnson was talking for victory in the *Laigh*, so it is useful to recall an earlier meditation, dating from 1760, on the Queen's fate. The occasion was a review of William Tytler's study of the 'casket letters', documents used as evidence against Mary over the charge that she murdered her second husband, Lord Darnley. There too we find Johnson treating loose talk of independence with some roughness. 'We live in an age in which there is much talk of independence', he begins, but if truth be told most people are easily suborned, and this affects the reputation of Mary Stuart. 'It has now been fashionable for near half a century to defame and vilify the house of Stuart, and to exalt and magnify the reign of Elizabeth. The Stuarts have found few apologists, for the dead cannot pay for praise; and who will, without reward, oppose the tide of popularity?' And Johnson goes on to applaud Tytler for 'a zeal for truth, a desire of establishing right, in opposition to fashion' and concludes by agreeing with the author that the casket letters were in all probability forgeries.[3] This is a spirited defence of truth, though it is a long way from being an expression of political support for the Jacobites. And this needs to be kept firmly in mind, for Johnson is all too easily imagined a Jacobite by friend and foe alike. Boswell tends to play up whatever sympathy for the Stuarts his friend may have had, while Horace Walpole, in his extremely hostile character of Johnson in the *Memoirs of the Reign of King George III* has had almost as much popular influence. 'With a lumber of learning and some strong parts, Johnson was an odious and mean character. By principle a Jacobite, arrogant, self-sufficient, and over-bearing by nature, ungrateful through pride, and of *feminine bigotry*, he had prostituted his pen to party even in a dictionary, and had afterwards, for a pension, contradicted his own definitions...'[4]

These sources and others like them have enticed people to fill the gaps in our knowledge of Johnson's life in the mid-1740s with an image of him as a Jacobite fellow traveller. A popular instance is John Buchan's *Midwinter* (1923), a novel where nostalgia for 'Old England' intersects with the brutal reality of the Forty-Five. In the course of the story we hear of a tutor named Samuel Johnson who, since his conversation consists largely of apt lines from the *Life* and the *Works*, we have no difficulty in identifying. When this Johnson's politics are questioned he responds, 'being neither solider nor statesman, I am not yet called to play an overt part in the quarrel, but I am a Prince's man inasmuch as I believe in the divine origin of the Christian state and therefore in the divine right of monarchs to govern. I am no grey rat from Hanover.' Later his resolve stiffens. When a Jacobite friend declares, after hearing that Prince Charles is beating a quick retreat from Derby, that he will follow the rebel army to Scotland, Johnson adds that he has 'been minded since this morning to get me a sword and fight in His Highness's army'.[5] And only the intervention of another historical character, General Oglethorpe, prevents him from being slaughtered on Drummossie Moor.

So much for popular fiction. If we turn to history, the picture is far more shadowy and considerably more complicated. Boswell tells us that, as an older man, Johnson regarded the Forty-Five as a 'noble attempt' (*Life*, III, 162). And he also reports that his friend was uncertain on a crucial matter. If merely 'holding up his right hand would have secured victory at Culloden to Prince Charles's army', Johnson 'was not sure he would have held it up; so little confidence had he in the right claimed by the house of Stuart, and so fearful was he of the consequences of another revolution on the throne of Great-Britain' (*Life*, I, 497–98).[6] But what of Johnson the younger man? We know far more about him than used to be the case a generation ago.[7] All the evidence points to Johnson being in London immediately before and after the defeat of the Jacobites at Culloden (16 April 1745), and we know what he was writing both before and after the battle.[8] *Marmor Norfolciense* (1739), Johnson's rather heavy-handed attempt at Scriblerian irony, is of little literary interest but has been seen recently to have strong political interest. In an influential essay on Johnson's political character Howard Erskine-Hill sees 'Jacobite sedition' in the piece and regards it as 'a Jacobite tract if ever there was one'.[9] *Marmor* consists of an ancient monkish rhyme, supposedly discovered near King's Lynn in Norfolk (and therefore associated with Sir Robert Walpole), and interpreted by a lumbering commentator. Amongst other things, the rhyme tells of a horse that shall drain the blood of a lion. The lion will lie 'melting in a lewd embrace', and when the horse drinks its blood 'nor shall the passive coward once complain' (Yale, x, 25). The commentary on these lines runs as follows: 'a horse is born in the arms of H————. But how then does the horse suck the lyon's blood? Money is the blood of the body politic' (Yale, x, 41). With the accession of George I, the Hanoverian horse became a part of the royal coat of arms, and here it is seen debilitating the 'Despotic' and 'lewd' English lion.

What politics are apparent in this commentary? Jacobite values, claims Erskine-Hill, for *Marmor* is 'crypto-Jacobite' in mode.[10] 'Crypto-Jacobite' is a familiar expression to students of eighteenth-century British history, though Erskine-Hill makes it more precise in setting it between 'constrained' and 'free' Jacobite writing. To clarify the notion a parallel with David Morgan's *The Country Bard* (1739) is explored. At first sight, we are told, this work appears to be merely 'a poem of routine political opposition to Walpole, less vehement than Johnson's *London*':

A close inspection of some of the detail in its footnotes, however, suggests crypto-Jacobitism. However, one would not have inspected the footnotes closely were it not for the fact that in 1745–46 Morgan joined the army of Charles Edward Stuart at Chester, advised the Prince himself, deserted him after the retreat from Derby, and was captured, condemned to death, and executed on Kennington Common with other Jacobites who had taken up arms for their cause. By comparison with his poem, his dying speech, printed and distributed to the crowd on his death, is an example of free Jacobitism. It reveals the principles which lay obscurely behind the innuendo of *The Country Bard*, though we should hardly have found them out if Morgan had not, briefly, joined the Regent of the man he considered his true king.[11]

So *The Country Bard* can be grasped as 'crypto-Jacobite' because of David Morgan's actions in the Forty-Five and his later testimony before being executed on Kennington Common on 30 July 1746 that the accession of the family of Hanover had brought about 'all our present ills, and the melancholy and certain prospect of the entire subversion of all that is dear and valuable to Britons'.[12] Were there trustworthy evidence that Johnson had acted as John Buchan fancied him to do, there would be good reason to claim *Marmor* as 'crypto-Jacobite' writing. (Even so, there would be room for doubt: Johnson could well have changed his mind over the interval from 1739 to 1745. An anti-government stance could have hardened into Jacobite sympathy.) Yet in the absence of definite evidence of Johnson's support for Charles Edward Stuart, even of actions and words far less dramatic than those of David Morgan, we are left to negotiate *Marmor*'s ironies in the contexts that are available to us.

Someone making a case for Johnson as a Jacobite, crypto- or otherwise, could reply that hard evidence for support of Charles Edward Stuart whether in action, conversation or coded letters is extremely hard to come by, and for an obvious reason. After the Fifteen, attainted rebels were liable to have their chattels and lands confiscated or, far worse, sentenced to be hanged, drawn and quartered.[13] If such evidence is required to identify someone as a Jacobite, then the number of Jacobites in England in the 1730s and 1740s would be very small indeed, far smaller than seems plausible.[14] All that one can do is examine all the circumstantial evidence, most of which is negative in kind: what is said or written about people rather than what they say or write themselves. The historian Jonathan Clark does precisely this, yet in doing so he moves from the bold assertion 'Johnson was a Jacobite' to the more modest claim that regarding Johnson as a Jacobite must be considered 'a realistic possibility', one that cannot be proven because 'Johnson was a political realist'.[15] To be sure, there is circumstantial evidence that needs to be carefully sifted. For example, we know that *Marmor* was attacked as Jacobite writing when it was reprinted in 1775, though Johnson had been accused of having regard for the Stuarts long before then.[16] Being called a Jacobite by a contemporary or by many contemporaries does not prove that Johnson was one; one expects outspoken celebrities to attract unfounded criticism and nasty slurs, especially once they are safely dead.

When applied outside the courts to an Englishman living at home, the word 'Jacobite' could mean different things at different times; and a good deal depended on who was calling whom a Jacobite. It was one thing to be a Tory after 1714, say, and to be called a Jacobite by Walpole; another to be an 'Old Interest' Tory and be called a Jacobite by a Tory of a different stripe.[17] Being a Jacobite could refer to an activity, like belonging to the Cycle Club or, going rather deeper, corresponding with James Francis Edward Stuart or meeting with Charles Edward Stuart (William King did both).[18] It could mean that one wrote for or regularly read *Fog's Weekly Journal* or a similar publication, or that one penned material to aid the cause. More vaguely, it could mean that one was seen drinking from a Jacobite glass or heard toasting 'To all those that dare to be honest.' Or being a Jacobite could refer to a range of passive commitments, dispositions or feelings which themselves might fluctuate in intensity over time and in different companies. It could mean privately regretting the constitutional violence of James II's exile while recognising its practical necessity. It could mean sympathising with the fate of the Old Chevalier while acknowledging the Hanoverian's right to the throne by long possession. The Johnson who emerges from *Marmor* seems more of an Oxford Tory than an active Jacobite.[19] He is consistent with Mrs Thrale's older 'Mr Johnson'.[20] The 'Dr Johnson' who emerges from Boswell's pages is also an Oxford Tory, though one whose moments of sentimental Jacobitism are set in italics. What I want to suggest, however, is that the discussion about whether Johnson was or was not a Jacobite, and if so of what kind, obscures an important issue.

Although Johnson flails the Hanoverian succession in *Marmor*, there is nothing in the commentary to suggest that the lion is ultimately to be preferred to the horse. *Marmor Norfolciense* was a risky piece to publish in 1739. Walpole was to remain strong, despite growing opposition, for another two years, and the great man was still quite capable of using the spectre of 'the Atterbury Plot' to encite fear of another Jacobite invasion.[21] Perhaps Johnson went into hiding for a short while. Certainly to the extent the satire criticised George II it would have aided the Jacobite cause. Like many of his contemporaries, Johnson strenuously objected to the weakening of England by George II's bleeding of funds to Hanover. The point had already been made in *London*: 'Lest ropes be wanting in the tempting Spring, / To rig another Convoy for the K—g'. The loyal Hanoverian commentator in *Marmor* says that construing money as the 'blood of the body politic' is a 'detestable' idea, one that 'can enter into the mind of none but a virulent Republican, or bloody Jacobite'. And the point of the irony, of course, is that any honest Englishman should be thinking critically of what George II is doing without sliding into either Jacobitism or Republicanism.

Not even in *Marmor* does Johnson endorse subordination in the sense of a divine right of kings to govern, one of the main planks of the Jacobite cause. And for written testimony to the contrary we need only turn to the 1753 preface to the index of the *Gentleman's Magazine*'s first twenty volumes. Here the Forty-Five is characterised as 'a Rebellion, which was not less contemptible in its beginning than threatening in its progress and consequences; but which, through the Favour of Providence, was crushed at once, when our Enemies abroad had the highest expectations from it . . .'[22] Or we may turn to the 'Introduction to the Political State of Great-Britain' (1756) where he writes how 'the necessity of self-preservation had impelled the subjects of James to drive him from the throne' (Yale, x, 142).[23] Nor, as we will see, does he uncritically entertain a doctrine of metaphysical subordination in which reality has set orders of being. That God is ontologically prior to human beings is no doubt one of Johnson's deepest and most unshakeable beliefs, and from it stems the oft-quoted quip 'the first Whig was the Devil' (*Life*, III, 326). Yet at heart this is a question of God being the absolute ground and origin of creation (a Christian doctrine) and not a question of ontic hierarchy (a philosophical speculation). Johnson's interest in subordination is centred on what is needed for the steady governance of a country, and while that requires the principle and the reality of an ultimate power it is no justification for absolutism. Imlac tells Rasselas that 'Oppression is, in the Abissinian dominions, neither frequent nor tolerated; but no form of government has been yet discovered, by which cruelty can be wholly prevented. Subordination supposes power on one part and subjection on the other; and if power be in the hands of men, it will sometimes be abused' (Yale, XVI, 32). In practice kings and queens rarely abuse their powers to the point of oppression, yet if that abuse becomes intolerable there is no divine injunction to prevent them from being overthrown and replaced by the next in line to the throne.

Or even by someone rather remote from 'the next in line', someone like Georg Ludwig, Elector of Hanover. The Act of Settlement (12 & 13 Will. III, c. 2), passed by the English Parliament in 1701, was framed in response to the death the previous year of William, Duke of Gloucester, an event which left no heir to the throne after the deaths of William III (who was unmarried) and Anne (who had no living children). The Act provided that the crown was henceforth to go to the granddaughter of James I, the Electress Sophia of Hanover and her heirs, if they remained Protestant. William died in 1702, Anne in 1714, shortly after Sophia. It was only a matter of time therefore until Sophia's son Georg Ludwig would be invited to take Anne's place. He was duly crowned on 20 October 1714, taking preference to fifty-six Catholics with better hereditary claims to sovereignty.[24] The significance of the coronation is nicely caught by Mary Countess Cowper in her diary entry for that day. 'I saw all the Ceremony, which few bodies did, and I own I never was so affected with Joy in all my Life; it brought Tears into my Eyes, and I hope I shall never forget the Blessing of feeling our holy Religion thus preserved, as well as our Liberties and Properties.' Protestantism protected liberty and property, Catholicism put them in jeopardy. It was not the first time that Parliament had bypassed closer heirs to the throne: the cases of Henry IV and Henry VII could be cited as precedents. 'One may easily conclude', Countess Cowper goes on to say, 'this was not a Day of real Joy to the Jacobites. However, they were all there, looking as cheerful as they could, but very peevish with Everybody that spoke to them.'[25] A Tory rather than a Jacobite, Johnson would not have disagreed with the Countess's stress on 'Liberties and Properties'. For him there is something more fundamental to the social order than the direct succession that is so necessary to Jacobitism, and that is the institution of property, real and personal. In the words of one of his sermons: 'Every man must easily discern that difference in property, is necessary to subordination, and subordination essential to government; that, where there is no property, there can be no motive to industry, but virtue; and that the bad, must then always be supported by those, whose generosity inclines them to provide for them' (Yale, xiv, 291). When thinking of what is essential to government, Johnson's emphasis is on property, not royalty.[26]

This emphasis will resonate as we follow Johnson through the Hebrides. But before going any further with him we need to know how Boswell stands on these issues. Of course he agrees with his friend that subordination is necessary for good government while also being drawn at times by those '*old Scottish* sentiments' to a certain Jacobitism. He differs widely from Johnson in his ideas of 'asiatic multiplicity', male succession, and other indices of patriarchy. And he also differs from Johnson, who hated slavery, on precisely that issue. Several weeks before his *Life of Johnson* appeared, Boswell published a bizarre verse pamphlet, *No Abolition of Slavery*, half apologia for romantic love and half attack on William Wilberforce's bill seeking to end the slave trade, which was then before the Parliament. Being a supporter of slavery was not a view he worked up for the sake of a poetic conceit. Far from it. In the *Life* itself we hear Johnson at Oxford toasting 'here's to the next insurrection of the negroes in the West Indies' and then, a little later, Boswell the narrator sharply marks his distance from his friend on this issue. 'To abolish a *status*, which in all ages GOD has sanctioned, and man has continued, would not only be *robbery* to an innumerable class of our fellow-subjects; but it would be extreme cruelty to the African Savages' (*Life*, iii, 200, 204). More generally, Boswell finds himself involved in scenes of subordination in a more extended sense of the word. Sometimes subordination is regarded negatively, as with the primacy of England over Scotland since the Union, a situation that continued to niggle him till death ('I attacked the Union and said the nation was gone', he tells his journal as late as 15 February 1790).[27] At other times, as with the elevation of Johnson over other company, he views subordination as a positive good. Not everyone agreed with him. Goldsmith for one objected to Boswell's 'making a monarchy of what should be a republick', and Robertson for another felt that the biographer-to-be went too far in venturing to worship their friend (*Life*, II, 257; III, 331).

Let us return to the scene in the *Laigh* underneath the Parliament in Edinburgh. It recalls the anxious scene in London where Boswell was introduced to Johnson. There Boswell was quickly trying to extricate himself from a conversational ditch into which he had slipped and then been elbowed further in by Tom Davies. '"Don't tell where I come from." – "From Scotland", cried Davies roughishly.' Boswell tries to clamber out by saying, none too brightly, 'Mr Johnson, I do indeed come from Scotland, but I cannot help it', only to receive the crushing retort, 'That, Sir, I find, is what a very great many of your countrymen cannot help' (*Life*, I, 392). Now, in Edinburgh, it seems as though Boswell is handed a golden opportunity to replay the famous conversation with the advantage of being on home ground only to lose, once again, to the powerful Englishman's quick wit and bow-wow manner. The victory over Boswell looks conclusive. But is it? Before using the name 'Boswell' too often we have to recognise that it picks out two subjects, an actor apparently inside the scene and a reporter apparently outside it. We have seen this earlier; it is one of Boswell's most winning literary ploys. Within the scene the politics at issue are starkly presented with each 'you' and 'we' drawing a firm line. Nothing could be more plain: Johnson *is* England, Boswell *is* Scotland. The characters play out an act of disunion while talking about the Union, and the play in no sense diminishes the seriousness of their views. Moving outside the scene, we pass from an ideological conflict between Johnson and Boswell to a conflict of authority between a character, Johnson, and the narrator, Boswell.

There can be no subordination without property, says Johnson, and no stable government without subordination. Throughout the ramble Johnson is concerned with real property, but more than that it is easy enough to identify a whole lexicon deriving from the Latin *proprius* used by both writers. Both the *Journey* and the *Tour* are concerned with proper place, proper names, propriety, and the connections these have with property. Yet we might be able to get further more quickly by tracing a twist in this chain. For in discussing Ossian, the Douglas Cause, Jacobitism and feudalism, the travellers are regularly faced with questions of forgery, adultery, the breaking up of property by money, and excess. These cases recur partly because of Boswell's probing of Johnson and partly because of what is inescapably before and around them at the time. Over the course of the century England had been slowly transforming itself from a society of court and patronage to a society of commerce and law. The Highlands were late in joining that change and since the middle of the century had been undergoing a violent transition from a 'natural' to a money economy. The ancient values that so interest the travellers occur in a divided medium of evaluation, between an old system of social subordination and a new system of monetary circulation. Motifs of property and money weave in and out of the tour, here merging with law and economics, there emerging amidst ethics and literature. Nor do they remain on the one level, since what presents itself as theme can elsewhere reveal itself as structure. While Johnson's *Journey* addresses relations between property and money, Boswell's *Tour* illustrates how cultural property is formed and distributed. I will take them in turn, devoting this chapter to the *Journey* and the next to the *Tour*.

'We came hither too late to see what we expected, a people of peculiar appearance, and a system of antiquated life' (*Journey*, 46). The tour is motivated, at least for Johnson, by a desire to experience a different form of society: it is a quest for anthropological knowledge. Early on, at St Andrews and Elgin, we see Johnson tracing the foundations of an earlier culture in the ruins of two Catholic cathedrals destroyed in the Reformation. As they go forward in their time, they go backward in Scotland's time, returning to a world that had been alien even to Lowland culture since the fourteenth century.[28] And that is exactly what they want. For Johnson the tour begins in earnest only when they enter the Highlands, and the moment is documented in a telling way. 'We went forwards the same day to Fores, the town to which Macbeth was travelling, when he met the weird sisters in his way . . . We now had a prelude to the Highlands. We began to leave fertility and culture behind us, and saw for a great length of road nothing but heath' (*Journey*, 18). Johnson then notes that the Highlands declare themselves by the sight of peat fires and the use of Gaelic, yet the division between Lowlands and Highlands is marked not so much by forsaking culture as by the naming power of a privileged literary culture. 'This to an Englishman is classic ground', he observes, for *Macbeth* is indeed an English classic, even though the characters and plot were taken from Scottish history and Scottish fable. In fact, as Johnson goes on to say, he and Boswell had not yet crossed the Hardmuir which is the traditional site where Macbeth is supposed to have met the witches. But the general point remains: what falls outside the dominant culture is already marked by it.

This habit of perceiving by way of cultural insides and outsides must be taken into account in any description of Johnson's travels. And so must this: the *Journey*'s 'I' works in at least two registers. One of these is empirical. Here is the Johnson who years earlier praised another traveller, Father Jerónimo Lobo, as 'a diligent and impartial enquirer' and who values him precisely because his *Voyage to Abyssinia* pours cold water on stories of Basilisks killing with their eyes, ostriches throwing stones at their hunters, and crocodiles shedding tears (Yale, xv, 3); and here too is the Johnson who brings to Scotland an oak stick with 'one nail . . . driven into it at the length of a foot; another at that of a yard' so that his measurements of caves, stones and monuments might be exact (*Tour*, 318). The other register is speculative: here we see Johnson brooding on problems that have long concerned him, connecting general ideas to particular events. And here it can be useful to step back and trace the paths that lead from the *Journey* to others. For some of Johnson's most general moral and legal views on property, worked out years before, find a permanent textual home only when incorporated into his reflections on Skye.

A case in point is one of Johnson's rare forays into metaphysics. Soame Jenyns' *Free Enquiry into the Nature and Origin of Evil* (1757) is one of the many eighteenth-century apologies for the Great Chain of Being, and Johnson's review of the book that same year in the *Literary Magazine* provides an incisive and passionate critique of the idea. Jenyns contends that reality is organised by way of three cardinal features: subordination, continuity and plenitude. Far from being original, the idea derives almost entirely from Bolingbroke and from Pope's expression of this idea. As Johnson points out, passages of Jenyns's study are little more than paraphrases of the *Essay on Man*, a poem about which Johnson had firm views. 'Never was penury of knowledge or vulgarity of sentiment so happily disguised', he writes. And more: 'When these wonder-working sounds sink into sense, and the doctrine of the Essay, disrobed of its ornaments, is left to the powers of its naked excellence, what shall we discover?'[29] Well, only commonplaces:

> Far as Creation's ample range extends,
> The scale of sensual, mental pow'rs ascends:
> Mark how it mounts, the Man's imperial race,
> From the green myriads in the peopled grass:
> What modes of sight betwixt each wide extreme,
> The mole's dim curtain, and the lynx's beam:

Of smell, the headlong lioness between
And hound sagacious on the tainted green...[30]

And so the poem goes on, for page after elegant page. The doctrine of metaphysical subordination is one that Johnson knew well, had thought about often, but finally found of no use to thinking or living: 'no system can be more hypothetical than this, and perhaps no hypothesis more absurd'.[31]

None of these reservations prevents Johnson from being impressed by a vision of natural subordination when he encounters it on his travels. Writing to Hester Thrale of the landscape near the Fall of Fiers he observes, 'at a bridge over the river which runs into the Ness, the rocks rise on three sides with a direction almost perpendicular to a great height, they are in part covered with trees, and exhibit a kind of dreadful magnificence. Standing like the barriers of nature placed to keep different orders of Being in perpetual separation' (*Letters*, II, 65–66). It is powerful, sublime even, but finally useless. As the Jenyns review reminds us, the terms of subordination make sense only when applied to society, for how can we speak intelligently of infinite space being high here and low there? Yet while society should be structured, there should be no confusion of the natural and the social. No individual should be regarded as naturally allocated a low station in life:

Though it should be granted that those who are *born to poverty and drudgery* should not be *deprived* by an *improper education* of the *opiate of ignorance*; even this concession will not be of much use to direct our practice, unless it be determined who are those that are *born to poverty*. To entail irreversible poverty upon generation after generation only because the ancestor happened to be poor, is in itself cruel, if not unjust, and is wholly contrary to the maxims of a commerical nation, which always suppose and promote a rotation of property, and offer every individual a chance of mending his condition by his diligence. (175)

There are two issues here. In the first place one can feel a pull between the property laws, as settled in England in the seventeenth century, and a more ancient sense of natural rights. How can this tension be resolved? The question leads us to the second issue: there is no conflict between social subordination and trade if a 'rotation of property' be encouraged. Quite clearly the interests of property (and hence stable government) and the demands of commerce (and hence the opportunity for wealth) must be allowed to find a balance.

Subordination and commerce have to accommodate each other in all kinds of circumstances. Johnson would have been alive to this as early as his Grub Street days, for it was a familiar theme of political discussion in a world where trade impinged at every level. Certainly a sense of this accommodation features in his writing of the parliamentary debates over the period 1740–43 when he was responsible for the reports published in the *Gentleman's Magazine* under the title 'Debates in the Senate of Lilliput'. Because Johnson wrote these speeches quickly, from rudimentary notes, it is never possible to distinguish firmly what certain Lords said in the House on a particular day and what Johnson himself thought about a topic as he later wrote about it at home. Here, though, the question of who said what is less pressing than the view of how commerce and government are seen to interact. One interesting example is the Lords' debate over the proposed Bill for Protecting and Securing Trade and Navigation (1742). The Hugo Castroslet (Lord Carteret) makes a general statement about subordination. 'Nothing, my Lords, is more necessary to the Legislature than the Affection and Esteem of the People, all Government consists in the Authority of the *Few* over the *Many*, and Authority, therefore, can be founded only on Opinion, and must always fall to the Ground, when that which supports it is taken away.'[32] That is a straightforward apology for hierarchy, yet when subordination appears in the debate over the Bill it is a matter of what Walter Jackson Bate has usefully called 'protective subordination', the use of a principle of order or regulation to protect a group's or individual's interest.[33] The Bill is concerned with protecting merchant ships by giving them a naval escort, and if this is to be feasible the trading vessels must give up certain liberties in order to secure themselves against enemy attack. The Hugo Devarlar (Lord Delaware) takes a dark view of human actions:

By the present Custom of Insurance, my Lords, the Merchant exempts himself from the Hazard of great Losses, and if he insures so much of the Value of the Ship and Cargo, that the Chance of arriving first at the Market, is equivalent to the remaining Part, what shall hinder him from pressing forward at all Events, and directing his Course intrepidly through Seas crowded with Enemies?

It is well known, my Lords, that there is, in a great Part of Mankind, a secret Malignity, which makes one unwilling to contribute to the Advantage of another, even when his own Interest will suffer no Diminution, nor is it predominant in Traders than in the other Classes of the Community, though it is exerted on different Occasions. (*Gentleman's Magazine*, xii, 665–66)

Lord Carteret responds by stressing the importance of rules that will protect both the good and the bad. 'Fixed and certain Regulations, are, therefore, my Lords, useful to the wisest and best Men; and to those whose Abilities are less conspicuous, and whose Integrity is at best doubtful, I suppose, it will not be doubted that they are indispensably necessary' (670–71). Without the protection of a tacit subordination, individual profit will suffer, to say nothing of the country's probable loss of wealth.

Everywhere one looks in Johnson's writings one finds the notion of unlimited freedom treated roughly. There must be some established control, a bottom line that cannot be crossed. In his 'Observations on a Letter from a French Refugee in America' (1756), Johnson dismisses the refugee's appeals to nature and Providence as so much cant. Such thinking 'would prove that no human legislature has a right to make any prudential laws, or to regulate any thing which before such regulation was indifferent'. Governments have such a right, and Johnson presents it as common sense: 'such is the state of society, that part must be sometimes incommoded for the advantage of the whole. Every nation forbids some importations or exportations, or regulates the buildings, plantations, and agriculture of its own people' (Yale, x, 174). Unregulated trade, like any free-for-all, can be dangerous, as another piece from 1756, 'Further Thoughts on Agriculture', makes manifest:

Commerce, however we may please ourselves with the contrary opinion, is one of the daughters of fortune, inconstant and deceitful as her mother; she chuses her residence where she is least expected, and shifts her abode, when her continuance is in appearance most firmly settled. Who can read of the present distresses of the Genoese, whose only choice now remaining, is from what monarch they shall solicit protection? Who can see the Hanseatick towns in ruins, where perhaps the inhabitants do not always equal the number of the houses; but he will say to himself, These are the cities, whose trade enabled them once to give laws to the world, to whose merchants princes sent their jewels in pawn, from whose treasuries armies were paid, and navies supplied? And who can then forebear to consider trade as a weak and uncertain basis of power, and wish to his own country greatness more solid, and felicity more durable? (Yale, x, 122)

Power based on trade will be weak and uncertain because it depends ultimately on rival nations and any number of accidents, here or there, which of course cannot be controlled or even predicted. Add to this the judgement that we simply do not know enough about 'the Theory of Trade', as Johnson had pointed out in his preface to *The Preceptor* (1748), and unrestricted commerce becomes a risky venture.[34] Far wiser then to attend first and foremost to agriculture, and now more urgently than ever, since the rapid growth of commerce has denuded the land of trees needed to build ships. (And unless things change, England will have to trade for timber.) The conclusion will surprise no one: 'By agriculture only can commerce be perpetuated; and by agriculture alone can we live in plenty without intercourse with other nations' (Yale, x, 125). In Johnsonian economics all speculation is constrained. All production is regulated from a centre of government that is supported by property and that in turn supports property. Commerce can and should flourish, but government must always reserve the right to intervene.

Years later, when travelling with Boswell, Johnson will test his preference for mercantilism over *laissez-faire* economics against the different exigencies of Highland life.[35] The two forces had already been engaging one another in Scotland for nearly a century before the journey. That the Forty-Five had a huge economic impact on Scotland is true, as David Loch saw, but it would not be accurate to say it forced Scotland into the world of modern commerce.[36] Economic conditions in the Highlands were gradually improved by the annexation of forfeited estates, and by their management by Commissioners. Yet Scottish merchants were enjoying improved access to English markets before Culloden.[37] Moreover, the possibility of economic exchange interfering with religious and political subordination had been in place in Scotland since 1681. It can be seen *in nuce* in two Acts passed that year in the Edinburgh Parliament: an 'Act acknowledging and asserting the Right of Succession to the Imperial Crown of Scotland' (13 August), and an 'Act for encouraging Trade and Manufactures' (13 September). The first Act endorses the Stuart succession. It begins:

The Estates of Parliament Considering that the Kings of this Realme deryving their Royall power from God almightie alone, doe succeid lineallie thereto According to the known degrees of Proximitie in blood, which cannot be interrupted suspended or diverted by any Act or Statute whatsoever, And that none can attempt to alter or divert the said Succession without involving the Subjects of this Kingdom in perjurie and Rebellion, And without exposing them to all the fatall and dreadful consequences of a Civil Warr...[38]

The second Act is set in a less passionate register, yet its opening words bear quotation:

Our Soveraigne Lord from his Princely cair for the Wealth and flourishing of this his ancient Kingdom, Considering that the importation of forreign Commodities (which are superfluous, or may be made within the Kingdom by encouragement given to Manufactures thereof) had exceidingly exhausted the money of the Kingdom, and hightened the Exchange to forreign places, So that in a short time the stock of money behooved to be exhausted and the trade therefore to fail...[39]

To bolster trade and increase the supply of money, the nation's new economic policy encouraged manufacturing by preventing Scottish merchants from dealing with familiar foreign markets. In their quest for new outlets they formed the Company of Scotland which would trade in Africa and the Indies, and when this company sustained heavy losses the Scottish merchants wanted access to English colonial markets. It was this desire for new opportunities for trade that became a powerful motive of local support for what the Scottish Jacobites most certainly did not want: the 1707 Act of Union with England.[40] Although it would become evident only decades later, the Jacobite values enshrined in the first Act were to be eroded by the exigencies acknowledged in the second Act.

This tension between subordination and property, on the one hand, and the encouragement of trade on the other, informs what Johnson sees in Scotland and how he sees it. In his *Journey* he writes of a 'reverence for property, by which the order of civil life is preserved', and there are times in the ramble when he likes to imagine himself as a Highland chief, actually possessing the islands of Inchkenneith and Isa. But when reverie yields to analysis, as it does in the *Journey*, he recognises that in modern society property needs to be taken in tandem with money, subordination allowed to engage with exchange. And so we find Johnson lamenting the rapid degeneration of the lairds 'from patriarchal rulers to rapacious landlords'. And rather than affirm subordination and the old patriarchal ways, even when taken by themselves, Johnson seems barely to regret the passing of a hierarchy that kept people in 'a muddy mixture of pride and ignorance' (*Journey*, 36, 73). It is interesting that nowhere in his book is there a mention of Culloden, nor anything about what he would have known very well, that feudal subordination was a crucial factor in the 1715 and 1745 rebellions and that it was in the direct interests of the Hanoverian line to have it dismantled as quickly and effectively as possible. Rather than focus on the indefeasible hereditatary rights of the Stuarts to the throne, Johnson is concerned with the natural rights of all men and women. Property has not so much to do with possessions as with enforceable rights to those possessions, and the only way for those born without property to secure natural rights without violence is by recourse to a legally sanctioned force – in this case, commerce. The supplement to nature turns out to be the best way of gaining natural rights. In this way the moral well-being of the tenants might be preserved and the threat of persistent emigration to America might be lessened.

Yet Johnson does not rest easily with this solution. What worries him is that the circulation of money may well exceed its supplemental role. 'Power and wealth supply the place of each other', he observes, and he wishes for an equitable balance between property and money: 'there are some advantages that money cannot buy, and which therefore no wise man will by the love of money be tempted to forego' (*Journey*, 77, 71). It would be a mistake to abolish all subordination in the name of exchange, for old social institutions of value in themselves can have hidden economic benefits. Hence the defence of those seemingly un-necessary beings, the Tacksmen, who once powerfully occupied 'a middle station, by which the highest and the lowest orders were con-nected' but whose dignity has now been lessened by the uses to which money are put. In former days it was the Tacksman's job to lease the Laird's property to tenants; he would secure the whole rent for the Laird in return for *tacks*, or subordinate possessions. Now, though, the people propose to eliminate the middleman and deal directly with the Laird.[41] A reasonable request? Not at all, says Johnson:

Those who pursue this train of reasoning, seem not sufficiently to inquire whither it will lead them, nor to know that it will equally shew the propriety of suppressing all wholesale trade, of shutting up the shops of every man who sells what he does not make, and of extruding all whose agency and profit intervene between the manufacturer and the consumer. They may, by stretching their understandings a little wider, comprehend, that all those who by undertaking large quantities of manufacture, and affording employment to many labourers, make themselves considered as benefactors to the publick, have only been robbing their workmen with one hand, and their customers with the other. (*Journey*, 71–72)

To attack hierarchy as such will not simply alter the social fabric, it will tear it. The real fear, then, is not how an individual will act in any given situation but what an alien system, imposing itself at tremendous speed, will do to an entire society. Presenting itself as a supplement, money may well supplant the whole economy, thereby transforming a system of life. As he observes in a sermon, 'property, if not virtuously enjoyed, can only corrupt the possessor' and, likewise, 'Trade may make us rich; but riches without goodness, cannot make us happy' (Yale, xiv, 254). While Johnson recognises an inherent violence in feudalism he also acknowledges dangers in commerce. They must be allowed to interact though not to exclude one another.

Let us return to the sentence that gave us our bearings last time and, keeping in mind Johnson's views of the relations of property and money, strike out on another path, one that will lead us to consider connections between literature and money. 'We came hither too late to see what we expected, a people of peculiar appearance, and a system of antiquated life' (*Journey*, 46). That the travellers wished to find 'a system of antiquated life' is one thing, but it is another thing to say that they 'came hither too late'. To be sure, by 1773 assimilation and migration had left their marks on the Highlands, and were to leave many more over the coming decades. Yet one important aspect of the tour, especially for Johnson, is the realisation that the Highlanders trust in a past that never was, that a contemporary nationalism has been posited as an historical origin. As we shall see in the following chapter, this turns on James Macpherson's hotly controverted 'translations' from the Gaelic of Ossian, whom he and many others held to be a third-century Scottish bard, fully the equal of Homer. Many rich themes intersect in the name 'James Macpherson', questions of nationalism and romanticism, forgery and translation. But I would like to approach these themes by way of two distinctions that organise a number of Boswell's and Johnson's observations while in Scotland. Throughout the tour the supposedly natural economy of the Highlands is loosely associated with an oral tradition. And in much the same way, the money economy, coming, as it does, from the metropolitan south, is leagued with a written tradition, one that is part and parcel of the world of booksellers and copyright, commerce and law.

It does not take Johnson long in the *Journey* to begin making observations about property and trade. Visiting the little island of Inch Keith gives him to think of how different the place would be were it as close to London as it is to Edinburgh. In that world, 'with what emulation of price a few rocky acres would have been purchased, and with what expensive industry they would have been cultivated and adorned'. And the towns of Kinghorn, Kirkaldy and Cowpar through which he then passes are viewed exclusively in terms of trade; they are 'not unlike the small or straggling market-towns in those parts of England where commerce and manufactures have not yet produced opulence' (2). By the time he reaches St Andrews his theme has become the proper relationship between commerce and learning, one sounded earlier in the century by that other memorable traveller Daniel Defoe.[42] It is only right that a wealthy trading nation should offer material support to literary societies and universities. That said, the university of St Andrews is well-placed with respect to trade, since it is as bad for students to live in a commercial centre (where they can be seduced by the love of money) as it is for them to be in a capital city with all its opportunities for dissolute behaviour. Where there is commerce, there is written learning; and only in those parts of the Highlands where money is new does one still find an oral tradition. Once in the Hebrides Johnson starts to show how unreliable oral accounts are, even when they concern the most ordinary of events, like making brogues. One day he is told that the islanders make them for themselves, the next day he is informed that brogue-making is a trade. And so he draws an inference: 'the traditions of an ignorant and savage people have been for ages negligently heard, and unskilfully related'. If oral testimonies could be tested for accuracy more faith could be placed in them, 'but such is the laxity of Highland conversation, that the inquirer is kept in continual suspense, and by a kind of intellectual retrogradation, knows less as he hears more' (*Journey*, 41). Written learning is another matter entirely, Johnson believed, for it does not vary and can always be inspected. Variation in textual transmission is not something he wishes to ponder.

Johnson nowhere determines a systemic relation between money and writing, and one would not expect him to do so. His cast of mind is of another order. To be sure, he makes general observations about money. Bennett Langton remembered him saying that a great merchant will spend money both because he has it and because he has 'enlarged views', whereas a country gentleman will be relunctant 'to lay out ten pounds' (*Life*, IV, 4). And he makes remarks to the effect that civilised values are generally associated with commerce and wealth and that where these are not found there is only 'a muddy mixture of pride and ignorance' (*Journey*, 73).[43] The view is not unique to Johnson; it was a common objection to fashionable Rousseauesque sentiments. Yet one can also find contemporary meditations on the relations between money and writing. A suggestive instance occurs in Gibbon's *Decline and Fall of the Roman Empire*, in an early passage that was composed in 1774, just one year after the tour. Gibbon writes there about German culture in the third century, and I would like to bring the historian into the discussion for a while partly because he presents a certain connection between money and letters very clearly and partly because his account meshes with Johnson's evocation of life in the Highlands. Like Johnson, Gibbon is drawn to the image of currency passing from a metropolitan to a primitive culture: 'The various transactions of peace and war had introduced some Roman coins (chiefly silver) among the borderers of the Rhine and Danube; but the more distant tribes were absolutely unacquainted with the use of money, carried on their confined traffic by the exchange of commodities, and prized their rude earthen vessels as of equal value with the silver vases, the presents of Rome to their princes and ambassadors.' No more than Johnson is Gibbon disposed to value a natural state of life. There are sentences in the *Decline and Fall* which would not seem out of place in the *Journey*: 'If we contemplate a savage nation in any part of the globe, a supine indolence and a carelessness of futurity will be found to constitute their general character. In a civilised state, every faculty of man is expanded and exercised; and the great chain of mutual dependence connects and embraces the several members of society.'

It is in terms of this long path from savagery to civilisation that Gibbon considers money:

The value of money has been settled by general consent to express our wants and our property; as letters were invented to express our ideas; and both these instititions, by giving a more active energy to the powers and passions of human nature, have contributed to multiply the objects they were designed to represent. The use of gold and silver is in a great measure factitious; but it would be impossible to enumerate the important and various services which agriculture, and all the arts, have received from iron, when tempered and fashioned by the operation of fire, and the dexterous hand of man. Money, in a word, is the most universal incitement, iron the most powerful instrument, of human industry; and it is very difficult to conceive by what means a people, neither actuated by the one nor seconded by the other, could emerge from the grossest barbarism.[44]

This requires some elucidation. Originally intended simply to represent our ideas, writing has helped mankind to increase them. And in exactly the same way, Gibbon says, money was designed to represent what we do or do not possess but has served to increase the store of possible possessions, namely the luxuries that embellish civilised life. So both writing and money seem to be for the good.

But the use of gold and silver as money is 'in a great measure factitious'. Interestingly enough, a small error has slipped into some modern editions of the *Decline and Fall*, so that the passage reads 'in great measure fictitious'.[45] With a shrug of the shoulders, one might say there is little difference between the two words. Johnson would have disagreed. If we look up the *Dictionary* we will find 'factitious' defined in the following way: 'Made by art, in opposition to what is made by nature'. Turning over the folio page we will find 'fictitious' defined as 'Counterfeit; false; not genuine' in the first instance, and then as 'Feigned; imaginary', and then, finally, as 'Not real; not true'. It is one of those occasions when Johnson has adopted a strict, almost fearful, response to the imaginary. He can be uneasy about what is made up, not what is made. Gibbon writes 'factitious' rather than 'fictitious' because his emphasis is on custom. Money is artificial; it is 'in a great measure' a social convention, and unlike iron has little real utility.[46]

And yet the idea of money can never be thoroughly cleansed of associations with counterfeiting, speculation and falsity. Although Gibbon was writing when England was enjoying a period of monetary stability he knew perfectly well that it had not always been so, and the qualification 'in a great measure' can remind us that however much the value of money is supported by a social agreement it is also underwritten by a local political power, not always the most secure of grounds in times of uncertain royal succession and war. This had been the case in Britain during the reign of William and Mary. The London merchants murmured amongst themselves that the King might not repay the debts incurred by the dispossessed Stuarts, and in 1694 they were loath to make him a loan – he had requested the large sum of £1,200,000 – so that England, along with Spain and Austria, might continue its war against France. But what did 'money' mean at the time? Not quite what it would come to mean for Gibbon or Johnson, for the very notion was in the midst of change.

One index of that change is John Locke's view of money as developed in several pamphlets on fiscal policy over the years 1691–95. The economic situation was as follows. Due to illegal clipping and general wear of the metal, the silver currency in circulation had deteriorated to such an extent that light coins could no longer be accepted at face value without an additional premium. Confidence in the currency had fallen to such an extent that in 1694 the Amsterdam Exchange moved strongly against the pound sterling. The Secretary of the Treasury, William Lowndes, suggested a devaluation of twenty per cent, which would mean there would be a fifth less silver in the pound than before. It was an easy and inexpensive solution, yet one that implied that the token value of money can be arbitrarily assigned. And that was its weakness, Locke objected. By his lights it was a mere paper solution, for in reality the exchange value of silver answered solely to the quantity of metal it contained.[47] A better policy, he thought, was to withdraw the silver coin in circulation and issue fewer newly minted coins with the full weight of silver in their place. With the 1696 Recoining Acts, this view eventually triumphed; it was an expensive policy decision, one that preserved the monetary standard at the hefty price of £2,700,000.[48]

The cost was met by taxes payable in good coin and, ironically, by something daringly new, notes drawable on the Bank of England, an institution established in 1694 by the London merchants in order to raise the million odd pounds required by the King. These notes were first issued to shareholders in the Bank, and for those who would accept them in lieu of coin they could be used as legal tender. The idea took. The King spent the money on the war, and more was later loaned to him: confidence grew in the use of this new kind of money – for that is what it became in effect – whose value did not answer to its weight. Needless to say, not every one approved of the introduction of paper money. As late as 1733 one can find Pope giving it a special place in a general satire on the abuse of riches, his 'Epistle to Allen Lord Bathurst'. Here questions of economics are raised and, in his carefully fashioned aristocratic way, debated wholly in terms of social morality. Following a venerable tradition, money itself is presented as morally dubious:

> What Nature wants, commodious Gold bestows,
> 'Tis thus we eat the bread another sows:
> But how unequal it bestows, observe,
> 'Tis thus we riot, while who sow it, starve.
> What Nature wants (a phrase I much distrust)
> Extends to Luxury, extends to Lust:
> And if we count among the Needs of life
> Another's Toil, why not another's Wife?
> Useful, I grant, it serves what life requires,
> But dreadful too, the dark Assasin hires:
> Trade it may help, Society extend;
> But lures the Pirate, and corrupts the Friend:
> It raises Armies in a Nation's aid,
> But bribes a Senate, and the Land's betray'd.[49]

The moral lesson is palpable: what can be used for good can also be abused for evil. Pope's unease with gold arises from it being regarded as a supplement to nature; it exposes an apparent lack in what should be sufficient and then, while filling it, introduces an excess that displaces it. What the couplets do not indicate, at least not on their glittering surface, is an anxiety over the rise of the moneyed man with respect to the landed interest. Only toward the end of the epistle, in the story of Sir

Balaam, does the anxiety become overt. For some time past a nation of aristocrats had been becoming in essential respects a nation of traders, and as the century wore on real property would lose economic and political importance while personal property would gain them. Joseph Addison was right when he observed in the *Spectator*, years before Pope wrote, that the British empire had long since been expanded by that subtle form of conquest, commerce.[50]

It is the conjunction of property and money that interests Johnson, not the relationship of nature and money, and his reflections on wealth are accordingly less romantic than those offered by Pope.[51] When we hear of money 'Trade it may help, Society extend', the voice is secure in English historical experience. Things are different on the borders of the Union. Travelling in the Highlands, Johnson sees how money does not so much extend the society around him as thoroughly transform it. 'Money confounds subordination, by overpowering the distinctions of rank and birth, and weakens authority by supplying power of resistance, or expedients for escape' (*Journey*, 94). Or, in the pungent words we have already heard, 'power and wealth supply the place of each other' (77–78). The society to which Pope and Bathurst belong has been diversified in both authority and wealth for some time. Not so the Highlands: 'the feudal system is formed for a nation employed in agriculture, and has never long kept its hold where gold and silver have become common' (94). Pope soon passes from the theme of money as morally dubious to the darker theme of paper credit as enabling political corruption on a grand scale: 'Gold imp'd by thee, *can* compass hardest things, / *Can* pocket States, *can* fetch or carry Kings' ('Epistle', ll. 567–68; my emphases). In his meditation on money and wealth, Johnson focuses on actuality rather than potentiality. Like Gibbon, he understands that money is 'in a great measure factitious', but when pondering economics in the *Journey* the slide from convention to falsity is not uppermost in his mind. Rather, it concerns him that there is insufficient 'philosophy of commerce' (106) in the Hebrides. By reason of their insularity, the inhabitants of Mull and Skye mistakenly suppose 'that the value of money is always the same' (130) and therefore do not grasp the significance of fluctuating foreign markets. If the islanders remain inattentive to the 'uncertain proportion between the value and the denomination of money' (118), the Hebrides will soon experience the hardships of inflation, as Europe already has.

Johnson may not have warmed to either *An Essay on Man* or 'Epistle to Allen Lord Bathurst', but there is no doubt of his admiration for Pope's verse. It comes within a hair's breadth of his esteem for Dryden's mighty line. Neither poet could have flourished in his art outside a lettered society, and the theme that a polite culture is fundamentally connected to writing is loudly sounded on several occasions in the *Journey*. On Raasay Johnson muses on Martin Martin, whose *A Description of the Western Islands of Scotland* (1703) had long ago prompted him to visit the Hebrides. Johnson regrets that Martin, an inhabitant of Skye, did not record the patriarchal life of the islands in the kind of detail that would now delight his readers. Something has vanished, and the cause of this impoverishment is quickly offered:

In nations, where there is hardly the use of letters, what is once out of sight is lost for ever. They think but little, and of their few thoughts, none are wasted on the past, in which they are neither interested by fear nor hope. Their only registers are stated observances and practical representations. For this reason an age of ignorance is an age of ceremony. Pageants, and processions, and commemorations, gradually shrink away, as better methods come into use of recording events, and preserving rights. (*Journey*, 52)

Literacy and pen and ink, are the 'better methods'. And they are still needed. The possibility that even the last traces of 'a people of peculiar appearance, and a system of antiquated life' could have been lost is quietly suggested. For Johnson notes, 'I have in *Sky* had some difficulty to find ink for a letter' (108).

Johnson had no sooner landed in Skye than he began to cast doubts on the value of oral history. He had indeed come a long way from Edinburgh where he and Boswell had visited the Advocates' Library and the *Laigh* underneath the Parliament where the written records of Scottish history are kept. There are no libraries and no signed assurances of any kind on Skye. Before leaving the island he was detained in Ostig by bad weather, and he took the occasion to write at length to Hester Thrale on his experience of the island. Safely back in London, he composed the book I have open before me now. In the passage at hand he draws on his Hebridean correspondence and writes about writing:

Books are faithful repositories, which may be a while neglected or forgotten; but when they are opened again, will again impart their instruction: memory, once interrupted, is not to be recalled. Written learning is a fixed luminary, which, after the cloud that had hidden it has past away, is again bright in its proper station. Tradition is but a meteor, which, if once it falls, cannot be rekindled. (*Journey*, 92)

Johnson enquires after the bards who were said to preserve local history, and for a while he is pleased with the knowledge he gains. 'They said that a great family had a *Bard* and a *Senachi*, who were the poet and historian of the house; and an old gentleman told me that he remembered one of each. Here was a dawn of intelligence' (92). Clouds soon darken the sun: 'Another conversation indeed informed me, that the same man was both Bard and Senachi. This variation discouraged me' (92). Why is he disappointed? Partly because oral testimony is unreliable – now he does not know if there were both storytellers and historians or simply storytellers – and partly because unless there is a distinction between the two there is likely to be a confusion of history and poetry. Truth is at stake.[52]

Several pages later, Johnson drops the distinction between Bard and Senachi and speaks only of the Bards. History, it seems, has been reluctantly discharged. Two paragraphs on the value of writing are worth quoting in full:

When a language begins to teem with books, it is tending to refinement; as those who undertake to teach others must have undergone some labour in improving themselves, they set a proportionate value on their own thoughts, and wish to enforce them by efficacious expressions; speech becomes embodied and permanent; different modes and phrases are compared, and the best obtains an establishment. By degrees one age improves upon another. Exactness is first obtained, and afterwards elegance. But diction, merely vocal, is always in its childhood. As no man leaves his eloquence behind him, the new generations have all to learn. There may possibly be books without a polished language, but there can be no polished language without books.

That the Bards could not read more than the rest of their countrymen, it is reasonable to suppose; because, if they had read, they could probably have written; and how high their compositions may reasonably be rated, an inquirer may best judge by considering what stores of imagery, what principles of ratiocination, what comprehension of knowledge, and what delicacy of elocution he has known any man attain who cannot read. The state of the Bards was yet more hopeless. He that cannot read, may now converse with those that can; but the Bard was a barbarian among barbarians, who, knowing nothing himself, lived with others that knew no more. (*Journey*, 96)

A language 'teems with books' only when there are booksellers to buy manuscripts, printers paid to set them in type, and people with ready money to purchase them and time to read them. In a culture with strong commercial interests literature can be circulated rapidly and effectively; its power and reach come from its superior access to history, right down to Latin and Greek classics, the greater number of literary exchanges that are possible, and the corresponding pressure to strike for original expression. There can be no originality, in any sense acceptable to

Johnson, in an oral culture that merely repeats its ancient poetry to itself.[53]

So not only is a dynamic culture essentially related to writing, but also writing is leagued with money. The abstract point that both writing and money are systems of conventional signs does not engage Johnson. The more concrete point, that there will be no polite literature without money, is the one at issue. We are told that 'the peculiarities which strike the native of a commercial country, proceeded in a great measure from the want of money' (94). Johnson sees very plainly that the patriarchy distinctive to the Highlands is being dismantled by money. And from this vantage point it can also be observed that the emergence of money marks the closure of the bardic tradition.

In a world like that of the ancient Highlands where oral tradition and patriarchy are important features, there is little need to raise the question of counterfeiting. By contrast, a world that exists in relation to money and writing, one that is slowly acknowledging the economic importance of intellectual and personal property as well as landed property, must look long and hard at forgery. As they travelled through Scotland in 1773, Johnson and Boswell were watching these two worlds converge. I turn now to consider their transit of Caledonia from this perspective.

CHAPTER 5

Cultural properties

'On Saturday the fourteenth of August, 1773, late in the evening, I received a note from him, that he was arrived at Boyd's inn, at the head of the Canongate. I went to him directly. He embraced me cordially...' (*Tour*, 21). Neither Johnson nor Boswell opens his recollection of the Hebridean ramble with this scene, and yet the jaunt begins here, with Boswell collecting his friend at the local coach stop. Or does it? If we are looking for the jaunt's true starting point, perhaps we should go back several months and focus on Boswell soliciting help in getting Johnson to stir from London. Invitations were sought from the Scottish chiefs Macdonald and MacLeod, and letters were written to James Beattie, Lord Elibank, William Robertson and Hester Thrale. Or perhaps we should go back decades earlier, before Boswell was born, and view the young Johnson in his father's bookshop engrossed in reading Martin Martin's *A Description of the Western Islands of Scotland* (1703). For Boswell, as he approaches Boyd's inn, it hardly matters who or what has helped to bring his friend up north. Seeing Johnson in Scotland is for him a tonic satisfaction. A line from his journal says it all: 'I exulted in the thought, that I now had him actually in Caledonia' (*Tour*, 21).

Something in that last phrase recalls another scene at another inn, Hayward's in London. It was privately performed on 12 January 1763, although the script was mostly written after the fact and with others in mind: his friend John Johnston of Grange and his older self.[1] At Hayward's, Boswell completes the seduction of Mrs Lewis, the beautiful young Covent Garden actress whom he calls 'Louisa' in the journal. Arriving at the inn, and feigning that his wife has just come to town, Boswell assumes the name of West Digges, the leading man in the

Edinburgh theatrical company. It was not an arbitrary or innocent choice of names. As a young man Boswell had been enchanted by the theatre, especially by actors and actresses, so much so that his father had removed him from its bad influence. He had learned English pronunciation from James Dance (alias Love), comic actor and assistant manager of the Canongate Theatre until he moved to Drury Lane in 1762; and in general players gave the young man models of polite behaviour. He addressed three poems to West Digges, and greatly admired his performance of Macheath in John Gay's *The Beggar's Opera* (1728), which was to remain one of his favourite roles and favourite plays.[2] It was a part he played now and again in London during 1762–3, as though he were living out Air xxii of the opera, '*Youth's the Season made for Joys*'.[3]

Only a month before bedding Louisa, Boswell had told his journal that he hoped 'by degrees to attain to some degree of propriety'. His guiding image was to be a composite: 'Mr Addison's character in sentiment, mixed with a little of the gaiety of Sir Richard Steele and the manners of Mr Digges' (*London Journal*, 62). Put more directly, the tyro wanted to embody a combination of Mr Spectator and Captain Macheath. Boswell hoped it would be a stable synthesis; it would not be and could not be. But that lesson lay ahead, as did his many evasions of it. Now, after supper at Hayward's, as the maid spreads fresh sheets upon the bed, the young man believes he must have hit upon the right image for himself. He muses, 'I could not help being somehow pleasingly confounded to think that so fine a woman was at this moment in my possession, that without any motives of interest, she had come with me to an inn, agreed to be my intimate companion, as to be my bedfellow all night, and to permit me the full enjoyment of her person' (*London Journal*, 138). Before very long, the young man would be unpleasingly confounded by signs of a visit from 'Signor Gonorrheoa', but let us leave the young man and the old Signor to their private negotiations.

'Having' Louisa in London and 'having' Johnson in Edinburgh are phased counterparts in Boswell's experience. The one person is a companion for the night, the other for three months; one is a sexual partner, the other a beloved father figure. With Louisa, Boswell signs the inn register with another's name: he plays at being an actor in order to possess an actress, and while making love 'could not help roving in fancy to the embraces of some other ladies' (*London Journal*, 139). Proper names and signatures are to be treated far more seriously in Johnson's company, and there Boswell listens while the great man thunders against James Macpherson's forgeries of Gaelic epics. When in London, Boswell possesses an actress who has recently played Queen Gertrude in *Hamlet*; in Scotland he accompanies a man who expresses contempt for tragic acting yet who he first saw, by the lights of a retired actor, as a Shakespearean character: Gertrude's dead husband, no less. And in that moment Boswell was cast as none other than Hamlet. Recall the occasion when the young Scotsman meets Johnson for the first time. Tom Davies 'announced his awful approach to me, somewhat in the manner of an actor in the part of Horatio, when he addresses Hamlet on the appearance of his father's ghost, "Look, my Lord, it comes"' (*Life*, i, 392).

In Mr Digges's room at Hayward's inn Boswell could scarcely believe that 'so fine a woman' as Louisa was 'at this moment in my possession'. A similar feeling of being slightly dazed by his good fortune comes over him ten years later when he writes to that consummate player, David Garrick, two weeks after their mutual friend had arrived up north. 'Here I am and Mr Samuel Johnson actually with me. Indeed as I have allways been accustomed to view him as a permanent London object, it would not be much more wonderful to me to see St Paul's Church moving along where we now are.'[4] Over a fortnight later, when the couple has got as far as Dunvegan in Skye, Boswell writes, this time with comic realism rather than comic surrealism, 'I was elated by the thought of having been able to entice such a man to this remote part of the world. A ludicrous, yet just, image presented itself to my mind, which I expressed to the company. I compared myself to a dog who has got hold of a large piece of meat, and runs away with it to a corner, where he may devour it in peace, without any fear of others taking it away from him' (*Tour*, 215).

In their different ways the scenes in London and Edinburgh have been carefully plotted in the hope of ending triumphantly, and both turn on acts of seduction and physical possession. We pass from a scene where a woman is regarded as sexual property to another where a friend is appropriated for purposes of symbolic consumption. In his journal Boswell gives the impression that having Johnson in Scotland is a private luxury. Yet the ramble is public from beginning to end. Thinking of Boswell's playful image of Johnson as St Paul's Cathedral, one could say that the 'permanent London object' is exhibited as a major piece of imported cultural property. These days the expression 'cultural property' is mostly used in law to designate a State's artistic, historical and monumental heritage.[5] Yet clearly the notion of cultural property exceeds legal codes. In earlier chapters I have discussed how Johnson is and is not a monument, how his times are and are not 'the Age of

Johnson', and how Boswell and his editors are involved in both constructions. Developing a national culture by reference to a 'great man', erecting monuments and statues, affixing plaques and coining tokens with his image, preserving houses in his name, and housing manuscripts: all these are of interest to heritage law. But where the law is concerned with the preservation of cultural property, I am more interested in its formation; and where the law attends to property, I propose to focus on acts of appropriation and expropriation.

Styling Johnson as cultural property is a complex act for Boswell, not only in its responses to Johnson but also in its selection of him. In a sense, the choice is an obvious one, for he is Dictionary Johnson, Mr Rambler, and the Idler. And yet he is not the sole living cultural authority for Boswell. From time to time Edmund Burke, David Garrick, Lord Kames, Pasquale Paoli and John Wilkes satisfy emotional and intellectual needs. The figure who interests me here, though, has a particular cultural authority for Boswell, and he shadows him before, during and after the Hebridean jaunt. I am half-thinking of James Macpherson, though more fully of Ossian. It is hard to distinguish them in all ways: the 'translations' were taken by many to be proper expressions of a culture – indeed, of all that is truly proper to the Highlands – and not simply the work of an individual writer. Boswell was an early believer in Ossian. He subscribed to Macpherson's tour of the Highlands in quest of a Scottish heritage in *Fingal*, and was so enthusiastic about the result that in 1762 he made a young woman whom he had just met, Kitty Gilpin, learn and repeat Ossian's address to the sun.[6] Here he is writing about Ossian to the Honourable Andrew Erskine on 17 December 1761: 'I will not anticipate your pleasure in reading the Highland bard; only take my word for it, he will make you feel that you have a soul.' And we get a sense of the intensity of that feeling by reading Erskine's response in his reply to Boswell of 10 January 1762:

It is quite impossible to express my admiration of his Poems; at particular passages I felt my whole frame tremble with ecstasy; but if I was to describe all my thoughts, you would think me absolutely mad. The beautiful wildness of his fancy is inexpressibly agreeable to the imagination; for instance, the mournful sound from the untouched harp when a hero is going to fall, or the awful appearances of his ghosts and spirits.[7]

If in the end the 'Sublime Savage' (*London Journal*, 265) is not chosen by Boswell as true cultural property, with all the authority appropriate to the role, it is partly because he thinks of Macpherson in terms of the rigid dyad of 'original' versus 'forgery' and partly because the poet offers him no opportunity to speak for him. The ancient monument that is Ossian attracts the Scot but not so much as does the monumental Johnson.[8] But before developing these thoughts I would like to say a little more about the styling of Johnson as cultural property.

Early in the previous chapter I contemplated Johnson and Boswell arguing with others in the *Laigh* beneath the Edinburgh Parliament. Now I would like to relate a story set just before that dispute. Less familiar than the episode with Louisa, this scene comes from an anecdote that Sir Walter Scott told John Wilson Croker, and it supplies the kind of detail that escaped Boswell, whether by accident or design. 'It was on this visit to the parliament-house', Scott writes, 'that Mr Henry Erskine (brother of Lord Erskine), after being presented to Dr Johnson by Mr Boswell, and having made his bow, slipped a shilling into Boswell's hand, whispering that it was for the sight of his *bear*' (*Tour*, 39 n. 4). Scott's Boswelliana are seldom reliable, yet it is true that Johnson was sometimes called a bear. Giuseppi Baretti, Edward Gibbon and William Mason all call him that – behind his back, of course – and he is figured as a bear in caricatures. An etching published in 1786, the year the *Tour* appeared, comes to mind. There Boswell is depicted as a monkey riding on the back of Johnson the bear.[9]

The difference between the guiding stories of this and the previous chapter, one traditional and one biographical, is illuminating. In the *Tour* Boswell relates a narrative that revolves around subordination; while in his letter to Croker, Scott recounts a tale of exchange. The moment Erskine's coin is accepted, even if in bad humour, Boswell must acknowledge that others see him as stage-managing a spectacle. Exactly what sort of spectacle Johnson is, and how Boswell serves as impresario, will concern us as we follow them once more through the Highlands. Before leaving the Edinburgh Parliament, it is worth our while to take a moment to ponder who leads whom in the ramble. Margaret Boswell's complaint about her husband fawning over their guest comes immediately to mind: 'I have seen many a bear led by a man; but I never before saw a man led by a bear' (*Life*, II, 269, n. 1). But the question of authority goes deeper than her disappointment with the poor figure her husband is cutting about town. And if pursued far enough it divides into two.

In Boswell's journal it is Johnson who usurps narrative authority. He waves aside 'the signed assurances of the three successive Kings of the

Hanover family, to maintain the Presbyterian establishment in Scotland', and then concludes the entire scene with a heavy thump: 'We'll give you that (said he) into the bargain.' (*Tour*, 41). In Scott's anecdote, seen from outside Boswell's consciousness – and with whatever shade of humour – it appears that Boswell is in charge of his friend and mentor. Re-reading the *Tour* itself, we can catch another process of exchange all too easily missed. Boswell allows Johnson to gain narrative command, yet in doing so he lays claim himself to narratorial authority.[10] He becomes the masterful writer who can afford to be laughed at and who even perhaps trades in such moves, overdrawing his account with the reader even before it has been properly established.

Let us briefly enter the world of eighteenth-century British law. 'Forgery is a stab to commerce, and only to be tolerated in a commercial nation when the foul crime of murder is pardoned.'[11] So observed Lord Mansfield in 1765. That same year William Blackstone began publishing his magisterial *Commentaries*, the fruit of his years as foundation Vinerian Professor of English Law at Oxford. When he turns to discuss forgery he reminds us that 5 Eliz. c. 14 (1562) required that a felon convicted of forgery was sentenced to stand in the pillory, have both ears cut off, nostrils slit and seared, the profit of lands forfeited to the crown, and thereafter to remain perpetually in prison.[12] 'Beside this general act', he goes on, 'a multitude of others, since the revolution (when paper-credit was first established), have inflicted capital punishment on the forging, altering, or uttering as true when forged, of any bank bills, or other securities…'[13] Several years later Robert Chambers, the second Vinerian Professor, makes rather more of the material that his predecessor set in parentheses. 'Forgery is one of the most dangerous and extensive evils to which men are subjected by the combinations of society and the regulations of civil life … a crime which the present state of the commerical world makes particularly dangerous.'[14] He is thinking of how much moveable wealth is tied up in bills of credit. And he had no doubts that forgery should be punishable by death.

Both legal pronoucements make sense in a world where property is considered another nature. Counterfeiting coins, title deeds and the like had been capital offences since 1634, but by the mid-1700s there were over 400 statutes relating to it.[15] To forge coins was high treason, a crime as serious as voluntarily fighting for a Stuart restoration. When notes of credit appeared alongside coins in the early decades of the eighteenth century the practice was not only satirised by Pope but also caused flickers of concern amongst tradesmen. Polite ethical worries were joined and outweighed by anxieties of commerce. If the use of gold and silver was 'in a great measure factitious', as Gibbon had put it, the circulation of banknotes brought the fictional nature of money to the fore. As late as 1758, in the case of *Miller* v. *Race*, the defendant pleaded that he had not paid on a banknote because it was not property. Lord Mansfield, who was hearing the case, rejected the argument. Banknotes, he said, were 'treated as Money, as Cash, in the ordinary course and transaction of Business, by the general Consent of Mankind'.[16] His view held sway. Yet it was not until late in the century that there was a general and deep confidence in paper money. Acts of parliament helped secure this increased trust: 7 Geo. 2., c. 22 (1734), 13 Geo. 2, c. 13, x. 11 (1742) and 13 Geo. 3, c. 79, s. 1 (1773) legislated against counterfeiting bills of exchange, counterfeiting or altering a bank bill and counterfeiting bank paper. All three were capital offences. The last act declared that, after 29 September 1773, any unauthorised person who shall 'by any Art, Mysterie or Contrivance, cause or procure the said Words, *Bank of England*, to appear in the Substance of any Paper whatsoever ... shall, for such Offence, be deemed and adjudged a Felon, and shall suffer Death as in cases of Felony, without Benefit of Clergy'.[17]

On 29 September 1773, Johnson and Boswell woke up in Ostaig on Skye. No mention is made of the new law by either man, and no one would expect them to recall it, deeply interested in the law though both parties were. Boswell was the son of a judge and was himself an advocate trained in Scottish law, and Johnson had helped Robert Chambers prepare his Vinerian lectures on English law at Oxford.[18] So it is no surprise that the tour as a whole is punctuated by discussions of literary property and literary forgery. In the year following the Caledonian journey the House of Lords will hear the case of *Donaldson* v. *Becket* and the question of literary property will be settled at long last. Lord Mansfield, that tireless defender of commerce, will be remembered as the most revered in law of those who defended the common law right of the booksellers. Neither before nor after 1773, however, will a Lord or a bookseller show the slightest legal interest in counterfeited poems. After all, whose property is invaded and what commerce is injured by falsely testifying that a poem was written by a dead man, or even by a legendary dead man? No one is going to be imprisoned or executed by misleadingly claiming to have recovered poems written in earlier centuries. Counterfeiting, here, seems to require discussion in terms of literary and social values rather than legal judgements, even if historical truth is at stake.

The travellers touch on this latter point whenever they talk about the supposititious blind Gaelic bard Ossian, whose name was once more in the air owing to the 1773 edition of his poems.[19] This *seanchaidh* was the son of Fingal, it was said, who in turn was chief of a clan in Argyllshire in the third century. For us, the story of Ossian goes back only to the middle of the eighteenth century when a young poet and family tutor, James Macpherson, was trying to make his way in the world. In 1758 he published *The Highlander*, a long poem set in the Scotland of yore that fused or confused history and legend. One can already detect in this piece of juvenilia an imperative that was to become important for Macpherson. The bards have a profound responsibility

> To keep in song the mem'ry of the dead!
> They handed down the ancient rounds of time,
> In oral story and recorded rhyme.[20]

Macpherson's creativity was to reveal itself in a more indirect fashion than original composition, however. He was encouraged to translate portions of Gaelic verse, and then to publish them. Accordingly, his *Fragments of Ancient Poetry Collected in the Highlands of Scotland, and Translated from the Gaelic or Erse Language* appeared in 1760. And this remarkable pamphlet marks his triumphant arrival in the world of letters.[21]

There had been growing literary interests in the Highlands for some years before Macpherson's first translations hit the bookshops. Edward Lhuyd's *Archeologia Britannica* (1707) is an isolated instance of philological scholarship in the area. Neither Oxford nor Cambridge was to pursue this kind of research for the rest of the century. In Scotland, the volumes of Allan Ramsay's *The Tea-Table Miscellany* and *The Ever Green*, all appearing in the 1720s, are an early index of a fascination with the oral verse of the Highlands. Not only were old songs gathered but also songs were composed and passed off as ancient.[22] And if we look at original poetry written south of the Tweed, we can see the Hebrides being imaginatively positioned in different ways. There is of course Johnson's image of the western islands in his poem 'London' (1738). Here life on the islands is evoked to satirise metropolitan existence under the Walpole administration:

> For who would leave, unbrib'd, Hibernia's land,
> Or change the rocks of Scotland for the Strand?

There none are swept by sudden fate away,
But all whom hunger spares, with age decay.
(Yale, VI, 48)

Ten years later, in 1748, one can see a quite different sensibility responding to the idea of the Hebrides. James Thomson was raised in Roxbur-
ghshire, near the English border, a long way from the Highlands. Yet in
'The Castle of Indolence' he evokes the romantic allure of the western
islands:

> As when a shepherd of the Hebrid Isles,
> Placed far amid the melancholy main,
> (Whether it be lone fancy him beguiles,
> Or that aerial beings sometimes deign
> To stand embodied to our senses plain)
> Sees on the naked hill, or valley low,
> The whilst in ocean Phoebus dips his wain,
> A vast assembly moving to and fro;
> Then all at once in air dissolves the wondrous show.[23]

This stanza was asterisked in 1756 by Joseph Warton in his influential
essay on Pope. 'I cannot at present recollect any solitude so romantic, or
peopled with beings so proper to the place, and the spectator', he wrote.
'The mind naturally loves to lose itself in one of these wildernesses, and
to forget the hurry, the noise and splendour of more polished life'.[24] And
it is this sense of the Highlands – melancholy, primitive and spectral –
that was to be intensified and ramified by Macpherson.

Macpherson's little collection of fragments appeared at just the right
moment. It caught the attention of men who mattered, and under the
patronage of several Edinburgh literati and powerful lairds Macpherson
travelled around the Highlands in 1760 and again in the following year in
search of more material. But before we follow the young man into the
wilds, we need to put a common misunderstanding about him to one
side. Time and again, Macpherson has been accused of deliberately
forging an epic poem, yet the historical facts are less cut and dried.
Unlike Thomas Chatterton, with whom he is often compared, Macpherson did not create an *oeuvre* that falsely claimed to have been written in
earlier times. There were no poems by Thomas Rowley composed in
Bristol in the fifteenth century. However, there was a corpus of
fianaigheacht before Macpherson was born. Not as much as enthusiasts at
the time testified: hopes that the *Leabhar Dearg* or Red Book of Clanronald
contained a wealth of Ossianic material were unfounded. Macpherson
did not forge a body of work in English; rather, he fabricated epic poetry

that was loosely, sometimes very loosely, based on traditional ballads. He was guilty of misrepresenting the ancient bards, not of making them out of thin air. Later in life he transposed his 'translations' into 'the original Gaelic', and did so with the intent of misleading people about the status of his earlier work. These were duly published, with a plain Latin translation, in 1807. But that whole mystification is another story.

There are three cycles of ballads circulating in Ireland and Scotland in the eighteenth century. In all likelihood as Macpherson travelled around the Highlands he heard ballads from the Cù Chulainn saga that looked back to the first century as well as from the third-century Finn saga. The two cycles had been kept distinct for generations, although in recent years the lines separating them had begun to blur. More boldly than others, and to the chagrin of the Irish, Macpherson transferred characters and events from the earlier into the later cycle.[25] He was accused, early on, of changing 'the name of Fionn MacCumhal, the Irishman, into Fingal' and of doing so in order to set up 'a Scotch king over the ideal kingdom of Morven, in the west of Scotland'.[26] Over the years Macpherson remained steady in claiming that, if there was any falsification, it had been done by the Irish, not him. 'The Irish historians have placed Cuchullin in the first century', he noted, and maintained that the old warrior truly belonged in the third century.[27] If Macpherson was not the first to expand the Ossianic canon in this way, his conception of Ossian may have been original. He was not looking so much for ballads as for 'one work of considerable length, and which deserves to be styled an heroic poem' – in other words, an epic.[28] So exactly how Macpherson understood epic poems to have been composed is worth some consideration.

It has been argued that the young poet was influenced by a view of Homer proposed by Thomas Blackwell, the eminent Grecian, and an early practitioner of historical criticism.[29] And doubtless he was. Blackwell was a powerful intellectual presence in the Aberdeen of the 1750s when Macpherson was a student at the university there. Two lines of influence are possible, and if both were followed the young poet would have had to negotiate a tension between them. There can be little doubt that Macpherson was impressed by Blackwell's leaguing of genius and the primitive: many people were. Perhaps also the young poet was inspired by another of the professor's ideas. For Blackwell and his followers, Homer was to be approached as a man in a particular historical situation. He was a weaver of tales from diverse sources, not a genius who originated everything that circulated under his name. It is possible that Macpherson conceived Ossian as being like this Homer. Just as Blackwell's Homer drew from the Egyptians, Greeks and Phoenicians, so too perhaps Ossian gathered stories from different places.[30] On this understanding, Ossian would not be the individual primitive genius that contemporary critics were to make him so much as the genius of the people of Scotland.[31]

If one is prepared to make a leap, an intriguing image of Macpherson comes into view. It could be that the young poet applied his understanding of Ossian to himself, and so felt justified in knitting together poetry from different heroic ballads in order to create the epic he believed had once existed. Certainly he writes of 'compleating the epic poem' *Fingal* and of collecting the 'broken fragments' of *Temora* and reducing it 'into that order in which it now appears'.[32] Yet at no time does he suggest that he is doing anything other than recovering the work of an individual, Ossian, the son of Fingal. The negotiation between 'individual genius' and 'genius of the country' would have been a subtle one with room enough for self-deception. At any rate, the epic poem *Fingal* was published in December 1761 with the quiet assistance of Macpherson's fellow Scot, Lord Bute, 'a certain noble person, the translator yet avoids to name ..., as his exalted station as well as merit has raised him above the panegyric of one so little known'.[33] Immediately popular, *Fingal* was quickly followed by *Temora* (1763), dedicated to the Earl of Bute, which was no less a success amongst those who were drawn to the new literary experience.

Written in a rhythmic prose that recalls English translations of the prophetic books of the Bible, the fragments and the epics seized the imagination of nearly all who read them. It was not a local or momentary craze. After reading the poems in Italian translation, Napoléon would approve *l'ossianique*, seeing there an heroic military ideal for himself and his men, while Goethe would find in the same work something altogether more tender and let it take root in young Werther's heart.[34] Here is a passage from the first gathering of fragments:

I sit by the mossy fountain; on the top of the hill of winds. One tree is rustling above me. Dark waves roll over the heath. The lake is troubled below. The deer descend from the hill. No hunter at a distance is seen; no whistling cow-herd is nigh. It is mid-day: but all is silent. Sad are my thoughts alone. Didst thou but appear, O my love, a wanderer on the heath! thy hair floating on the wind behind thee; thy bosom heaving on the sight; thine eyes full of tears for thy friends, whom the mist of the hill had concealed! Thee I would comfort, my love, and bring thee to thy father's house.[35]

One person whose imagination was not gripped by this style of writing was Samuel Johnson. Some of his most brutal throwaway lines are reserved for Ossian. Even so, a passage from his *Journey* indicates both how close and how distant he was to something in or behind the passage we have just read:

I sat down on a bank, such as a writer of Romance might have delighted to feign. I had indeed no trees to whisper over my head, but a clear rivulet streamed at my feet. The day was calm, the air soft, and all was rudeness, silence and solitude. Before me, and on either side, were high hills, which by hindering the eye from ranging, forced the mind to find entertainment for itself. Whether I spent the hour well I know not; for here I first conceived the thought of this narration. (31)

At first glance, it might seem as if Johnson is alluding to Macpherson's fragment. But the scene was a romantic commonplace, as Johnson signals. And in any case he moves quickly from nature ('clear rivulet') to culture ('the thought of this narration'), making it plain that *his* narration is not to be a romance. The contrast between romance and history is a familiar Johnsonsian theme, although here the two are at first kept apart only by his book's on-going and rather laboured joke about the lack of trees in Scotland.

Johnson's attitude to romance is equivocal, to say the least, for he seems to have been as attracted to tales of adventure and chivalry as he was disturbed by their 'wild strain of imagination' (Yale, III, 20) that could lead a soul away from reason and reality.[36] Establishing the truth about the distant past is beset with difficulties, he knew, for trustworthy records were few and far between. There would always be a margin of fable in any history of a country's origins. What raised his ire, however, was any deliberate confusion of romance and history; and that was precisely the fault he attributed to Macpherson's 'translations' of Ossian. Those poems evoke an age 'in which the giants of romance have been exhibited as realities'. And the deduction is obvious. 'If we know little of the ancient Highlanders, let us not fill the vacuity with *Ossian*' (*Journey*, 99). The student of history needs to develop a healthy distrust of what he or she is told, especially when there is no contemporary evidence to support it. Oral history is of doubtful value: 'The traditions of an ignorant and savage people have been for ages negligently heard, and unskilfully related. Distant events must have been mingled together, and the actions of one man given to another' (*Journey*, 41).[37] Poetry, especially oral verse passed down from generation to generation, must be regarded as unreliable evidence. And of course deliberate mystification must be rejected with contempt.

Macpherson was not the first or the last counterfeiter to cross Johnson's path, and it is worth taking a moment to distinguish his situation from the others. One of Johnson's London friends, George Psalmanazar, was well known as the author of *An Historical and Geographical Description of Formosa* (1704) which deliberately gave a false account of the island.[38] William Lauder made fradulent claims in an attempt to discredit *Paradise Lost*, and imbroiled Johnson in the affair to the extent that he contributed a preface to the misleading *Essay on Milton* (1749).[39] Both Psalmanazar and Lauder composed literary fakes, and consequently injured no one's property. What Johnson called 'the stability of possession, and the serenity of life' (Yale, xiv, 310) were not affected by either man.[40] Yet both stability and serenity were upset by a case of counterfeiting in which Johnson interested himself well after the Hebridean tour. In 1777 William Dodd forged the signature of Philip Stanhope, the fifth Earl of Chesterfield, on a bond in order to gain the princely sum of £4200. Johnson helped him, arguing in effect that a crime against property was not a crime against nature. In their different ways, all three men publicly repented, while Macpherson retracted nothing. 'All truth is valuable', Johnson wrote late in life, 'and its value is not decreased when it comes late.[41] At no time did Macpherson offer what Johnson regarded as simple and decisive evidence: the manuscript from which he translated *Fingal*.

There has been considerable debate whether there were Gaelic originals of the Ossianic poems that could be consulted in manuscript. A history of the debate would pass from responses to Johnson's *Journey* to the *Report* of the Committee of the Highland Society of Scotland (1805); it would touch on the argument between William Shaw and John Clark, pause over unfriendly source criticism like Malcolm Laing's and wishful criticism like Patrick Graham's, weigh national pride and scholarly embarrassment over the Gaelic 'originals' of Ossian published in 1807, and would end, though not conclude, with exchanges in modern journals. For a long time the discussion generated more heat than light. What were the doubters, deflators and debunkers of Ossian really looking for? There could be no third-century manuscripts and no third-century regular epics originating in the Highlands, but would sixteenth- and seventeenth-century manuscripts of heroic ballads have satisfied them, or even James Macpherson's transcriptions of ballads he heard in the Highlands?[42] Johnson took an extreme position in the debate, maintaining that there were no Gaelic manuscripts of any kind, and he was sharply answered by Donald MacNichol.[43] Almost certainly Macpherson had early sixteenth-century Gaelic manuscripts in his possession, one of them being the Book of the Dean of Lismore, and perhaps Macpherson had once believed or hoped that this was the epic poem he was looking for.[44] Whether he deposited these manuscripts in Thomas Becket's book shop in 1762, as has been believed, is far from certain. It is more likely that he allowed the transcripts he had taken in the Highlands, texts written in his peculiar Gaelic orthography and unlikely to be readily understood, to be consulted by the curious.[45] Johnson may have been mistaken about there being no old Gaelic manuscripts, yet he was very likely correct to think that Macpherson had left none at Becket's shop.

Johnson's contemporaries had different stakes in the publication of the Ossianic poems, although all the most deeply interested – Blair, Gray, Hume, Montagu and Walpole – were concerned about authenticity as well as literary merit. The intense excitement about these prose poems can be sensed in one of Gray's letters to Thomas Wharton. There he talks of 'these Specimens of antiquity, if it be antiquity: but what plagues me is, I can not come at any certainty on that head. I was so struck, so *extasié* with their infinite beauty, that I write into Scotland to make a thousand enquiries.' The letters he gets in return from Macpherson do not resolve the matter; they seem the work of an unskilful deceiver: 'in short, the whole external evidence would make one believe these fragments (for so he calls them, tho' nothing can be more entire) counterfeit: but the internal is so strong on the other side, that I am resolved to believe them genuine, spite of the Devil & the Kirk. it is impossible to convince me, that they were invented by the same Man, that writes me these letters. on the other hand it is almost as hard to suppose, if they are original, that he should be able to translate them so admirably.'[46]

Like all the interested parties of the day, Johnson and Gray agree that there are two main issues to resolve. The first is a question of historical fact. Should the poems be signed, as it were, 'Ossian' or 'James Macpherson'? The second issue turns on literary value. Do the poems have high aesthetic merit? But there is a third question which is not stated directly but which organises the debate as a whole, namely whether these two issues can be considered independently or whether they must be taken together. To regard them independently is to concede the possibility that a counterfeit artwork can have high aesthetic value, while to consider them as dependent is to deny that possibility out of hand. Gray appears to suggest that aesthetics are free standing; he testifies to the poems' 'infinite beauty' while being uncertain about their historical authenticity. Yet he will not go so far as to separate literary value from historical fact. He must be assured of their origin. With this in mind, Gray wrote to an unidentified correspondent to whom he aired his suspicions about the poems' authorship. The letter was shown to David Hume who at the time believed the translations to be genuine and who responded in detail to the poet's worries and stilled them for a while. In this letter of 1760 Hume distinguishes the authenticity and the antiquity of the poems. Belief in their antiquity is a matter of probability, he says, although he finds Macpherson's reasonings on that head quite convincing. Of their authenticity he has no doubts: 'certain it is, that these poems are in every body's mouth in the Highlands, have been handed down from father to son, and are of an age beyond all memory and tradition'. His uneasiness at this point is limited to the claim that Ossian had composed an epic according to a regular plan. 'None of the specimens of barbarous poetry known to us, the Hebrew, Arabian, or any other, contained this species of beauty; and if a regular epic poem, or even any thing of that kind, nearly regular, should also come from that rough climate or uncivilized people, it would appear to me a phenomenon altogether unaccountable.'[47]

This is a strong reservation, and one Hume was prudent to make: we now know that *Fingal* draws on a number of heroic ballads, not on a regular Gaelic epic.[48] And yet Hume is pleased to find a man of Gray's refined taste approving the bardic fragments; it is a reassurance that he himself has not fallen victim to 'national presuppositions'.[49] Like Gray, Hume finds the poetic fragments beautiful but will not dissociate that judgement from his provisional belief in their historical authenticity. This is all the more clear when the spotlight falls on *Fingal*, the longed-for epic that would ground Scotland as the heroic poems of Homer, Virgil and Milton had grounded Greece, Rome and England. The improbability of such a poem originating in the Highlands had worried Hume from the beginning. In 1763, by which time the philosopher's suspicions over Ossian had grown, he writes to Macpherson's strongest promoter Hugh Blair about the poems in translation. 'It is vain to say, that their beauty will support them, independent of their authenticity: No; that beauty is not so much to the general taste as to ensure you of this event; and if people be once disgusted with the idea of a forgery, they are thence apt to entertain a more disadvantageous notion of the excellency of the production itself' (*Letters of David Hume*, I, 399). And in time he will confirm this view himself. By 1775, in an essay he will leave unpublished, he argues that the poems are forgeries and talks of *Fingal* as a 'tiresome, insipid performance' whose verse is 'harsh and absurd in the highest degree'.[50] What was once considered a matter of beauty has become a literary curiosity, proof that an ancient pedigree will blind men's eyes to true literary value. Compare the later judgement of the poems to one communicated to Blair from Paris in 1763. 'I have met here with Enthusiasts for Ossian's Poetry; but there are also several Critics who are of my Opinion, that, tho' great Beauties, they are also greater Curiosities, and that they are a little tedious by reason of their Uniformity' (*Letters of David Hume*, I, 418–19).

Hume's commitment to the charms of Ossian fades over the years but at no point does he stray from his general epistemological position as outlined as early as 1739 in *A Treatise of Human Nature*. The relevant passage occurs in his discussion of belief which he takes to be a 'lively idea associated with a present impression'. To exemplify this definition he distinguishes reading a narrative as fiction from reading it as fact:

If one person sits down to read a book as a romance, and another as a true history, they plainly receive the same ideas, and in the same order; nor does the incredulity of the one, and the belief of the other hinder them from putting the very same sense upon their author. His words produce the same ideas in both; tho' his testimony has not the same influence on them. The latter has a more lively conception of all the incidents. He enters deeper into the concerns of the persons: represents to himself their actions, and characters, and friendships, and enmities: He even goes so far as to form a notion of their features, and air, and person. While the former, who gives no credit to the testimony of the author, has a more faint and languid conception of all these particulars; and except on account of the style and ingenuity of the composition, can receive little entertainment from it.[51]

Everything turns on the status of those two 'as's in the first sentence, and before long Hume recognised it was equivocal. There is a difference between someone who reads a narrative arbitrarily as romance or history and someone who follows generic signs and customs of reading in approaching it as one or the other. So liveliness cannot remain the sole modifier of belief; it must be one term amongst others that give some body to context. In an appendix to the *Treatise* Hume concedes that 'an idea assented to *feels* different from a fictitious idea, that the fancy alone presents to us: And this different feeling I endeavour to explain by calling it a superior *force*, or *vivacity*, or *solidity*, or *firmness*, or *steadiness*' (629). At first this emphasis on feeling seems a weak way of telling reality from fiction, yet when Hume goes on to say that feeling renders ideas 'the governing principles of all our actions' his reasoning is on firmer ground. People will act (or at least think they should act) on what they believe to be true in fact, and will not act on what they believe to be fictional.

Clear-cut as it seems, the distinction between history and romance cannot be applied to all writings with equal confidence. To take a contemporary example, Ellis Cornelia Knight's *Marcus Flaminius, or a View of the Military, Political, and Social Life of the Romans* (1793) was read variously as history and as romance. After reading it Horace Walpole exclaimed, 'there is so much learning and good sense well digested, such exact knowledge of Roman characters and manners, and the barbarian simplicity so well painted and made so interesting, that it is imposible not to admire the judgement and excellent understanding of the authoress' – before registering a caveat, 'though as a novel, which it can scarce be called, it is not very amusing'. At the same time the *Monthly Review* disparaged Knight's grasp of Roman history while applauding it as a fine work of fiction.[52]

There was no polemical exchange over the literary status of *Marcus Flaminius*. For the generation that first read *Fingal, Temora* and the other Ossian poems, however, any equivocation of history and romance could not be left without comment. The matter turned on historical documentation and national pride, not on differences between historical and fictional writing. It has recently been proposed that 'If the poems were not *exactly* what Macpherson ... said they were, they could not be received as literature at all', 'there could be no such thing as a "both-at-once" or "either–or" reading', and it was left to a later generation 'to attend aesthetically to works which they knew to have been written for more or less practical or extraliterary purposes'.[53] This overstates the case a little. When replying to Johnson's claim that the Ossian poems are contemporary works Donald MacNichol appeals to an 'either–or' reading. And he believes he has an inescapable conclusion:

But what is the consequence of this hasty and absurd declaration? After all that has been said upon the subject, the Poems must still be considered as the production either of Ossian or Mr Macpherson. Dr Johnson does not vouchsafe to tell us who else was the author; and consequently the national claim remains perfectly entire. In labouring to deny their antiquity, therefore, the Doctor only plucks the wreath of ages from the tomb of the ancient bard, to adorn the brow of the modern Caledonian. For the moment Mr Macpherson ceases to be admitted as a translator, he instantly acquires the title to the original. – This consequence is unavoidable, though it is not to be supposed Dr Johnson intended it.[54]

It is a stroke that Johnson would not have felt. For he maintained that the poems were not only contemporary productions but also of very low literary quality.

One anonymous commentator of the day argued that if James Macpherson had claimed the poems as his own only the credulous and ignorant would have believed him, for *Fingal* has too many 'internal marks of antiquity'.[55] Hugh Blair would have agreed.[56] Many others, though, would have admired the poems more wholeheartedly if only their worries about historical antiquity could be allayed. Putting aside Johnson's claim that there were no old Gaelic manuscripts, could there still be a way of giving historical context to the poems? Well yes, in principle – a theoretical principle, not a moral one – by offering a revisionary history of Scotland, one that maintained Fingal was Scottish rather than Irish. Macpherson may not have forged English poetry, as Chatterton had done, but he did forge a Gaelic epic and, before that, a national tradition. He did so by rewriting Irish and Scottish history. Ferdinando Warner was the first to draw attention to anachronisms in the poems. Writing to 'Lord L—', Warner judges that 'tho' the Poems have taken their Heroes from the Irish History, yet that, like other Poems, they are worked up without any Regard to Truth as it pleased the Fancy of the Composer'. His conclusion turns on a *reductio ad absurdum*:

And unless we will suppose that All the Writers of Irish Affairs thro' several succeeding Ages, have agreed in the same wicked Design of imposing upon Posterity with a heap of Lies and Forgeries, these Objections are enough surely to convince your Lordship, and every other impartial Person, that the Poems are so far from being the genuine History of the Times they treat of, that they contain no History at all of that ancient and once famous People.[57]

Macpherson was unmoved. In his notes to Ossian's poems he claims that Roderic O'Flaherty's *Ogygia* (1685) and Geoffrey Keating's *Foras Feasa* (c. 1634) are greatly in error, and maintains against Warner that the Irish 'begun to appropriate Ossian and his heroes to their own country'.[58]

When travelling in the Highlands, Johnson was aware that Macpherson was appealing to a past that had never been, though he does not seem to have known the extent of the error. He did not know, for instance, of any relation between James Macpherson and the Reverend John Macpherson who had entertained the 'translator' in 1760 when searching for ancient manuscripts.[59] Johnson and Boswell had dipped into John Macpherson's *Critical Dissertations on the Origin, Antiquities, &c., of the Ancient Caledonians*, which had appeared in 1768, seven years after *Fingal*. The travellers had good reason to acquaint themselves with the book, for it had been praised and used by Thomas Pennant whose *Tour in Scotland* (1769) Johnson admired. His approval, however, did not extend to the Reverend Macpherson's essay: 'you might read half an hour, and ask yourself what you had been reading: there were so many words to so little matter, that there was no getting through the book' (*Tour*, 206). If he had known that James Macpherson had contributed the preface, he might have thought more about the book's content than its style. We read in the preface that, in the seventh and eighth centuries, 'the sennachies and sileas of Ireland made then a property of the Scots of Britain, and, secure of not being contradicted by an illiterate, and I may say, an irreligious race of men, assumed to themselves the dignity of being the mother-nation'. And in the work itself we learn that the author will endeavour to show 'that the Scots of Ireland went originally from Scotland'.[60] Having read this, Johnson may well have agreed with Joseph Ritson's later verdict in the *Bibliographia Scotia*, that 'these dissertations ... wil [*sic*] be rejected, with indignation and contempt, by the enlighten'd antiquary'.[61] And for an excellent reason, because they concoct a context that legitimates *Fingal* and the romantic traditions it evokes, a context which, as it happens, was in turn confirmed by James Macpherson in his *Introduction to the History of Great Britain and Ireland* (1771).[62]

What we have in the work of the two Macphersons is a closed circuit of text and context, each promoting the other. John Macpherson defends the authenticity of Ossian. 'The candid part of the nation, though some of them perhaps were at first prejudiced against the genuineness of the work, have been agreeably surprised to find that their suspicions were absolutely groundless.'[63] Then James Macpherson endorses 'the late very ingenious Dr Macpherson', noting his indebtedness to his account of 'the dispute between the British and the Irish Scots' and steadily argues for 'the British extraction of the old Irish'.[64] Indeed, the history proposed by John Macpherson confirms the antiquity of Ossian so fully that James Macpherson declares he does not need to cite his own translations:

The perfect agreement between Ossian and the genealogical system we have established, has placed his æra beyond the commencement of the popular opinion of the Hibernian descent of the Scots; which was old enough to be placed in a period of remote antiquity by Bede, who flourished in the beginning of the seventh age.[65]

This revision of history is accomplished so neatly and so plausibly that even the scrupulous Gibbon was taken in. 'In the dark and doubtful paths of Caledonian antiquity', he writes, 'I have chosen for my guides two learned and ingenious Highlanders, whom their birth and education had peculiarly qualified for that office.'[66]

In the work of the two Macphersons we see the forging of a Highland tradition, an inscription of values promoted in the fashionable pre-romantic poetry of the age – directness, intensity and naturalness – as an origin shimmering in the mists of history. The moment of Ossian had been well prepared for by the Forty-Five and by a long-standing interest in Scottish folk poetry; but in this picture all half-tones are dropped out, leaving only the stark figure of James Macpherson. Johnson was not in a position to expose all the dissimulation involved, and history proves that others had already repudiated Ossian in convincing detail.[67] But Johnson went to the heart of the matter. Ossian was not a reflection of a national culture, as readers at home and in Europe were to think, but a medium for the presentation of an imaginary relationship with a national culture.[68]

Scotland's independence had been less and less of a political reality for some time: in 1603 the crown of Scotland was joined with that of England, in 1707 Scotland lost its independent parliament in the Legislative Union, in 1715 the attempt at a Stuart restoration failed, and in 1745 all Jacobite hopes were dashed. Thereafter Scotland mourned the nationhood it had lost, and the very elements that were suppressed by Hanoverian power were displaced and intensified as literature and 'authentic' tradition. No sooner were Highland clothes proscribed by Westminster in 1746 than the clan tartans began to appear.[69] In the decades following Culloden there comes to be a prizing of the Highlands, their cultural values and their oral poetry. Not that Johnson stood wholly outside or beyond the conflict. His distaste for *Fingal* is bound up with an anxiety over what we would now call romanticism, but there are other elements in play that need to be identified.

In their own ways both Johnson and Boswell distinguish true from false cultural property. As we shall see in a moment, Boswell tends to elide this polarity with another, between Johnson and Ossian – or, better, a spirit that Macpherson misses closely in Ossian – and not always with complete intellectual or emotional success. For his part, Johnson vigorously rejects the romanticised heritage that people find in Ossian, while affirming the values of a written literature. Indeed, he displays those values as he travels around Scotland, although he would be the last to notice it. His judgements on oral verse have all the weight of authority, though they are not always persuasive:

In an unwritten speech, nothing that is not very short is transmitted from one generation to another. Few have opportunities of hearing a long composition often enough to learn it, or have inclination to repeat it so often as is necessary to retain it; and what is once forgotten is lost for ever. I believe there cannot be recovered, in the whole *Earse* language, five hundred lines of which there is any evidence to prove them a hundred years old. Yet I hear that the father of Ossian boasts of two chests more of ancient poetry, which he suppresses, because they are too good for the *English*. (*Journey*, 97)

Students of oral poetry, familiar with the makings of the *Eddas* and the *Niebelungenlied*, may reject Johnson's premises and fault his reasoning; while scholars of Highland verse may indicate bards of the *Gaidhealtachd* who were able to recite thousands of lines of verse. It is hard to know what Johnson would accept as evidence of a poem's age in an oral culture or even what 'evidence' might mean here. And were one to satisfy Johnson on that score, he would still need to be convinced of the value of what had been preserved. Oral poetry can never excel, he thinks, because it moves in too narrow a compass. He had made the point to Anna Seward when discussing Stephen Duck and Thomas Chatterton: 'No man can coin guineas, but in proportion as he has gold.'[70] And he disparaged the poetry of St Kilda for similar reasons: 'it must be very poor, because they have very few images' (*Life*, v, 228).

If Boswell is prepared to indulge Macpherson more than Johnson does, it is partly because he feels sentimentally attached to a Highland community that has sustained itself by telling and hearing tales from Ossian. There were times when, privately and publicly, he regretted that Scotland had lost its independence and as a consequence 'all national dignity'.[71] His response was an emotional one, early and late. As he said in one disputation, 'Sir, the love of our country is a sentiment. If you have it not, I cannot give it you by reasoning.'[72] This is the Boswell who once planned to edit a Scots dictionary, who was affected by the bagpipes, who felt 'oatmeal in the blood', who defended feudalism, and who dressed up as a Highlander.[73] Once in the role of romantic laird,

however loosely worn, another system of property comes into view, one
very different from that in current operation. After all, the stories woven
into *Fingal* belonged not to a bookseller but to the clans, and had helped
to hold them together for generation on generation. In Macpherson's
hands, these stories are themselves concerned with property and propriety, with rights to land and the right to love. As Macpherson himself
reminds us, his first epic looks back to a time before commerce and
private property.[74] *Fingal* tells of Ireland being invaded by Swaran, King
of Lochlin, of Fingal coming to the aid of Cuchullin, the chief of the Irish
tribes, and expelling the Danes from the country. To this sombre tale of
invasion and restoration the translator adds the love narrative of Agen-
decca and Fingal, itself a story of familial borders and their trans-
gression.

Sometimes Johnson and Ossian form a polarity in Boswell's imagination, with Johnson represented as authentic cultural value. Other
times, they are viewed by way of differences. For Boswell's response to
them is not always constant. He never entirely frees himself from an
attachment to an independent Scotland. Despite his claim to be a
'citizen of the world' (*Tour*, 20), he is entranced by the circulation of
literature, culture and nationhood that we would now call an aesthetic
ideology and that is sharply seen in Ossian and the works defending it.
Witness for example Boswell's sporadic sympathy for Highland romance and the new romantic writing. And yet this warm feeling for
home is balanced (or more than balanced) by an overwhelming respect
for Johnson's critical powers and a longing to succeed in England. 'I was
born for England', he writes on 18 May 1778.[75] Why does he think so?
Partly because there is 'a better *spirit of office*, more propriety of behaviour, and a more civilized mildness of manners on the south of the
Tweed than on the north . . .', and partly because Johnson was, as he
said, his 'great SUN'.[76] Both this national pride and this admiration for
England are felt in Sir Walter Scott's story of Henry Erskine slipping
Boswell a shilling for the sight of his bear. The image of Johnson as bear
is common enough, as we have seen, and he is also occasionally pictured
as a giant, an elephant, an oddity, almost a monster (*Life*, ii, 66, 348,
347). In a century when giants and midgets were publicly exhibited at
Bartholomew Fair and other places, not to mention more exotic creatures such as a boneless girl, a man with one head and two bodies, and a
young man with hedgehog bristles all over his body, the sight of Johnson
would not be without effects.[77] What makes Johnson a spectacle, however, is more to do with Boswell than with his friend's striking features
and eccentric manner.

Just as Johnson's 'I' slips from register to register in the *Journey*, so Boswell moves between roles in the *Journal*. Sometimes he is an impresario, a showman touring the country with a wonderful act. Edward Topham saw this first hand during his stay in Edinburgh. Johnson, he says, 'was looked upon as a kind of miracle in this country, and almost carried about for a shew. Every one desired to have a peep at the Phenomenon; and those who were so happy as to be in his company, were silent the moment he spoke, lest they should interrupt him, and lose any of the good things he was going to say.'[78] At other times, Boswell is more of a collector intent on curiosities. He clearly enjoys showing 'Dictionary Johnson' to luminaries and friends. He has, after all, managed to shift an English cultural monument to Scotland. And yet it is not only Boswell who devours Johnson. The great author and John Bull figure is symbolically consumed by the people of Scotland. He is marked as Boswell's property, yet placed to advantage so he may be admired. 'This man is just a *hogshead* of sense', testifies one Highlander, while another calls him 'a *dungeon* of wit' (*Tour*, 341, 342). The impresario smiles, accepting the implied tribute; the collector treasures the memory and the unusual expressions.

There is never any doubt that Johnson remains within a space carefully organised and monitored by Boswell. The tour's path is smoothed by letters of introduction, family connections and respect for Lord Auchinleck. Boswell's act of appropriation in bringing his friend to Scotland is only partly a symbolic consumption, it is also a production: Johnson is given room to re-create himself, develop new ideas, new friendships and a new book. Always, Boswell is the medium of transaction: he supplies Johnson with opportunities to observe, talk and write. And the biographer is well aware of the role he must play:

I looked on this Tour to the Hebrides as a copartnership between Dr Johnson and me. Each was to do all he could to promote its success; and I have some reason to flatter myself, that my gayer exertions were of service to us. Dr Johnson's immense fund of knowledge and wit was a wonderful source of admiration and delight to them: but they had it only at times; and they required to have the intervals agreeably filled up, and even little elucidations of his learned text. I was also fortunate enough frequently to draw him forth to talk, when he would otherwise have been silent. The fountain was at times locked up, till I opened the spring. (*Tour*, 278)

The manuscript journal is even more pointed. There the Highlanders observe that it is always Boswell who 'set him a-going' (*Hebrides*, 244).

So the copartnership consists of a grand text being called into being, then adorned with commentary. Boswell sees himself as a necessary auxiliary, and the vision was not to change. In a sense it could not change, for his transactions continually express a desire to render Johnson and all he stands for valuable. Writing to his old friend William Temple on 4 April 1775, he says, 'Mr Johnson has allowed me to write out a Supplement to his Journey. But I wish I may be able to settle to it.' And on 10 May he continues, a little dejectedly, 'Dr Johnson does not seem very desireous that I should publish any Supplement. Between ourselves, he is not apt to encourage one to *share* reputation with himself.'[79] If the copartnership works only within tight bounds, falling away the moment publication is whispered, Boswell's conception of himself as supplement remains. It can be read in his epigraph from Pope once Johnson was safely dead and that fuller supplement, Boswell's journal of the tour, could appear in print:

> O! while along the stream of time, thy name
> Expanded flies, and gathers all its fame,
> Say, shall my little bark attendant fail,
> Pursue the triumph and partake the gale?
>
> (*Tour*, title page)

To speak 'in the name of Johnson', as Boswell claims to do, is in fact a doubled project. He must of course speak *of* the great Cham, representing his words and acts to the world at large; and Boswell is proud that Johnson reads, corrects and authenticates his journal while on tour. At the same time, Boswell appropriates Johnson's name to himself, displacing the master's proper idiom to his own journal. The supplement is dangerous: the biddable young friend becomes the great biographer whose literary fame can eclipse that of his subject.

Boswell is often praised for giving us an accurate picture of Johnson. Yet he does not simply represent the great man, he arranges opportunities for him to appear as a great man. He travels with a friend, to be sure, but also with a world of moral and aesthetic value that a part of him longs to inhabit and, in doing so, to distance himself from Scotland.[80] The *Tour* records many instances in which he cues his friend into a conversation. 'I talked of the difference of genius, to try if I could engage Gerard in a disquisition with Dr Johnson' (*Life*, v, 93); and he elsewhere reflects that he leads 'as one does in examining a witness, – starting topicks, and making him pursue them' (*Life*, v, 264).[81] Johnson is a fund, but the credit must circulate; he is a fountain that must be opened; and he is a text requiring elucidation. This project of presenting Johnson consists now of leading him to talk, now of placing him in appropriate contexts so that the talk will be profitable. 'To see Dr Johnson in any new situation is always an interesting one to me', Boswell notes, and he is especially adept at fabricating these situations (*Life*, v, 132). Indeed, from the meeting with Lord Monboddo at the start of the tour to the argument with Lord Auchinleck at the end, we see Boswell place Johnson in one new context after another. In order to capture Johnson's uniqueness, his peculiar idiom and singular mind, Boswell must trace a process of repetition and social interchange. Boswell is always 'curious' to discover how his friend will act and what he will say. A collector, Boswell wishes mainly to collect the same thing, Samuel Johnson, over and over, always the same and always different. There is a pleasure in seeing Johnson removed from his proper place, London, and negotiating cultural differences, and there is a pleasure, too, in having Johnson's greatness repeatedly confirmed, showing him to exceed the bounds of any given occasion. All in all, Johnson is prime cultural property, bringing kudos to Boswell, while at the same time buttressing his sense of self, as any acquired property does.

Edmund Burke once testified to Boswell's skills as a social negotiator, observing of the famous dinner at Dilly's that brought the arch-enemies Johnson and Wilkes to the one table, that 'there was nothing to equal it in the whole history of the *Corps Diplomatique*' (*Life*, III, 79). One could say that, in bringing Johnson to Scotland, Boswell performed another extraordinary act of cultural diplomacy. The spectacle of a small Scotsman happily leading a large Englishman across the Highlands turns the Union into a show for all to see. For the Boswell who longed for Scottish independence mostly gave way to the Boswell who saw the advantages of being a north Briton, and who contemplated writing a history of the Union.[82] The Caledonian jaunt was not the first time that Boswell had personally tried to represent the Union. On 13 August 1764, when visiting the court of Brunswick, he imbues a dance with the hereditary princess with political significance: 'Accordingly I danced with Her Royal Highness, who danced extremely well. We made a very fine English minuet – or British, if you please, for it was a Scots gentleman and an English lady that performed it.'[83] A month later in Berlin he records an even more literal attempt to embody the Union: 'I breakfasted with Burnett on Scots oatmeal pottage and English porter. This is one of the best methods that can be taken to render the Union truly firm' (*Grand Tour*, 98). Nor would the Hebridean tour be the last time when Boswell tried to achieve the Union. After Johnson's death, he would try, unsuccessfully, to live it out in his body. 'I was vexed that I could not unite Auchinleck and London fully, yet I indulged hope.'[84] In the *Tour*, though, we see the Hebridean ramble publicly signify the act of Union at its most politically orthodox, England being supplemented by Scotland.[85]

I would like to end this meditation on Johnson and Boswell's travels by taking that last thought a little further. In my opening chapter I pointed out that Boswell conceived the *Life* as allowing Johnson to speak after his death. Were all to go according to plan, the biographer would merely fill the chasms that Johnson had left in his autobiography; and so the preservation of English cultural property would fall to a Scot. All does not go quite as planned, however, and Boswell interlaces stretches of two autobiographies, Johnson's and his own. Stepping back several decades from the time when Boswell was writing on Johnson, we can see James Macpherson similarly attempting to preserve a Highland heritage by making a dead bard speak. We know a good deal how Boswell wrote his biographies. But how did Macpherson compose *Fingal, Temora* and the rest?

The question can be answered in dark tones. Thinking of Macpherson's heroes like Fingal Malcolm Laing proposes that,

In appropriating those heroes to the Highlands of Scotland, he found a convenient chasm in the history of Britain under the Romans, and connected Fingal with Caracella in 208, and with Carausius the usurper in 286, in order to ascertain his era without recourse to Ireland, and to escape detection during the intermediate period.[86]

This view of Macpherson composing by filling chasms can be presented far more gently. While Laing was offering his judgement the Highland Society appointed a Committee to look into the whole question of the authenticity of Macpherson's work. In their *Report*, published in 1805, they offer the following observations about Macpherson's method. The Committee is 'inclined to believe', they say,

that he was in use to supply chasms, and to give connection, by inserting passages which he did not find, and to add what he conceived to be dignity and delicacy to the original composition, by softening incidents, by refining the language, in short by changing what he considered to be too simple or too rude for a modern ear, and elevating what in his opinion was below the standard of good poetry.[87]

And in our own day we find Macpherson's approach presented in similar terms. Thus Howard Gaskill: 'he exploits a large gap in Scottish pre-history to conjure up, Tolkein-like, a fantasy third-century Gaelic world with its own customs, traditions and endless genealogies'.[88] If we accent the softer accounts of the situation, a comparison may be ventured. Boswell may well work firmly in an economy of mimesis, which Macpherson does not, but in terms of composition both writers work in an economy of means: the biographer steps into the background to allow the great man to complete his autobiography, the poet retreats in order to present himself as translator. There is another point of similarity. Macpherson writes as a Scot to let a lost Scottish society speak, and believes he can do so only by giving it a tone of epic grandeur. A generation later, another Scot, Boswell, writes to let a dead Englishman speak, and not just any man south of the Tweed but an English monument.

When composing his epics, Macpherson gazes back before 1707 and before 1603 as though neither date existed to find a culture he regards as proper to the Highlands, and he does so by conjuring a bard in whose name he must speak. William Mason pokes fun at this in an ode:

> Say, Johnson! where had been Fingal,
>   But for Macpherson's great assistance?
> The chieftain had been nought at all,
>   A non-existing non-existence.
> Mac, like a poet stout and good,
> First plung'd, then pluck'd him from oblivion's flood,
> And bad him bluster at his ease,
> Among the fruitful Hebrides.
> A common poet can revive
> The man who once has been alive:
> But Mac revives, by magic power,
> The man who never liv'd before.
>   Such *hocus-pocus* tricks, I own,
> Belong to Gallic bards alone.[89]

In truth, the 'magic' has as much to do with politics as poetry. In their romantic imaginings *Fingal* and *Temora* implicitly oppose the very idea of Britain and the systems of exchange and property that are inextricably a part of it. In the *Life* and *Journal* this new world is embraced, though, to be sure, with reservations and with looks backwards and sideways. It is in these books, and not simply in the drama of Boswell exhibiting Johnson, that the Union is shown as symbolically fulfilled. And it is done above and beyond the highest hopes of the English.

CHAPTER 6

Everyday life in Johnson

Johnson composed his elegy 'On the Death of Dr Robert Levett' (1783) only a year before his own demise. It is one of his most piercing works, and holds a special place in his canon. Coming very late in his writing life, the elegy condenses many of the concerns of his periodical essays, fiction and verse. It is not simply a powerful act of compression, a final summation of a lifetime's wisdom: one or two familiar Johnsonian themes are delicately adjusted, and for once we hear him speak in a public voice of a domestic companion. Experience of old age has scarcely softened his central theme of the vanity of human wishes. We are told in no uncertain terms that we are 'condemn'd to hope's delusive mine', and the generality and weight of the line are wholly familiar to his readers. Even so, there is something in these stanzas that I feel only in a handful of his most private and heart-rending letters and prayers. It is as though all that is condensed in his petition 'let my life be useful, and my death be happy' (Yale, 1, 66) is re-cast in the third person and in the past: Levett's life was useful, his death was happy. One could call this quality 'emotion' or 'experience', but it would be inadequate and misleading to rest there, and words like 'directness' and 'personal' are hardly sufficient in themselves. All these qualities may be found in Johnson's most magisterial prose, if one is open to finding them. In this poem, though, we observe the human situation not 'with extensive view', as from an icy peak, but narrowly and at ground level. We are used to Johnson uttering grim truths about human kind with compassion for individual men and women, but here a valued companion of many years is reviewed with 'affection's eye'.

Robert Levett (1705–82) was an unlicensed practitioner of medicine. He met Johnson in 1746 at Old Slaughter's Coffee House in St Martin's Lane, and lived with Johnson on and off thereafter, becoming a permanent guest in 1762, first in Johnson Court and then in Bolt Court. He was not the only recipient of Johnson's generosity, and the household to which he belonged was far from being a scene of domestic bliss. 'We have tolerable concord at home, but no love', Johnson wrote to Hester Thrale. 'Williams hates everybody. Levet hates Desmoulins and does not love Williams. Desmoulins hates them both. Poll loves none of them' (*Letters*, III, 140). And yet some rituals survived the chaos. Each day the two men would breakfast together, with Levett pouring tea for Johnson and then eating his left-over crusts of bread. Much has been written about this household, especially in recent years, but its economy is only of tangential concern to me here and now.[1] I am not so much interested in how the Levett of art squares with the Levett of life. Rather, I am intrigued by something to which the poem alludes but does not represent, something that straddles the wavy and broken line between art and life. I will call this quality 'dayliness' or 'everydayness', without attempting to distinguish them for the time being. It seems to appear in the opening stanza and be developed more strongly toward the end of the elegy:

> Condemn'd to hope's delusive mine,
>   As on we toil from day to day,
> By sudden blasts, or slow decline,
>   Our social comforts drop away.
>
>   . . .
>
> No summons mock'd by chill delay,
>   No petty gain disdain'd by pride,
> The modest wants of ev'ry day,
>   The toil of ev'ry day supplied.
>
> His virtues walk'd their narrow round,
>   Nor made a pause, nor left a void;
> And sure th'Eternal Master found
>   The single talent well employ'd.
>
> The busy day, the peaceful night,
>   Unfelt, uncounted, glided by:
> His frame was firm, his powers were bright,
>   Tho' now his eightieth year was nigh.
>
>   (Yale, VI, 314–15)

Nine times out of ten people are curious about Robert Levett only because they think that in finding out more about him they will learn more about Johnson's domestic life. It would be wishful thinking to see the elegy lend itself to this desire in the phrase 'from day to day'. From the very beginning of the poem the everyday is discounted in favour of a biblical sense of the day as the theatre of work and salvation. We are reminded that as sons of Adam we must toil for everything, including hope, and the thrust of the elegy is that Levett was exemplary in performing his duties, both as a doctor and as a Christian. This emphasis continues in the evocation of Levett supplying the 'modest wants of ev'ry day' by the 'toil of ev'ry day'. It is as though any number of biblical verses are folded into the stanza: 'Give us this day our daily bread', 'Consider the lilies of the field . . .', 'Sufficient unto the day is the care thereof' . . . Levett's days and nights passed 'unfelt' and 'uncounted' not because he lived in a stupor but because he was blessed. In dedicating himself fully to others he lived without regret or anxiety, leaving no void for those in need or in himself.

The general direction of this reading seems unavoidable, and yet there is something else astir in the poem. Coming close to the words on the page but then withdrawing from them is an awareness of Levett's everyday life. This occurs because we are reading a poem that, rightly or wrongly, we expect to have traces of biography and autobiography. After all, we know that Levett was a long-time companion of the author. And yet it is hard to see how, for Johnson, there could be such a thing as a biographical poem. In *Rasselas* Imlac tells us that 'the business of a poet . . . is to examine, not the individual, but the species; to remark general properties and large appearances: he does not number the streaks of the tulip, or describe the different shades in the verdure of the forest' (Yale, XVI, 43). While taking this in, we may remember another passage that begins in precisely the same way. Johnson is speaking to Boswell: 'the business of the biographer is often to pass slightly over those performances and incidents which produce vulgar greatness, to lead the thoughts into domestick privacies and display the minute details of daily life, where exterior appendages are cast aside . . .' (*Life*, I, 32). 'On the Death of Dr Robert Levett' prizes the demands of poetry over those of biography, attending to 'large appearances' rather than 'minute details of daily life'. We read of 'the busy day, the peaceful night' but see nothing in particular of either, just as we gain no nuanced sense of what was involved in 'the toil of ev'ry day'.

Johnson's poem omits not only details about Levett but also a sense of his everyday life. The distinction is important but not immediately obvious. Thanks mainly to George Steevens's unsigned article in the *Gentleman's Magazine* for February 1785 we know some particulars about the man: his thin build, his swarthy complexion, his taste for the bottle.[2]

None of these details is offered in the elegy partly because the genre of lyric poetry forbids it, and partly because for Johnson one would have to have many talents, not just the one, to merit them being recorded. We recall the following passage from the 'Life of Browne':

> Of every great and eminent character, part breaks forth into publick view, and part lies hid in domestick privacy. Those qualities, which have been exerted in any known and lasting performances, may, at any distance of time, be traced and estimated; but silent excellencies are soon forgotten; and those minute pecularities which discriminate every man from all others, if they are not recorded by those whom personal knowledge enables to observe them, are irrecoverably lost.[3]

At first we might think that Levett's everyday life consisted of innumerable details, and considered objectively that is surely correct. Yet our lived experience of the everyday is different. At most we have only a highly selective consciousness of it, and by and large we do not recall many particulars but a general wash of habitual activity. Could it be that Levett's days and nights pass without being counted or felt because it is in the nature of everydayness not to be sharply registered?

If we remain open to this possibility in the poem it is largely because Johnson seems to encourage it. He addresses himself time and again to what he called 'the general surface of life' (Yale, II, 262). In the *Rambler* and elsewhere we find a 'psychopathology of everyday life', and that is one reason why Johnson continues to be read with attention.[4] His biographies, essays, fiction and poetry are of value not simply in making sense of literature, in entertaining us, or in giving us a finer appreciation of English, but in helping us to live day by day. As he observed to Lord Monboddo when calling upon him in Scotland, 'I esteem biography, as giving us what comes near to ourselves, what we can turn to use' (*Tour*, 79). Admirers of Johnson esteem their man in similar terms, and not just with his biographical essays in mind. And often enough, too, they look beyond Johnson to the general surface of life in the eighteenth century, and enjoy the many pleasures afforded by books such as *The Georgians at Home*, *Daily Life in England in the Reign of George III*, and *Daily Life in Johnson's London*.[5] The desire to know how ordinary people two centuries ago worked and relaxed in their weekly round has been with us, and has been met by cultural historians, since the late nineteenth century. Only under the influence of Sir Lewis Namier, with his overly strict insistence that historians admit solely the hard evidence of written records and the severe logic of familial self-interest, was there a waning of interest in everyday life in eighteenth-century England.

Yet 'ev'ry day' is not a common expression for Johnson, especially when used as an adjective. Far from it, in fact: the elegy for Levett is one of the few times he uses the word. In the twentieth century expressions like 'everyday life' and 'everyday knowledge' are familiar, and even the abstract noun 'everydayness' is heard from time to time. But these tend to be apprehended rather than comprehended: too transparent to require narrow definition yet not linked to concepts that can readily be given. What is the daily? What is the everyday? What roles do they play in Johnson's writings and in writing about Johnson? And how to they fit into a consideration of the culture of property? An obvious place to start pondering these questions would be Johnson's *Dictionary*. But if one looks up 'everyday' there one is bound to be disappointed: it has no entry. There is 'daily', which means 'Every day; very often'. And there is 'quotidian', which means 'Daily; happening every day'. It seems that we should already know what 'every day' means.

Turning to the *Oxford English Dictionary*, one sees that James Murray and his colleagues spend half a column delineating the different meanings that 'everyday' has acquired. We are told that as a substantive it means 'each day in continued succession' and that when used in dialect it designates 'a week-day, as opposed to Sunday'. The substantive has been in use since Chaucer. Only in the seventeenth century, though, do persons and things begin to be regarded as everyday. Three classes of meaning can be distinguished in the word's adjectival sense:

1. Of or pertaining to every day, daily; also, pertaining alike to Sundays and week days.
2. Of articles of dress: Worn on ordinary days or week-days, as opposed to Sundays or high-days. Also fig. *Every-day self.*
3. To be met with every day; common, ordinary. Of persons and their attributes: Commonplace, mediocre, inferior.

The third meaning of the word comes into play only in the middle of the eighteenth century. To illustrate it, the editors of the *OED* begin by citing William Shenstone. In 1763, the year of his death, we find the poet quoted as writing that 'things of common concern ... make no slight impression on everyday minds'. The sentence is more illuminating when more fully given. It is drawn from a set of numbered observations 'On Writing and Books' written, though not published, some years before he died. How is it that truly brilliant works are composed? Unlike other people, 'men of genius forget the things of common concern, unimportant facts and circumstances, which make no slight impression in every-day minds'.[6]

One man of genius who did not forget things of common concern was Samuel Johnson. Anyone who has at least a causual acquaintance with his writings would agree that he testified time and again to the significance of what is common and to the daily as the arena of moral and religious struggle. The daily is not always the mediocre. As good a text as any for this theme might be taken from a letter Johnson wrote to Giuseppi Baretti on 20 July 1762. He had just returned from a visit to Lichfield. 'Moral sentences appear ostentatious and tumid', he writes, 'when they have no greater occasions than the journey of a wit to his own town: yet such pleasures and pains make up the general mass of life; and as nothing is little to him that feels it with great sensibility, a mind able to see common incidents in their real state, is disposed by very common incidents to very serious contemplations' (*Letters*, 1, 207). This does not exhaust the meaning of the everyday for Johnson, however, and lest we lose sight of it, let us listen to more of what the editors of the *OED* tell us about the word. After the quotation from Shenstone we are given a line from Johnson, from his *Life of Akenside* (1781): 'this was no every-day writer'. Is this Johnson using the word as an adjective? No: if we check the biography in question we discover it is Pope's estimation of Akenside as given to Dodsley.[7] The adjectival sense of 'every-day' plainly occurs in speech before mid-century. But there are other quotations, so we read on. After seeing the name 'Johnson' it is with a feeling of inevitability that we look down the column and find that the very next citation comes from Boswell's *Life of Johnson*: 'every-day knowledge had the most of his just praise'.

In an earlier chapter I pointed out how Boswell was happy to include material from other people when erecting his monument to Johnson's memory. This is not what has happened here: the editors of the *OED* cite J. W. Croker's 1831 edition of the *Life* which, as we have seen, interpolates whole texts by other hands into Boswell's narrative. So the words 'every-day knowledge had the most of his just praise' could have been quoted without mentioning Boswell at all, and it would have been tactful to have done so. For these words were written by an intimate of Johnson's whom Boswell could never charm, try as he might, and are contained in a memoir of their mutual friend that he disparages in his biography. I am thinking of Hester Lynch Piozzi and her *Anecdotes of the Late Samuel Johnson, LL.D* (1786).[8] Here, returned to its context, is the full sentence the *OED* uses to illustrate the meaning of 'every-day':

Useful and what we call every-day knowledge had the most of his just praise. 'Let your boy learn arithmetic dear Madam', was his advice to the mother of a rich young heir: 'he will not then be a prey to every rascal which this town swarms with: teach him the value of money, and how to reckon it; ignorance to a wealthy lad of one-and-twenty, is only so much fat to a sick sheep: it just serves to call the *rooks* about him.'[9]

The *OED* does not indicate that everyday knowledge is lightly contrasted with useful knowledge. In the passage itself the shading remains uncertain, since Hester Piozzi does not positively distinguish them. And her careful phrasing ('what we call') quietly makes us aware that the expression 'every-day knowledge' is a relatively new idiom. In all likelihood it has only recently worked its way into polite society from the language of tradesmen and is only now finding its way into print.[10]

How best to deal with what life throws in our path is an immemorial concern, and we are well used to hear Mr Rambler advising us to regulate our lives before it is too late. But before assimilating the everyday to wisdom literature, we need to separate two threads which are frequently tangled together when 'every' and 'day' are used by Johnson or with him in mind. There is the Johnsonian theme of making the most of each day, usually presented in biblical rather than Horatian accents, and often cast in the negative: we must avoid or overcome lassitude and laziness. We think of the motto that Johnson had inscribed on the dial-plate of his watch: Νμξ γαρ ερχεται, 'the night cometh, when no man can work' (John 9.4) (*Life*, II, 57). We recall *Rambler* 134, the great essay on procrastination, and we summon the image of him lying in bed all morning before breakfasting with Levett. Yet to seize the day, to place time under the glare of eternity, is not the same as to contemplate the everyday. This is not a biblical concept; it is secular through and through. As we have seen, in its adjectival sense at least the word was a new one in the eighteenth century. It makes sense for us to approach it from a historical perspective.

In early modern times, the common and the ordinary were slowly being set in a new relation. Rather than appearing in the broad horizon of 'every year', in the steady rhythm of the seasons, they were also becoming visible in the more narrow arena of the 'every day'. According to Samuel Kinser, in the passage from the medieval to the early modern world, 'feudal–military–chivalric models of action and achievement not only became politically impossible, they lost their attraction'. The ordinary became charming, and to clinch the point Kinser asks us to recall paintings of domestic and quotidian scenes by Vermeer, Chardin and Watteau. We might add that even when the ordinary was grubby or dangerous it was still of interest, as novels by Defoe, Fielding and Smollett amply show. Johnson's remarks on these narratives in the *Rambler* are to the point:

The works of fiction, with which the present generation seems more particularly delighted, are such as exhibit life in its true state, diversified only by accidents that *daily* happen in the world, and influenced by passions and qualities which are really to be found in conversing with mankind. (Yale, III, 19; my emphasis)

The ordinary would gain political weight, Kinser says, become 'calculable as an accumulation of days, as everydayness', only in the middle of the nineteenth century when politics had become oriented by 'economic everyman'. Why? Because in ordinary man 'rested the power to produce and consume, revealed now as the ultimate strength of the nation'. And so it is only in the nineteenth century that we find 'the fusion of the ordinary with the everyday'.[11]

Suggestive as it is, this historical narrative does not tell us all we need to know. It may tell us what the ordinary is, and how it changes, but it neither identifies the everyday nor acknowledges the meshing of the ordinary and the everyday that the *OED* suggests was already happening in the eighteenth century. When can one detect the first signs of the everyday? It is tempting to return to the teens of the eighteenth century and cite some lines from Swift's 'A Description of the Morning' (1709) or 'A Description of a City Shower' (1710). More appropriate, though, are these lines from John Gay's 'Trivia; Or, the Art of Walking the Streets of London' (1716):

> For Ease and for Dispatch, the Morning's best:
> No Tides of Passengers the Street molest.
> You'll see a draggled Damsel, here and there,
> From *Billingsgate* her fishy Traffic bear;
> On doors the sallow Milk-maid chalks her Gains;
> Ah! how unlike the Milk-maid of the Plains!
> Before proud Gates attending Asses bray,
> Or arrogate with solemn Pace the Way;
> These grave Physicians with their milky Chear,
> The Love-sick Maid and dwindling Beau repair;
> Here Rows of Drummers stand in martial File,
> And with their Vellom-Thunder shake the Pile,
> To greet the new-made Bride. Are Sounds like these,
> The proper Prelude to a State of Peace?

Now Industry awakes her busy Sons,
Full charg'd with News the breathless Hawker runs:
Shops open, Coaches roll, Carts shake the Ground,
And all the Streets with passing Cries resound.[12]

The narrator stylishly guides us about town in different weathers, both
day and night, advising us all the while about narrow streets, the right
coats and shoes to wear, when to take a cane, which direction to take, to
whom to give or refuse the wall and, depending on who we are, which
kind of person to avoid.

Is this the everyday? Not quite: Gay identifies and addresses the
ordinary – or, more precisely, the manners suitable to ordinary occasions in a growing and sometimes lawless metropolis: nasty encounters with Mohocks and Scowrers are vivid memories for those with split
nostrils and 'burned' bottoms. In Walpole's London even walking the
streets must be judged an art, and the poem responds to the situation
with art, even to the point of framing the everyday so heavily it vanishes
altogether. And yet Gay's mock-georgic comes to mind for a good
reason. It hints that the everyday begins to be reckoned in the city, in
walking about town, on the street, in being jostled and jolted by 'the
rushing Throng'.[13] Speed is a prominent trait: one does not find the
everyday in the rhythms of a life ruled by the rhythm of planting and
harvest.[14] One finds it in a culture where experience has come to be
calibrated in hours and minutes, not just days, and where one's time is
treated as personal property.[15] The everyday cannot be found in any
one occupation or place in town, it is trivial yet important, and seems
neither to begin nor to end but always to be there. It will not be easy to
specify the everyday more narrowly, but if we are to try we have to look
ahead in the century. And to do that we must retrace our steps.

It is true, as Hester Piozzi says, that Johnson had a very large store of
useful knowledge. Amongst his books were William Payne on trigonom-
etry, Henry Rowland on vegetation, Richard Bradley on gardening and
Robert James on fevers.[16] He could speak about book binding and
butchery, cooking and commerce; he could read several modern lan-
guages, find his way through problems of geometry and use tables of
interest; he knew about brewing and boxing, law and machinery, and a
great deal more. He was a poet who knew the trades. It is also true that
we readily associate him with the everyday. The word has become
familiar, outgrown all need to be prefaced by a half-apologetic 'what we
call', and yet it does not point to a clear and distinct concept. When we

think of Johnson from the perspective of the everyday we usually do so in a casual and vague manner. We set out on the right track when separating Johnson's everyday life from a sense of the quotidian in his writing, but this sense is hard to locate. There is a reason for this: the everyday has become the ground against which people and events cut figures, and it recedes as we approach it in search of a positive definition.

'The everyday: what is most difficult to discover.' So begins an essay by one of the most subtle commentators on the topic, Maurice Blanchot. He goes on to claim that the constitutive trait of the everyday is 'being *unperceived*'.[17] And this puts it well. In another letter to Baretti, this time dating from 10 June 1761, Johnson explains why everyday life is so elusive: 'it must be remembered, that he who continues the same course of life in the same place, will have little to tell. One week and one year are very like another. The silent changes made by time are not always perceived; and if they are not perceived, cannot be recounted' (*Letters*, 1, 196–97). Johnson is thinking here of his everyday life, not 'the everyday' as such; and we need to be aware of the distinction. My everyday life may be difficult to discover, but in principle it can be brought to light. I need to be minutely attentive to what I do, or to have others closely monitor my deeds for a while. '*The* everyday' is a different matter: despite the definite article, it is not an ensemble of personal habits and routines but many heterogeneous, dispersed points of activity and inactivity; and consequently it cannot be grasped and positively known. Several people have written at length and with insight on aspects of the everyday without drawing this distinction and without saying just what they take the word to mean, or even indicating that anything needs to be said on the subject. It is as though they presume that they and their readers already know what the everyday is but are unable to conceptualise it or believe that doing so would be beside the point.[18]

They are not wholly wrong. One can know how to use a word without being able to detail its meanings, and 'everyday' is a difficult word to pin down because it is usually defined negatively. The everyday, we tell ourselves, is not touched by the heroic, the marvellous, the monumental or the philosophical; and if we think harder, we might say that it is neither cumulative nor systemic. My everyday life is habitual and repetitive, and consequently needs to be defamiliarised in order to be perceived. And all we hear of *the* everyday, Michel de Certeau suggests, are 'poetic or tragic murmurings'.[19] This is beautifully put, if rather oddly conceived: what is the prose of the world if not the everyday? Yet I retain the word 'murmurings', which nicely captures the elusiveness of the everyday, its perpetual rumbling in the background of our lives, and the impossibility of making it speak in a single, articulate voice. If the everyday is ground rather than figure – an indistinct and shifting hubbub as Johnson leaves his chambers, walks along the Strand, dines in a chop house, takes tea with a friend, writes a letter, meets friends in a tavern – then it will be nothing more than a mix of accidents and habits. It may be very familiar but is unlikely to be known. The word 'everyday' would simply name a rattle bag of innumerable things that are dispersed, fragmentary and unrelated.

On this account the everyday cannot be analysed: there is no truth proper to it. Now Johnson can be read with this conception of the everyday in mind. Life, he tells us, is more a matter of endurance than enjoyment. For one thing, we must put up with any number of accidents over which we have no control and some of which will inevitably bring misfortune in tow. Thus *Rambler* 150:

As *daily* experience makes it evident that misfortunes are unavoidably incident to human life, that calamity will neither be repelled by fortitude, nor escaped by flight, neither awed by greatness, nor eluded by obscurity; philosophers have endeavoured to reconcile us to that condition which they cannot teach us to mend, by persuading us that most of our evils are made afflictive only by ignorance or perverseness, and that nature has annexed to every vicissitude of external circumstances, some advantage sufficient to over-balance all its inconveniences. (Yale, v, 32–33; my emphasis)

Yet nature does not supply all we need in order to live. We must look above it, and seek help outside philosophy. For Johnson, Christianity reveals an ethic that limits disappointment. If we take our religious obligations seriously, we will do as well as we can. But if we neglect them, avoidable misery will surely disrupt the surface of life. *Rambler* 81 tells us that Jesus's precepts rectify 'the direction of daily conduct' (Yale, IV, 61). And in an early sermon Johnson stresses the point. Each day is charged with moral significance:

Nor are these obligations more evident than the neglect of them; a neglect of which *daily* examples may be found, and from which *daily* calamities arise. Almost all the miseries of life, almost all the wickedness that infests, and all the distresses that afflict mankind, are the consequences of some defect in these duties. (Yale, XIV, 5; my emphases)

'Almost all': there are sorrows that not even the most pious of human beings can overcome. There is the consciousness, first of all, that so little of life is truly lived. So much time is taken up with repetitive actions,

deeds performed almost automatically, that experience itself is devalued. In reflecting on this we pass from the activity of the 'daily' to the
passivity of 'the everyday'. *Rambler* 8 approaches the notion from behind, as it were. There we are told that 'if all the employment of life were
crowded into the time which it really occupied, perhaps a few weeks,
days, or hours would be sufficient for its accomplishment, so far as the
mind was engaged in the performance' (Yale, III, 41). A long life can be
almost completely consumed by the everyday, with little being won even
in the name of everyday knowledge. To this should be added an
experience that was not fully available to Gay: the loss of selfhood on the
street, the feeling of being slowly dissolved in the anonymity of the
crowd:

While we see multitudes passing before us, of whom perhaps not one appears to
deserve our notice, or excites our sympathy, we should remember, that we
likewise are lost in the same throng, that the eye which happens to glance upon
us is turned in a moment on him that follows us, and that the utmost which we
can hope or fear is to fill a vacant hour with prattle and be forgotten. (Yale, V,
84–85)

The distinction between 'daily' and 'everyday' is broader and deeper
than it first seems. If the daily is fraught with significance, the everyday is
bent to insignificance. Part of the tension of reading the *Rambler* or the
Lives of the Poets, let alone Boswell's *Life*, lies in seeing how Johnson
struggles with these two forces.

So we can imagine reading and writing about 'Johnson and the
everyday' in a world where the everyday has no identifying trait. One
can approach the topic from another angle, however, and argue that the
everyday works against and around a definite sense of the proper.
Indeed, everyday life would mark a temporary escape from the culture
of property. Taking a hint from De Certeau, we could conceive the
everyday topographically, and be on the lookout for 'places of power'
with 'points of concentration "proper" to them', and take care to note
how these discourses of control are subverted by everyday practices.[20]
To be sure, we can begin to picture Johnson from this perspective.
Although in age and death he became a figure of immense cultural
authority, he had no place proper to him for most of his life. Of course, if
we are asked to look for institutions or places of social power with which
he was associated, we can certainly find them: Pembroke College, St
Clement Danes, the offices of the *Gentleman's Magazine* and Streatham, to
list only a handful. Johnson may have passed through all these places

and exerted considerable influence in the latter two, but he did not employ the strategies of the powerful.

Can we locate him, then, around and against these places, in the world of the city at large, developing a practice of everyday life on other people's property? Yes, although we pass from what the quotidian meant for Johnson to his everyday life. It is easy enough to recall him wandering around London with no place to call his own. When Johnson recalls Richard Savage in the late 1730s, he is also remembering himself as one of his friends:

> He lodged as much by Accident as he dined and passed the Night, sometimes in mean Houses, which are set open at Night to any casual Wanderers, sometimes in Cellars among the Riot and Filth of the meanest and most profligate of the Rabble; and sometimes, when he had no Money to support even the Expenses of these Receptacles, walked about the Streets till he was weary, and lay down in the Summer upon a Bulk, or in the Winter with his Associates in Poverty, among the Ashes of a Glass-House.[21]

This is indeed a culture of the powerless, as de Certeau would call it, though in such destitution there is little room for the creative tactics he associates with the quotidian. We move closer to that world when picturing Johnson the Grub Street writer who must catalogue a library, write journalism, concoct parliamentary debates, and translate this and that merely to survive. All this is familiar to readers of Johnson; but when we relate this activity to particular alleys and streets, all we have before us is a list. The associations, feelings, habits and memories that made up Johnson's everyday life are no longer there.

Before continuing, it is worth reminding ourselves that Johnson believed that sites of power have little direct influence on daily life. In the words of the couplet he contributed to Oliver Goldsmith's poem 'The Traveller': 'How small of all that human hearts endure, / That part which laws or kings can cause or cure'.[22] It would be a mistake to read these lines as electing private over public space, an inner world over the outer, or individual over collective experience. These are attitudes that belong to the century following Johnson's. Besides, the everyday cannot be subsumed under any or all of these polarities. It crosses them all, and effects a focal shift that partly defines the subject of modern biography:

> The mischievous consequences of vice and folly, of irregular desires and predominant passions, are best discovered by those relations which are levelled with the general surface of life, which tell not how any man became great, but

how he was made happy; not how he lost the favour of his prince, but how he became discontented with himself. (Yale, II, 262)

Everydayness is more closely leagued with happiness and unhappiness than with greatness. Yet perhaps it takes hold at a lower level than either, in the bid to accommodate oneself to the world simply in order to survive.

The main difficulty of talking about the quotidian has been the absence of a truth proper to it. It has no unique features or traits that can be reassembled, and conceiving it by way of a creative relation to a place does not take us where we would like to go. What is valuable in de Certeau, however, is his emphasis on everyday life as a series of acts of appropriation. Perhaps we would get further more quickly if we attend to these acts and ask what is appropriated or not appropriated in the everyday. There are very different answers to this question, and getting a sense of them may lead us away from Johnson for a while. Yet maybe that will help us understand him the better. In the hope that this is so, let us take our bearings from one of the earliest and most searching accounts of the everyday. In *Being and Time* (1927) Martin Heidegger questions what everydayness means for human being – or in his vo- cabulary, *Dasein. Alltäglichkeit*, everydayness, is placed in quotation marks, as though to hold it in suspension while under examination. ' "Everydayness" ', he writes, 'means the "how" in accordance with which *Dasein* "lives unto the day" ["in den Tag hineinlebt"], whether in all its ways of behaving or only in certain ones which have been prescribed by Being-with-one-another'.[23] So while everydayness refers to the calendar it cannot be reduced to the passage of one day suc- ceeding another. It is not merely that our circumstances are temporal, our very being is given by time; and although we may transcend the rule of the calendar now and then we will always return to let it organise our lives. What it means to *be* a finite entity capable of wondering about being is a question that Heidegger pursues early and late, but here I cannot follow him at all closely. One thing I can take from him, however, is an understanding that 'everyday' points in two directions, to the diurnal rhythm of the calendar and to a structure of being. The word denotes a punctual reference and a category.[24]

Let us try to make better sense of this category. Heidegger argues that while the everyday is familiar to us as individual beings it remains opaque at the level of human being. We need to shift our analysis from the ontic to the ontological, and when we do this we discover that our everyday life is inauthentic. In our everyday lives we relate to one another in deficient ways, both in reducing other people's integrity by regarding them in terms of their social or work function and, more subtly, in allowing ourselves to substitute for them and to be substituted for by them. In our workaday lives we have in effect no proper name and our experience is not our property: it belongs to the 'They' or the 'Everyone'. *Dasein*'s condition is liable to be worse in the city than in the country because the city is dense with work and its consequent pressures to conform and be lulled into anonymity.[25] 'Being', in the modern age, has become no more than 'being produced' and 'being consumed', and it requires something not unlike a religious conversion for a person to embrace authentic human being. It is a grim conclusion that this authenticity means actively seeking a profound awareness of one's essential finitude. Death, here, is not a notional truth, not something that happens to others. Only by existentially recognising that no one can die for me, by appropriating my mortality, do I transcend inauthentic everyday existence. Finitude is not merely a property of being human: my death is proper to me.

Do these ideas bring any aspect of Johnson into sharper focus? He was not so much anxious about death as about Judgement after death. The thought of human finitude greatly distressed him, to be sure, though not as much as did the blank fear that he may be damned for all eternity. That said, the conjunction of the Englishman and the German has a point. To use the distinction I have been developing in this chapter, both writers regard the daily as authentic and the everyday as inauthentic, while conceding that everydayness is integral to human being. It is at heart a religious vision, and while their theologies may be very different both men are centred in Protestantism. Thereafter, they part company. Heidegger proposes an account of human being without recourse to a moral vocabulary – even 'authentic' is used analytically, not evaluatively – while Johnson believes this to be undesirable and impossible. Heidegger deplores the alienation that has become part and parcel of modern everyday life, yet Johnson strives to redeem everyday life, if not 'the everyday', to turn it to use whenever possible. We can see more clearly what is involved here if we turn for a moment to another understanding of appropriation and, with it, a different account of the everyday.

Marx believed there was a nature 'proper' to human beings, and sought to find its essence in labour. And when doing so he construed labour by way of social relations, not ontological categories.[26] Later

Marxists would see less and less reason to develop a metaphysical doctrine of man, and would come to view social relations as a matrix of forces that are formed in history and can therefore be changed in history. Under capitalism these social relations have become alienated. Marx explained why as early as 1844, when distinguishing the right to private property from the right to appropriation:

Man appropriates his comprehensive essence in a comprehensive manner, that is to say, as a whole man. Each of his *human* relations to the world – seeing, hearing, smelling, tasting, feeling, thinking, observing, experiencing, wanting, acting, loving – in short, all the organs of his individual being, like those organs which are directly social in their form, are in their *objective* orientation, or in their *orientation to the object*, the appropriation of the object, the appropriation of human reality... Private property has made us so stupid and one-sided that an object is only *ours* when we have it – when it exists for us as capital, or when it is directly possessed, eaten, drunk, worn, inhabited, etc., – in short, when it is *used* by us.[27]

A society organised around private property will be sure to generate an alienated everyday life. For in everyday life people appropriate the environment around them in order to preserve themselves and reproduce themselves as individuals.[28] In a culture of private property, however, the social relations that comprise this world are radically askew: no one can appropriate himself or herself as a whole person.

The immediate response to this is an obvious one. Eighteenth-century English society was solidly grounded in private property. In the town and the country people would acclaim England as the blessed land of both liberty and property, and do so with feeling, but the courts and the government looked more jealously on the latter. 'We talk loudly of PROPERTY in *England*', Defoe wrote in 1709, 'and when we are before the Parliament, we should more particularly talk of it – For 'tis the Language of the Place, 'tis the Darling of the *House*. – *Their Laws* have been made to *preserve it* – Traytors have been Impeach'd for *Invading it*...'[29] The emphasis was not to change as the century wore on. For Marx, everyday life in Johnson's time would have been grossly alienated; but there is more to be said on the subject than this. Later Marxists have called for further distinctions than that between property and appropriation in order to understand everyday life. Henri Lefebvre, for one, discriminates between appropriated and dominated space. There are acts in which domination is twinned with appropriation, he says, and a student of eighteenth-century London in search of examples could point to cathedrals and courts, barracks and great houses. And there are acts in which appropriation occurs without domination: the goatherd's hut that Johnson and Boswell visit near Inverness, the Shakespeare festival that David Garrick organises at Stratford, Johnson's early morning jaunt down the Thames with Beauclerk and Langton.[30] On Lefebvre's understanding, modernity is the era when space tends to be dominated and not merely appropriated. If we credit this, Johnson's London would be squarely in the modern age.

For all their many differences of stance and substance, Heidegger and Lefebvre agree to set the everyday in tension with modernity, and to look with nostalgia on the life of peasants and villagers. In a village a balance is struck, Lefebvre thinks: public space may be dominated by and for the community, while leaving private space to be appropriated by the family. This ideal of everyday life becomes for him a means of developing a critique of modernity. And so we have passed from regarding the everyday as having no essential trait, to being a category, to being a critical concept. I am not interested in assessing Lefebvre's account of the everyday, or in judging the extent to which it is utopian. All I wish to suggest, after bringing Marx and Lefebvre into the discussion, is that since the word came into use everyday life has been prized only as experienced in the past. It is a past everyday that is used to criticise the present, and it may well be a past that has never been a present. Now everyday life is bad, we say, it is completely devalued; but back then it was better. Now we cannot see how we appropriate the world about us and live our everyday lives; we must look back.

In chapter three I quoted George Birkbeck Hill's confession that he valued the *Life of Johnson* not because it memorialised a great man but because it preserved an entire literary era, one that was blessedly free from 'those troublesome doubts, doubts of all kinds, which since the great upheaval of the French Revolution have harassed mankind (*Life*, I, xxxi). It would be a mistake to dismiss Hill's remark with a smile, or to observe that Boswell wrote the *Life* in the shadow of the Revolution, which he regarded with horror. Boswell's art gives us the sense of a teeming literary environment, and when reading his *Life* and journals we glimpse the last light of a world about to be changed forever. It may be that the quotidian can never be brought sharply into focus, not even by a Boswell, a Frances Burney or a Thrale, but more than any other writer it is Boswell who gives us the impression of everyday life.

What counters, opposes or resists the everyday? If we take the word to denote those activities that enable the whole person to maintain and reproduce himself or herself as an individual, then the best answer I know is 'the tendency towards homogenisation'.[31] Boswell felt the subtle attraction of this force, instructing himself time and again to 'be *retenu*', but as a man and more so as a writer he kept failing to succumb to it. W. H. Auden identifies one aspect of this when reflecting on the *London Journal*. 'Like every ordinary man, Boswell wanted desperately to become a conventional man; that is to say, to lose his humanity and become a mechanical doll. What makes him so extraordinary is that this transformation, which most ordinary men go through with the greatest ease, was entirely beyond his powers.'[32] Boswell was indeed fascinated by the diversity of the life around him, as well as of the life within him. Whether he was one soul or many selves intrigued and frightened him by turns. Of more interest to me in this chapter is Boswell as a writer. Here, too, he is quite unable to be conventional: a controlled excess marks his style. This has many aspects. One is that the everyday and the non-everyday are held in tension in his writing, especially when Johnson is the subject.

In order to begin thinking about this, we need to recognise that in the *Journal of a Tour* and the *Life* Boswell presents Johnson in the first sense the *OED* gives to 'everyday': 'each day in continued succession'. Composed in 'scenes', and mostly adapted or taken directly from his diaries, Boswell's biographies are structured to reveal how Johnson lives day by day. Before we can get anywhere, then, we need to consider what was involved in writing those diaries. For Johnson, a man would be well advised to keep a diary for all sorts of reasons. The reasons for keeping a business diary are not necessarily the same as for keeping a travel or a personal diary. In some circumstances a diary could be of value for a future biographer or for historians, while for the writer himself a personal diary was also a means of personal moral surveillance. This latter concern comes quickly to the surface in a conversation about diaries recorded in the *Life*. It begins with Johnson disagreeing with Hester Thrale. She has just suggested that small things may as well be forgotten.

JOHNSON. 'No, Madam, a man loves to review his own mind. That is the use of a diary, or journal.' LORD TRIMLESTOWN. 'True, Sir. As the ladies love to see themselves in a glass; so a man likes to see himself in his journal.' BOSWELL. 'A very pretty allusion.' JOHNSON. 'Yes, indeed.' BOSWELL. 'And as a lady adjusts her dress before a mirror, a man adjusts his character by looking at his journal.' (*Life*, III, 228)

Before one notices it the rationale for keeping a diary has changed from reviewing one's mind to adjusting one's character. Using a diary to chart moral and spiritual progress had been a common practice among Puritans in the previous century. One thinks of the journal kept by the Reverend Henry Newcome from 1661 to 1724.[33] The practice was kept up by Methodists and Quakers in the eighteenth century. A diary, the dissenters thought, served as a mirror; and Boswell's conceit is an elegant gloss on this. At the time of making the remark he may have believed he was doing what they had done, and at other times he may have half-believed it. Yet it is closer to the truth to say that he put his diary to more immediate ends than the Puritans did with their journals.

Like many another before and after him, Boswell uses his journal to render fresh experience comprehensible to himself, to make it truly *his*, by carefully calibrating it day by day. This is most clearly seen in 1762–63 when London is for him a space of distraction, enchantment and pleasure. The city is excessive in the present and its past, and the parvenu can make sense of it only by setting it in the grid of his daily sallies. Also, though, Boswell uses the journal to relive what had already happened in the most economic way possible, and – at times – to shape what was to occur so it would have as much vivacity as possible. Where Johnson conceives a diary as an instrument of regulation, Boswell employs it as a means of intensification. And where Johnson imagines a diary as an aid to reflection, Boswell uses it as a theatre for self-dramatising. In the early journals especially, life is a performance. It is partly scripted in memoranda he would compose each morning:

Breakfast on fine muffins and [enjoy] good taste of flour. Have hair dressed, and if the day is moderate, to go Whitehall Chapel and Lady B.'s. But if it be cold, stay in comfortable and write journal, short this week, and account of 4 volume of Hume. Have Erskine today and tell him the story and inspirit him. Pray remember – and mark it on separate paper – how happy you now are in the full enjoyment of liberty. Summer will come when all Scots will be gone. Then you'll grow more English and fine.[34]

Boswell hopes to encounter himself in these terms later in the day. If all goes well, he will appropriate a self he has already expropriated. But no script can guarantee this meeting of present and future selves, and so the performance must be partly improvised on the streets, chapels and houses that he names. And finally the experience is written up in dramatic terms, sometimes even with dialogue and stage directions.

After Boswell's journals had been discovered and studied, Frederick Pottle observed, 'it is now James Boswell whom we are in a position to know more thoroughly than any other human being'.[35] The Scot may not analyse himself as thoroughly or as eloquently as Rousseau does, and he may not write as evenly or as lushly as Pepys does; but his journals give us a fuller and more continuous account of a life than do the writings of the other two. This may very well be true, but does knowing Boswell as thoroughly as we do mean that we also know his everyday life? To answer this question we need to follow a little debate about what makes good journalising that is conducted in the diaries themselves. Here is Boswell writing on 17 March 1776, trying to catch up on missing a few days' entries, and reflecting on the act as he writes:

I am fallen sadly behind in my journal. I should live no more than I can record, as one should not have more corn growing than one can get in. There is a waste of good if it be not preserved. And yet perhaps if it serve the purpose of immediate felicity, that is enough. The world would not hold pictures of all the pretty women who have lived in it and gladdened mankind; nor would it hold a register of all the agreeable conversations which have passed. But I mean only to record what is excellent: and let me rejoice when I can find abundance of that.[36]

The economy of mimesis seems to be overturned here: life should fall into line with the representation of it. Yet Boswell is not making a philosophical point about the relative priority of representation to presence, no more than he is contemplating a conversion of facts ('can record') and values ('should live'). His concern is with opportunities for self-representation in a busy life. In this internal debate the thought of recording everything is rejected. One wants to preserve the figure, not the ground – or at least not all of it.

If we leap ahead to March 1783, we find Boswell retouching the same image in *Hypochondriack* no. 66. A new detail is added:

Sometimes it has occured to me that a man should not live more than he can record, as a farmer should not have a larger crop than he can gather in. And I have regretted that there is no invention for getting an immediate and exact transcription of the mind, like that instrument by which a copy of a letter is at once taken off.[37]

Such a transcription would record both figure and ground – the whole ground – what is vividly experienced each day along with the everyday. He regrets there is no instrument; but it was not always so. On 8 March 1778 he tells his diary something else when reflecting on the previous day. What worries him now is that there is too much to record:

I wish I could learn to keep my journal in a neat, short manner ... I think too closely. I am too concave a being. My thoughts go inwards too much instead of being carried out to external objects. I wish I had a more convex mind. And yet the happiness of a rational being is reflection. But I am too minute. I am continually putting the Roman praetor's question, '*Cui bono?*' to every incident of life, to each part of a whole.

We see here why the everyday appears to one side or slightly out of focus in Boswell's journals. For at heart, the everyday is not a matter of detail but of repetition, speed and plurality; it does not fall into a part–whole relationship, for it can never form a unity. Boswell indeed can and often does play the role of 'the savourer of life's incidents and accidents, the connoisseur of the casual', as Peter Steele has finely put it.[38] And as the balance of this comment suggests, all Boswell's experience is referred to an organising and judging consciousness, one that is often breaking into self-consciousness. His is not a *journal intime* of the kind that was to flourish in the following century, especially on the continent. Yet in reading his journals at a stretch it is as though we pass from the naive to the sentimental not once but many times. The experience has distinct pleasures for the reader. However, as soon as a diarist tries to see how a day's events hang together, his or her everyday life is in danger of being overlooked, reduced or suppressed.

It is worthwhile remembering that Boswell does not always look for unity, even when he is selecting, as he inevitably does, details of what has happened over the course of a day. There is an untidiness in his journals that one does not find in Pepys, scraps of information that do not fit into a narrative, moments when this concave being flexes outwards and becomes convex. A case in point would be the 'Dialogue at Child's' that the young cub vowed to include each Saturday in his *London Journal*. The passage interrupts the drama of his growing intimacy with Louisa:

1 CITIZEN. Pray, Doctor, what became of that patient of yours? Was not her skull fractured?
PHYSICIAN. Yes. To pieces. However, I got her cured.
1 CITIZEN. Good Lord.
Enter 2 CITIZEN *hastily.* I saw just now the Duke of Kingston pass this door, dressed more like a footman than a nobleman.
1 CITIZEN. Why, do you ever see a nobleman, dressed like himself, *walking?*
2 CITIZEN. He had just on a plain frock. If I had not seen the half of his star, I should not have known that it was him. But maybe you'll say that a half-star is sometimes better than a whole moon. Eh? ha! ha! ha![39]

Boswell scripts this chit chat as a scene, but its dramatic form is not as important as its function in the journal: to give an effect of the everyday continually going on around him. There are different voices and tones, and they come from different places; they do not intersect with our interests or projects, and they appear to have no consequence at all.

I turn now to how Johnson is figured by Boswell. We must be careful to distinguish two things. First, Boswell's Johnson cuts across the everyday: he is extraordinary, monumental. Second, Boswell gives an impression of Johnson's everyday life; and it is this aspect that I wish to explore. Early on in the *Life* we are told that the biography will follow the calender; it does so from year to year and, once Boswell meets Johnson, slows down, sometimes proceeding at the pace of day to day. What is worthwhile in the work, the author feels, is the interlacing of diverse perspectives, the public and the private, the world of speech and the world of writing:

Indeed I cannot conceive a more perfect mode of writing any man's life, than not only relating all the most important events of it in their order, but interweaving what he privately wrote, and said, and thought; by which mankind are enabled as it were to see him live, and to 'live o'er each scene' with him, as he actually advanced through the several stages of his life. (*Life*, I, 30)

It has been noticed before now that the words in quotation marks are not given in full. They come from Pope's 'Prologue to Mr Addison's Tragedy of *Cato*', and there the poet tells us that the tragic muse wishes 'To make mankind, in conscious virtue bold / Live o'er each scene, and be what they behold'.[40] What happens when the second half of the line is dropped by Boswell? An ambiguity is opened, Paul Alkon tells us: we may either identify with Johnson, becoming him 'while seeing him represented', or we may re-live the scene ourselves by being transformed 'into moral equivalents of the hero'. This has implications for reading the *Life* itself. It may be regarded as exemplary biography, with the usual moral justification, or it may be approached as something quite new, a biography whose authenticity turns on experience.[41] And of course it may be both.

I think this interpretation misses what is being said. Boswell's style of biography allows readers not simply to view Johnson as though on stage, but to be his intimate companion. One will '"live o'er each scene" *with him*' (my emphasis) and not *as* him. We will live with him 'as he actually advanced', that is, moving with him as interested contemporaries. We may see Johnson as a hero, as some of his friends did at times; and if we are so disposed, we may even identify with him, though that is not a requirement of the biography. Then again, seeing him up close we may regard him in many other ways, depending on the circumstance – as affectionate, hilarious, gluttonous, inconsiderate, kind, monstrous, rude and so on – as his companions and friends surely did. In other words, unlike *Cato* the *Life* puts us in touch with the subject at the level of his everyday life.

Even today the friendship of Johnson and Boswell is commonly conceived in legendary terms, as though the Scot was always in the Englishman's company and recorded his words and deeds day by day. Croker was the first to point out in his 1831 edition of the *Life* that, in the context of Johnson's entire life, Boswell saw his friend and mentor rarely. After doing some arithmetic, he concludes that '*little less than an hundredth part* of Dr Johnson's life occupies *above one half* of Mr Boswell's works'.[42] It was of course the justification for the kind of edition he prepared, and I have already discussed it in chapter three. Croker's figures may be inaccurate but his general point remains: Boswell chronicles Johnson's life only in some seasons and only over fifteen trips to England.[43] Now the fact that Boswell did not see Johnson every day or every month or even every year creates chasms in his narrative that must be filled in order to maintain the illusion of completeness and continuity. Whether he fills them, and how he fills them, give rise to debates over the status of the *Life* as biography.

If we are concerned with reading Boswell rather than improving him, it is likely that other things will come to mind. One of these is the phenomenon of repetition in the *Life*. Over the years Boswell tends to meet with Johnson in the Spring Recess of the Edinburgh court, and more often than not Johnson is at home in London. It is valid to argue, as Alkon does, that while reading the biography or even while merely recalling it we can form 'an inescapable impression of the same day taking place over and over again', of being returned to a Johnson who seems impervious to time.[44] Here the lack of information about Johnson, the fact that our knowledge of him centres on a handful of days that seem endlessly to recur, has the strange effect of making us believe we know his everyday life. But what we know is repetition rather than routine.

Were there to be a quintessential moment in the *Life* it would be Spring in London. Boswell has just attended the solemn service at St Paul's, and is paying Johnson a visit. Perhaps Johnson wishes to be quiet, perhaps he wishes to talk with Boswell: if so, the conversation is likely to converge on religious matters. The Johnson who appears before us is the great Christian apologist, and when other people appear – Mr Allen the printer, Mr Lowe the painter, Dr Scott of the Commons, Anna Williams – they make little impression on us. Johnson occupies the foreground or, better, his conversation does. And all the details we know about him tend to gather in this image. We recall Johnson with his little wig, reading a Greek New Testament, stroking Hodge, drinking tea. In truth Boswell shows us very little of Johnson's everyday life; but the sheer familiarity of the image, brought about by a repetition that accumulates rather than disperses, almost convinces us that we know it very well indeed. It is not there in the pages we have read; and not finding it can be a surprise. All we have is an aura of the everyday: a sense that Johnson has just been moving through his house, reading in his chair, eating his dinner, scraping orange peel, writing a letter, talking with Mrs Desmoulins or Dr Levett, and a sense too that as soon as we make our bows he will resume doing these same things.

CONCLUSION

'Property, contract, trade and profits'

Lewis Namier once grandly observed that 'every country and every age has dominant terms, which seem to obsess men's thoughts. Those of eighteenth-century England were property, contract, trade, and profits'.[1] Someone unprepared to follow Namier in taking such an extensive view might say that he is running different things together. This person might be tempted to quote Edmund Burke's distinction between property as 'sluggish, inert, and timid' and ability as 'a vigorous and active principle'.[2] And he or she might then ask, what are 'contract, trade, and profits' if not the lawful struggles of ability against the interests of landed property? Namier would doubtless concede that estates were sluggish in eighteenth-century England and defend himself by pointing out that as the century wore on property became less a matter of land than of moveable wealth: banknotes, bills of credit, stock. This association of property and paper is the main reason why so many acts of parliament under the Hanoverians were passed concerning forgery, and why the punishments set for these crimes were so severe. There was no rigid distinction between 'property', on the one hand, and 'contract, trade, and profits', on the other. Appropriations and expropriations of ability and resources, both local and foreign, brought a teeming world of commerce into being, and from time to time this new wealth came to be invested in landed property. Seen correctly, Namier's remark lets us glimpse one aspect of a central force in eighteenth-century Britain, a tension between property and appropriation or, if one prefers to accent the negative, between property and expropriation.

In the preceding chapters I have tried to be aware of this broad tension while focusing intently on Samuel Johnson. In no way does Johnson simply or singularly embody the great shifts and pulls of property and appropriation that characterise his times. In explaining the genesis of 'the Age of Johnson', I have remained sceptical about its use in literary studies. Yet Johnson is taken, time and again, to represent both his age and his countrymen. I have been interested in how Johnson has been monumentalised by James Boswell and others, how he has become a national heritage, and how this influences what we can inherit from him. Boswell's Johnson is a seductive figure in whom readers make deep emotional investments, and he is an example of the complex acts of appropriation and expropriation that characterise Boswell as a biographer. The figure and the example are closely bound together. Yet if 'Boswell's Johnson' is a kind of property, one with its own critical and editorial history, the reactive move of seeking a 'Johnson without Boswell' does not so much escape questions of property as draw property lines too closely around Johnson.

One of the most determined questing for 'Johnson plain', Donald Greene, has rightly insisted on the independence, perspicacity and wisdom of Johnson's writings, and rather less persuasively has bemoaned Boswell's power to distract us from reading them. It is true that the *Life* does not always take us where we imagine it will, to the Samuel Johnson who wrote so much and so well, and that it frequently returns us to our guide: James Boswell. A biography may appear to be a convenient passage to the man or woman who interests us, but it almost always doubles back and asks us finally to value it for its own sake. I suspect that not very many who enjoy a biography of Charles James Fox ever seek out his *Speeches in the House of Commons*, splendid though the six volumes are. How many of us, actors included, who are delighted by a life of David Garrick feel that the next step is to read *The Lying Valet* or *Miss in Her Teens?* Or, more pointedly, one wonders if many readers of James Clifford's *Young Samuel Johnson* and *Dictionary Johnson* went on to read the *Life of Savage* or the *Rambler*. I am inclined to think that the chances are that many of Clifford's admirers put his book down and chose another biography from the shelves.

It is a pity that so much of the brilliant prose and lively drama of two hundred and fifty years ago is left unread or unperformed, but it is a mistake to think that a fine biography will ever lead us to these texts by its own lights. Greene would like a biography of Johnson the author rather than Johnson the talker, and proposes that we use the moralist's writings to regulate the accidents of his conversation. But Johnson is not simply the property of the 'serious student', as Greene would have it, and a biographer must recognise first and foremost that Johnson is a man before he is an author. As Mr Rambler himself tells us, 'for many reasons a man writes much better than he lives' (Yale, III, 75). Boswell knew this, his *Life* shows it, and this is one reason for its popularity amongst serious students and lay readers. At times Boswell may well be, as 'Peter Pindar' said in a verse epistle, a 'haberdasher of small ware' but the satirist was perfectly right to concede in advance that he was 'charming'.[3] To resist this charm and demythologise Boswell, to show that he actually saw Johnson on at most 425 days out of the twenty-two years they knew each other, is a useful piece of work.[4] If this makes us more attentive of the chasms in the *Life*, as it surely does, it also makes us more likely to admire the art of the biography in giving such an illusion of a complete and coherent Johnson. When we turn to James Clifford's biographies of Johnson, so admired by Greene, we will be grateful for his scholarship and grace, but we will quietly measure his art against Boswell's and find it lacking.

In reading and re-reading the *Life of Johnson* I have been struck by how powerfully it is governed by an economy of death. Boswell first saw Johnson as a ghost, first thought of writing his friend's life while stretched out on a grave, and introduces his book by telling us that he plans to let the dead Johnson speak directly to us in 'his own minutes, letters, or conversation' (*Life*, 1, 29). The usual economy of death is that the deceased does not leave the grave; it is fit and proper to stay dead. For Boswell, however, Johnson has two tombs, one in Westminster Abbey and one in the *Life*. In the first tomb one does not speak, in the second one speaks endlessly, though with the help of someone to 'explain, connect, and supply' (*Life*, 1, 29). Of all Johnson's critics, it is Thomas Carlyle who has been most sensitive to this economy. The man of letters is a very curious kind of hero, he tells us. 'He, with his copy-rights and copy-wrongs, in his squalid garret, in his rusty coat; ruling (for this is what he does), from his grave, after death, whole nations and generations who would, or would not, give him bread while living...'[5] Intellectual property survives the tomb and true literary authority can sometimes survive it far longer. What is so captivating about the *Life* is that it preserves two completely different sorts of literary authority, Johnson's and Boswell's. Of course, Johnson's authority as a critic can be experienced only in reading his 'Preface to Shakespeare' or his 'Life of Dryden', to name two of my favourites, but Boswell's task was to write a life, not an appreciation of criticism.

The 'economic acts' by which Boswell determines the law of Johnson's tomb, appropriates his idiom and abridges his life by leaving chasms, are only part of what has interested me in writing this book. Johnson has become a national heritage, a cultural property, yet I have been equally fascinated by how property was understood by him and his times. Others have attempted to distil a Johnsonian economics from his social and political writings, making comparisons or contrasts with Bernard Mandeville, Adam Smith and others. I have tried to follow Johnson over a short but concentrated period, from August to November, 1773, when he travelled about Scotland with Boswell. Here we see Johnson concerned with entailed property and the idea of 'proper place'. We overhear him and Boswell talking about appropriation and expropriation, about the Hanoverian vanquishing of the Jacobites and the consequent breakdown of feudal life by the introduction of money. Years before Johnson headed north, the Highlands had embarked on its troubled passage from a 'natural' to a money economy. By 1773 the old world of social subordination was being engaged by a new world of economic exchange, and in his *Journey to the Western Islands* Johnson broods on what he sees, testing and refining his general economic and political views.

One of the most appealing aspects of Johnson is his steady emphasis that all general views must be tested by daily experience. We live day by day, both in and against the everyday, and the most common economic acts – appropriating the world about us simply to maintain ourselves as ourselves – are often the least familiar to us. Always, there is a pressure to conform, to become 'proper', someone else, one of the crowd. We read Boswell partly because of the sense he projects of everyday life more than two hundred years ago, partly because he crosses that world in such a singular and vivacious way. And we read Johnson partly because he gives us strength to maintain our individuality, even when it is sharply at variance with his own. In his own words, 'what is nearest us, touches us most' (*Letters*, 1, 345).

Notes

1 William Blackstone, *Commentaries on the Laws of England*, 4 vols. (Oxford: Clarendon Press, 1765–69), II, 2. The lectures were first delivered in 1753, and Blackstone was appointed to the Vinerian Chair in 1758.

2 Blackstone, *Commentaries*, II, 3.

3 Daniel J. Boorstin maintains that, for Blackstone, property is 'the primary value of the whole system', *The Mysterious Science of the Law: an Essay on Blackstone's 'Commentaries'* (1941; Gloucester, MA: Peter Smith, 1973), 167.

4 The Lockean basis of Blackstone's lectures is plain. He observes that property 'improved and meliorated by the bodily labour of the occupant, which bodily labour, bestowed upon any subject which before lay in common to all men, is universally allowed to give the fairest and most reasonable title to an exclusive property therein', *Commentaries*, II, 5. At other times, though, as when he meditates on the source of law, and locates it in the State's power, one can detect the influence of Hobbes.

5 John Locke, *Two Treatises of Government*, ed. Peter Laslett (Cambridge University Press, 1967), 305–6.

6 The expression 'possessive individualism' is of course C. B. Macpherson's. See his *Political Theory of Possessive Individualism* (Oxford University Press, 1962), 3 and 263–64.

7 The Act was repealed nearly a hundred and fifty years later. See 21–22 Vic., c. 26 (1858). H. T. Dickinson notes that 'it often cost several thousand pounds to win a seat, even in the smaller boroughs', *The Politics of the People in Eighteenth-Century Britain* (New York, NY: St Martin's Press, 1995), 15. Paul Langford indicates how expensive this really was. 'If an income of £50 is treated as the minimum at which it was possible to aspire to membership of the middling rank, then one in five of all families was entitled so to be considered, divided more or less equally between town and country...', *A Polite and Commericial People: England 1727–1783* (Oxford: Clarendon Press, 1989), 62. Finally, Linda Colley indicates the hold that men of property had on parliament: 'Whereas fewer than sixty mercantile MPs were elected to the House of Commons at each general election between 1714 and 1770,

members of the landed élite made up over 75 per cent of the Commons'
membership as late as 1867. Peers of the realm, who formed the bulk of
every British cabinet until the early twentieth century, were also, almost
invariably, men with landed estates to their name', *Britons: Forging the Nation
1707–1837* (New Haven, CT: Yale University Press, 1992), 61.

8 See the opening pages of Dickinson's *Liberty and Property: Political Ideology in
Eighteenth-Century Britain* (New York, NY: Holmes and Meier, 1977).

9 James Harrington, *The Commonwealth of Oceana and a System of Politics*, ed. J. G.
A. Pocock (Cambridge University Press, 1992), 13.

10 Douglas Hay makes the point sharply: 'the Glorious Revolution of 1688
established the freedom not of men, but of men of property': Douglas Hay *et
al.*, 'Property, Authority and the Criminal Law', in *Albion's Fatal Tree: Crime
and Society in Eighteenth-Century England.* (New York, NY: Pantheon Books,
1975), 18.

11 See 'From the *Craftsman*, 25 July', *Gentleman's Magazine*, July 1741, 378.

12 See Ian R. Christie, *Wilkes, Wyvill and Reform: the Parliamentary Reform Movement in British Politics, 1760–1785* (London: Macmillan, 1962), 32–33.

13 James Boswell, *The Life of Johnson, Together with Boswell's Journal of a Tour to the
Hebrides and Johnson's Diary into North Wales*, ed. George Birkbeck Hill, rev.
and enl. L. F. Powell, 6 vols. (Oxford: Clarendon Press, 1934–64), IV, 97. All
further references to the *Life* will be incorporated into the text, as *Life* and
references to the *Journal of a Tour* will be referenced as *Tour*.

14 Edmund Burke, *Reflections on the Revolution in France and on the Proceedings in
Certain Societies in London Relative to that Event. In a Letter to Have been Sent to a
Gentleman in Paris* (London: J. Dodsley, 1790), 74–75.

15 See Christie, *British 'non-élite' MPs, 1715–1820* (Oxford: Clarendon Press,
1995), 47.

16 See Langford, *Public Life and the Propertied Englishman 1689–1798* (Oxford:
Clarendon Press, 1991), 294–95.

17 Daniel Defoe, *The Original Power of the Collective Body of the People of England,
Examined and Asserted* (1702; London: R. Baldwin, 1769), 16.

18 Arthur Wellesley Secord, ed., *Defoe's Review*, 22 vols. (Facsimile Text Society
14. New York, NY: Columbia University Press, 1938), V (vol. 13), 632.

19 See Leon Radzinowicz, *A History of English Criminal Law and its Administration
from 1750*, vol. 1: *The Movement for Reform* (London: Stevens and Sons, 1948), 4.

20 See Ronald Paulson, *Breaking and Remaking: Aesthetic Practice in England,
1700–1820* (New Brunswick, NJ: Rutgers University Press, 1989), 257.

21 Peter Linebaugh, *The London Hanged: Crime and Civil Society in the Eighteenth
Century* (Cambridge University Press, 1992), xxi. The change begins in the
late seventeenth century. The point is effectively made, in quite different
ways, by G. E. Alymer's reading of seventeenth-century legal dictionaries,
'The Meaning and Definition of "Property" in Seventeenth-Century England', *Past and Present*, 86 (1980), 87–97, and Macpherson in 'The Meaning
of Property', his introduction to *Property: Mainstream and Critical Positions*
(Toronto: University of Toronto Press, 1978), 1–13, esp. 7.

22 A good deal has been written in this area since 1930 when Paschal Larkin published his *Property in the Eighteenth Century with Special Reference to England and Locke* (1930; rpt. New York, NY: Howard Fertig, 1969). I am indebted in particular to Dickinson, *Liberty and Property: Political Ideology in Eighteenth-Century Britain*, Langford, *Public Life and the Propertied Englishman*, Macpherson, ed. *Property: Mainstream and Critical Positions*, James Raven, *Judging New Wealth: Popular Publishing and Responses to Commerce in England, 1750–1800* (Oxford: Clarendon Press, 1992), and Mark Rose, *Authors and Owners: the Invention of Copyright* (Cambridge, MA: Harvard University Press, 1993).

23 I have in mind two remarkable studies by Marc Shell: *The Economy of Literature* (Baltimore, MD: The Johns Hopkins University Press, 1978) and *Money, Language, and Thought: Literary and Philosophic Economies from the Medieval to the Modern Era* (Berkeley, CA: University of California Press, 1982).

24 I take the distinction from Pierre Bourdieu, *The Field of Cultural Production: Essays on Art and Literature*, ed. and intro. Randal Johnson (London: Polity Press, 1993), 40.

25 Bertrand H. Bronson, *Johnson Agonistes and Other Essays* (Berkeley, CA: University of California Press, 1965). Bronson's 'The Double Tradition of Dr Johnson', from which I have quoted, was first published in 1951.

26 See, in particular, James L. Clifford, *Young Samuel Johnson* (London: Heinemann, 1955) and Thomas Kaminski, *The Early Career of Samuel Johnson* (New York, NY: Oxford University Press, 1987).

27 Even a highly selective list of these works would make a very long note. As an indication of the variety of Johnson's writing and reading, see two books by Robert DeMaria, Jr, *The Life of Samuel Johnson: a Critical Biography* (Oxford: Blackwell, 1993) and *Samuel Johnson and the Life of Reading* (Baltimore, MD: The Johns Hopkins University Press, 1997).

28 Marshall Waingrow, ed. *James Boswell's 'Life of Johnson': an Edition of the Original Manuscript in Four Volumes*, 1: *1709–1765* (New Haven, CT: Yale University Press, 1994).

29 Thomas B. Macaulay, 'Essay on Boswell's "Life of Johnson"', *Edinburgh Review*, 54 (1831), 1–38. Also see Macaulay's essay on Johnson in *Encyclopedia Brittanica*, 7th edn. (1830–42). For the rehabilitation of Boswell's reputation see George Birkbeck Hill, ed. James Boswell, *The Life of Samuel Johnson* (Oxford: Oxford University Press, 1887), 6 vols; Chauncey Brewster Tinker, ed., *Letters of James Boswell* (Oxford: Clarendon Press, 1924), 2 vols; and the trade edition of The Yale Editions of the Private Papers of James Boswell (1950–89). Pottle was involved with all volumes of the project except the last, *Boswell: The Great Biographer 1789–95*, ed. Marlies K. Danziger and Frank Brady (New York, NY: McGraw-Hill, 1989), which is is inscribed 'In memory of Frederick A. Pottle Boswellianissimus 1897–1987'.

30 Claude Rawson, 'The Night I Didn't Get Drunk', review of *Boswell: The English Experiment 1785–1789*, *London Review of Books* (7 May 1989), 18. Given Rawson's distaste for Boswell, it is an irony that he is now the General Editor of the Yale Editions of the Private Papers of James Boswell.

I THE MONUMENT

1 For instance, although Johnson was known to be the author of *The Rambler* the first edition of it to bear his name was published two years after his death, in 1786, as the first volume of Harrison's British Classics.

2 A familiar line was to recall Johnson's definition of 'pension'. See for example *The North Briton*, 12 (21 August 1762), 68–69. For further instances see Helen Louise McGuffie, *Samuel Johnson in the British Press, 1749–1784: a Chronological Checklist* (New York, NY: Garland, 1976).

3 David Garrick, 'On Johnson's Dictionary', in *The Poetical Works of David Garrick*, ed. George Kearsley, 2 vols (London: George Kearsley, 1785), II, 506. A line in jingoism can be found in Garrick's writings of the day: see his prologue to Arthur Murphy's *The Apprentice* (1756). As a further index of the English feeling against the French see Samuel Foote's farces *The Englishman in Paris* (1753) and *The Englishman Returned from Paris* (1756). That Johnson himself felt less than heroic is suggested by his poem 'ΓΝΩΙ ΣΕΑΥΤΟΝ' written after revising and enlarging the *Dictionary* in 1772.

4 *The World*, 100, 28 November, 1754 in Alexander Chalmers, ed. *The British Essayists, with Prefaces Historical and Biographical* (London: C. and J. Rivington, et al., 1823), XXIII, 196. On Dodsley's relations with Lord Chesterfield as Johnson's patron and contributor to *The World*, see Harry M. Solomon, *The Rise of Robert Dodsley: Creating the New Age of Print* (Carbondale, IL: Southern Illinois University Press, 1996), 162–67.

5 *The Rambler*, eds. W. J. Bate, J. M. Bullit and L. F. Powell. The Yale Edition of the Works of Samuel Johnson. All references to *The Rambler* in the text will be to this edition and referenced as Yale, III, IV or V.

6 When it first appeared in print, the word was 'chum'. See however *The Letters of Tobias Smollett*, ed. Lewis M. Knapp (Oxford: Clarendon, 1970), 75 n. 2.

7 Oliver Goldsmith, *The Bee*, in *Collected Works of Oliver Goldsmith*, ed. Arthur Friedman, 5 vols. (Oxford: Clarendon Press, 1966), I, 447–48. All further references to Goldsmith's works will be to this edition.

8 Richard C. Cole, ed. with Peter S. Baker and Rachel McClellan, and assistant James J. Caudle, *The General Correspondence of James Boswell, 1766–1769*, 2 vols. The Yale Editions of the Private Papers of James Boswell, Research Edition, Correspondence, vol. V (New Haven, CT: Yale University Press, and Edinburgh University Press, 1993), I, 108. All references to Boswell's correspondence will be to this edition unless otherwise noted.

9 Samuel Johnson, *A Dictionary of the English Language*, 2 vols. (London: J. and P. Knapton, et al., 1755). All further references to the *Dictionary* will be from this edition.

10 Cf. Boswell's story of Johnson's views on the reception of *Irene*, 'When asked how he felt upon the ill success of his tragedy, he replied, "Like the Monument"', *Life*, I, 199.

11 *Lives of the English Poets*, George Birkbeck Hill, ed. 3 vols. (Oxford: Clarendon Press, 1905), I, 2.

12 Marshall Waingrow, ed. *The Correspondence and Other Papers of James Boswell, Relating to the Making of the 'Life of Johnson'*. The Yale Editions of the Private Papers of James Boswell, Research Edition, Correspondence, vol. II (New York, NY: McGraw, 1969), 26.

13 Samuel Johnson, *Rasselas and Other Tales*, ed. Gwin J. Kolb. The Yale Edition of the Works of Samuel Johnson (New Haven, CT: Yale University Press, 1990), XVI, 119. All further references to Johnson's writings will be to this edition unless otherwise noted and referred to in the text as Yale, XVI.

14 This should not be taken to imply a disregard for monuments. Consider the following remark: 'A contempt of the monuments, and the wisdom of antiquity, may justly be reckoned one of the reigning follies of these days, to which pride and idleness have equally contributed', *Sermons*, ed. Jean Hagstrum and James Gray. The Yale Edition of the Works of Samuel Johnson (New Haven, CT: Yale University Press, 1978), 82. This work is referred to in the text as Yale, XIV.

15 Sir Joshua Reynolds, 'A Journey to Flanders and Holland' in his *Literary Works*, ed. Henry William Beechey, new and improved edn, Bohn's Standard Library, 2 vols. (London: Henry G. Bohn, 1852), II, 190. A full account of the St Paul's monument is given by Peter Martin, 'Edmond Malone, Sir Joshua Reynolds, and Dr Johnson's Monument in St Paul's Cathedral', *The Age of Johnson*, 3 (1990), 331–51.

16 There are two monuments in Lichfield: one in the Cathedral, erected in 1793, and another in the Market Place, raised in 1838. A third statue was built in 1910 in the churchyard of St Clement Danes, London. See *Life*, IV, 464–72.

17 See W. P. Courtney and D. Nichol Smith, *A Bibliography of Samuel Johnson* (1915; rpt. Oxford: Clarendon Press, 1951), 161. We are still without an entire edition of Johnson's *Works*, even though the Yale editions promise to become the standard reference when complete. New additions to the Johnson canon continue to be made well into the twentieth century. See Donald J. Greene, 'The Development of the Johnson Canon', in *Restoration and Eighteenth-Century Literature: Essays in Honour of Alan Dugald McKillop* (Chicago, IL: University of Chicago Press, 1963), 407–27.

18 George Birkbeck Hill, ed. *Johnsonian Miscellanies*, 2 vols. (Oxford: Clarendon, 1897), II, 19.

19 John Wain, ed. and intro., *Johnson on Johnson: a Selection of the Personal and Auobiographical Writings of Samuel Johnson (1709–1784)*. Everyman's Library (London: Dent, 1976).

20 Edmond Jabès, *The Book of Resemblances*, trans. Rosemarie Waldrop, 3 vols (Hanover, NH: Wesleyan University Press, 1991), II, 39.

21 Isobel Grundy makes the point well: 'Johnson's phrases and sentences often sound more assured, but his paragraphs and whole essays more tentative, than those of other writers', 'Samuel Johnson: Man of Maxims?', in her edited collection, *Samuel Johnson: New Critical Essays* (London: Vision, 1984), 29.

22 In 1758, while a member of the Royal Society for the Encouragement of Arts, Manufactures and Commerce, Johnson served on a committee investigating prostitution. See D. G. C. Allan and John L. Abbott, '"Compassion and Horror in Every Human Mind": Samuel Johnson, The Society of Arts, and Eighteenth-Century Prostitution', in *The Virtuoso Tribe of Arts and Sciences: Studies in Eighteenth-Century Work and Membership of the London Society of Arts*, ed. D. G. C. Allan and John L. Abbott (Athens, GA: University of Georgia Press, 1992), 28. It is perhaps worth noting that Misella would be imagined by Johnson as no older than twenty-two and as young as twelve or thirteen. London prostitutes seldom lived long into their twenties. See Lawrence Stone, *The Family, Sex and Marriage in England, 1500–1800* (New York, NY: Harper and Row, 1977), 618.

23 These quotations are taken from Allen Reddick's *The Making of Johnson's Dictionary, 1746–1773* (Cambridge University Press, 1990), 177.

24 Charles Cowden Clarke, ed. *The Poetical Works of Edmund Waller and Sir John Denham* (Edinburgh: James Nichol, 1862).

25 H. Bunker Wright and Monroe K. Spears, eds. *The Literary Works of Matthew Prior*, 2 vols. (Oxford: Clarendon, 1959), I, 177.

26 Suggestions for an English academy had been made by Addison, Defoe, Dryden, Evelyn, the Earl of Roscommon and Sprat. See Reddick's *The Making of Johnson's Dictionary*, 14. That the idea lingered on after mid-century can be seen in a letter by Smollet to John Moore of 3 August 1756. There he writes of 'an extensive Plan which I last year projected for a sort of Academy of the belles Lettres, a Scheme which will one day, I hope, be put in Execution to its utmost Extent', *The Letters of Tobias Smollet*, 46. Nothing is known of Smollet's plan.

27 Herbert Davis, ed. *The Prose Writings of Jonathan Swift*, 14 vols. (Oxford: Blackwell, 1973), IV, 14. All further references to the *Proposal* will be incorporated into the text.

28 The first to notice this was John Oldmixon, *Reflections on Dr Swift's Letter to the Earl of Oxford about the English Tongue* (Los Angeles, CA: Augustan Reprint Society, 1948). Herbert Davis remarks on the 'political overtones' of Swift's letter in his introduction to vol. IV of the *Prose Writings*. The entire question is discussed by Lennard J. Davis in his essay, '"Upon Mouldering Stone": Swift's Politics of Language', *The Age of Johnson*, 2 (1989), 42–43. I am indebted to Davis's analysis.

29 'This, my Lord, is my idea of an English dictionary, a dictionary by which the pronunciation of our language may be fixed, and its attainment facilitated; by which its purity may be preserved, its use ascertained, and its duration lengthened', *The Plan of a Dictionary of the English Language* (London: J. and P. Knapton, *et al.*, 1747), 32.

30 On the roles of the quotations in the *Dictionary* see Robert DeMaria, Jr, *Johnson's Dictionary and the Language of Learning* (Chapel Hill, NC: The University of North Carolina Press, 1986) and Allen Reddick, *The Making of Johnson's Dictionary*.

31 *Lives of the Poets*, I, 232–33; III, 16.
32 I am indebted to Jacques Derrida's analysis of the expression *déjà-pas-encore* in his 'L'âge de Hegel', *Du droit à la philosophie* (Paris: Galilée, 1990).
33 I return to this question in chapter four. Also see Donald Greene's *The Politics of Samuel Johnson*, 2nd edn (Athens, GA: University of Georgia Press, 1990), xxix–xvii.
34 This is the *Secunda Scaligerana*, published before the *Prima Scaligerana* (1669) but compiled after it. I am indebted for this date and for information about ana to the article, 'Ana' in the *Encyclopaedia Britannica*, 11th edn (Cambridge University Press, 1910–11).
35 'Instead of melting down my materials into one mass, and constantly speaking in my own person, by which I might have appeared to have more merit in the execution of the work, I have resolved to adapt and enlarge upon the excellent plan of Mr Mason in his Memoirs of Gray' (*Life*, I, 29).
36 The remark appears in a letter of 16 March 1791 sent from Dorothea Gregory Alison to Mrs Montagu. It is quoted by B. R. McElderry, Jr, 'Boswell in 1790–91: Two Unpublished Comments', *Notes and Queries*, 9: 7 ns, 268.
37 Oliver Goldsmith, *The Citizen of the World*, in *Collected Works of Oliver Goldsmith*, II, 57.
38 'He thought slightingly of this admired book [Hervey's *Meditations*]. He treated it with ridicule, and would not allow even the scene of the dying Husband and Father to be pathetick' (*Life*, V, 400).
39 Joseph Addison, Sir Richard Steele, *et al.*, *The Spectator*, ed. Gregory Smith, intro. Peter Smithers, 4 vols. Everyman's Library (London: Dent, 1945), I, 78.
40 A distinction drawn by Hugh Blair is very much to the point here. 'A great difference there is between being serious and melancholy; and a melancholy too there is of that kind which deserves to be sometimes indulged', *Sermons*, 5 vols. (London: T. Cadell and W. Davies, 1815), II, 366, sermon xiii. Also consider Blair's remarks in 'On Death': 'In whose eye does not the tear gather, on revolving the fate of passing and short-lived man? Such sensations are so congenial to human nature, that they are attended with a certain kind of sorrowful pleasure. Even voluptuaries themselves indulge a taste for funeral melancholy. After the festive assembly is dismissed, they choose to walk retired in the shady grove, and to contemplate the venerable sepulchres of their ancestors', vol. III, 86, sermon v.
41 Frederick A. Pottle, ed., *Boswell's London Journal, 1762–1763*. The Yale Editions of the Private Papers of James Boswell (London: Heinemann, 1950), 270, 57. All quotations from Boswell's journals will be taken from this edition, referenced in the text as *Journal*. Boswell speaks of the 'admired meditations' of Hervey in his second *Hypochondriack*. See Margery Bailey, *The Hypochondriack: Being the Seventy Essays by the Celebrated Biographer James Boswell, Appearing in the 'London Magazine', from November 1777 to August 1783 and Here First Reprinted*, 2 vols. (Stanford, CA: Stanford University Press, 1928), I, 113.

42 Edward Carpenter, ed. *A House of Kings: the History of Westminster Abbey* (London: John Baker, 1966), 252.

43 Goldsmith, *The Citizen of the World*, 62.

44 Frederick A. Pottle, ed. *Boswell on the Grand Tour: Germany and Switzerland* (London: Heinemann, 1953), 114.

45 *Ibid.*, 115–16. Boswell first lets it be known that he proposes to write Johnson's life in a letter to Garrick on 10 September 1772.

46 Bronson, 'The Double Tradition of Dr Johnson'.

47 Waingrow, ed. *The Correspondence and Other Papers of James Boswell*, 519.

48 *Ibid.*, 111, 96, 112.

49 R. J. Mackintosh, ed. *Memoirs of the Life of the Right Honourable Sir James Mackintosh*, 2 vols (1835; rpt. Boston, MA: Little, Brown and Co., 1853) I, 92.

50 Irma S. Lustig and Frederick A. Pottle, eds. *Boswell: the Applause of the Jury, 1782–1785* (London: Heinemann, 1982), 272.

51 *Ibid.*, 271.

52 Johnson was not pleased with the idea, which reminded him of his death. A similar incident occurred on his travels through Wales with the Thrale family. Three years after a visit to Gwaynynog, the Reverend Robert Myddelton erected an urn to mark Johnson's visit to his parish. 'Mr Myddelton's erection of an urn', wrote Johnson to Hester Thrale, 'looks like an intention to bury me alive. I would as willingly see my friend, however benevolent and hospitable quietly inured. Let him think for the present of some more acceptable memorial', *The Letters of Samuel Johnson*, ed. Bruce Redford (Princeton, NJ: Princeton University Press, 1992) 5 vols., III, 68–69. Boswell liked to imagine having statues cast of people he knew or admired. He wished to have a statue made of Paoli when the great man looked particularly grand one day, and he also contemplated erecting a monument to his ancestor Thomas Boswell on Flodden Field where he died in battle. (Nothing came of either project.) However, after Johnson's death, Boswell became a member of the Friends to the Memory of Dr Johnson, the group which arranged subscriptions for a monument to Johnson which was eventually erected in St Paul's Cathedral.

53 Waingrow, ed. *The Correspondence and Other Papers of James Boswell*, 263.

54 *Monthly Review*, 7 (1752), 131. Hill's authorship is attested by Benjamin Christie Nangle, *The Monthly Review, First Series, 1749–1789: Indexes of Contributors and Articles* (Oxford: Clarendon Press, 1934). Howard D. Weinbrot documents the feeling of a chasm at the death of Dryden. See his *Britannia's Issue: the Rise of British Literature from Dryden to Ossian* (Cambridge University Press, 1995), 122 n. 12.

55 Hill, ed. *Johnsonian Miscellanies*, 2 vols. (Oxford: Clarendon Press, 1897), I. 275 n. 2.

56 *Ibid.*, 275–76. Also see I, 305–6.

57 Anon., *An Ode on the Much Lamented Death of Dr Samuel Johnson* (London: J. Rozea, 1784), 8–9. Peter Pindar pokes fun at this kind of reaction to

Johnson's death at the beginning of 'Bozzy and Piozzi'. See John Wolcot, *The Works of Peter Pindar, Esq.* 3 vols. (London: J. Walker, 1794), I, 327–71.

58 Anon., *Johnson's Laurel: or, Contest of the Poets* (London: S. Hooper, 1785), 38–50.

59 Cf. *Life*, III, 268.

60 Rev. Samuel Martin, *An Epistle in Verse, Occasioned by the Death of James Boswell, Esquire, of Auchinleck*. Addressed to the Rev. Dr T. D. (Edinburgh: Mundell and Son, 1795), 47–48, 59–62.

61 Joseph W. Reed and Frederick Pottle, eds. *Boswell: Laird of Auckinleck, 1778–1782* (London: Heineman, 1977), 134.

2 'THE AGE OF JOHNSON'

1 William Roberts, *Memoirs of the Life of Mrs Hannah More*, 2 vols. (London: R. B. Seeley and W. Burnside, 1836), I, 313. Alexander Chalmers makes a similar remark, 'his death formed a very remarkable era in the literary world', and also observes, 'it was his singular fate that the age, which he contributed to improve, repaid him by a veneration of which we have no example in the annals of literature', *The Works of the English Poets, from Chaucer to Cowper; Including the Series Edited, with Prefaces, Biographical and Critical, by Dr Samuel Johnson: and the Most Approved Translations*. 21 vols. (London: J. Johnson et al., 1810), XVI, 568, 567.

2 Sir John Hawkins, *The Life of Samuel Johnson, LL.D*, 2nd edn. (London: J. Buckland et al., 1787), 580. Cf. John Hoole's account: 'Sir John further asked if he would make any declaration of his being of the church of England; to which the Doctor said *"No!"'*, *Johnsoniana*, 169.

3 More, *Johnsoniana*, 299. For example, see *Life*, II, 106; III, 153; IV, 422 n. 2. Hume's death was also contrasted with Hooker's by George Horne in an anonymous letter to Adam Smith published in 1777. See *Gibson's Three Pastoral Letters. Horne's Letters on Infidelity, and to Adam Smith* (New York, NY: New York Protestant Episcopal Press, 1831).

4 Reverend William Agutter, *On the Difference Between the Deaths of the Righteous and the Wicked, Illustrated in the Instance of Dr Samuel Johnson, and David Hume, Esq.* (London: J. Richardson, 1800), 8. Agutter misses the point closely: Johnson was not terrified by death but by the thought of judgement after death.

5 Hill, *Johnsonian Miscellanies*, I, 209.

6 *Johnsoniana*, 113.

7 Arthur Murphy, 'An Essay on the Life and Genius of Samuel Johnson LL.D.', in *The Works of Samuel Johnson, LL.D.*, 6 vols. (Dublin: Luke White, 1793), I, 3. Murphy's essay was first published in 1792.

8 For an account of literary fame in the eighteenth century, see Leo Braudy, *The Frenzy of Renown: Fame and its History* (New York, NY: Oxford University Press, 1986).

9 Lars E. Troide, ed. *The Early Journals and Letters of Fanny Burney* (Oxford: Clarendon, 1988), I, 217. All further references to Burney's early journals

and letters will be to this edition.

10 Lars E. Troide and Stewart J. Cooke, eds. *The Early Journals and Letters of Fanny Burney* (Oxford: Clarendon Press, 1994), III, 100, 103.

11 For a thorough discussion of this, see Annette Wheeler Cafarelli, *Prose in the Age of Poets: Romanticism and Biographical Narrative from Johnson to De Quincey* (Philadelphia, PA: University of Pennsylvania Press, 1990).

12 Ben Jonson, *Poems*, ed. Ian Donaldson (Oxford University Press, 1975), 308–09.

13 Northrop Frye, for instance, seeks to define the latter half of the eighteenth century without reference to Johnson: 'the age of sensibility, when the sense of literature as process was brought to a peculiarly exquisite perferction by Sterne, and in lesser degree by Richardson and Boswell', 'Towards Defining an Age of Sensibility', *ELH* 23: 2 (1956), 145.

14 A. S. Turberville, ed. *Johnson's England: an Account of the Life and Manners of His Age*, 2 vols. (Oxford: Clarendon Press, 1933), I, v.

15 Turberville, *English Men and Manners in the Eighteenth Century* (1st edn. 1926; New York, NY: Oxford University Press, 1957).

16 G. M. Trevelyan, *History of England* (1st edn. 1926; London: Longmans, 1956), 506.

17 James Engell, ed. *Johnson and His Age*. Harvard English Studies 12. (Cambridge, MA: Harvard University Press, 1984), vi. Donald Greene had earlier rejected the labels 'the Age of Reason', 'the Age of Neoclassicism', 'the Augustan Age' and 'the Enlightenment' for the eighteenth century in Britain. See his 'The Study of Eighteenth-century Literature: Past, Present and Future', *New Approaches to Eighteenth-Century Literature: Selected Papers from the English Institute*, ed. Phillip Harth (New York, NY: Columbia University Press, 1974), 25–26.

18 Paul J. Korshin, ed. *The Age of Johnson: A Scholarly Annual* (New York, NY: AMS Press, 1987), I, v.

19 I am indebted for information about these courses and about book collectors to Frederick A. Pottle's *Pride and Negligence: the History of the Boswell Papers* (New Haven, CT: Yale University, 1982), 73f.

20 Wilmarth Sheldon Lewis, 'Introduction', *The Age of Johnson: Essays Presented to Chauncey Brewster Tinker*, ed. Frederick W. Hilles (New Haven, CT: Yale University Press, 1949), xii.

21 C. B. Tinker, 'Samuel Johnson; the Unaccountable Companion', in his *Essays in Retrospect: Collected Articles and Addresses* (New Haven, CT: Yale University Press, 1948), 34.

22 James Kinsley, ed. *The Poems of John Dryden*, 4 vols. (Oxford: Clarendon Press, 1958), IV, 1765.

23 Maurice Mandelbaum, *The Anatomy of Historical Knowledge* (Baltimore, MD: The Johns Hopkins University Press, 1977), 22.

24 Jeffrey Barnouw defends the notion of historical period, maintaining that 'a holistic conception of the character of an age which is to be tested and refined (or rejected) in close readings of texts by writers who, on any

account, would have to be considered central to their times', 'Johnson and Hume Considered as the Core of a New "Period Concept" of the Enlightenment', *Studies on Voltaire and the Eighteenth Century*, 190 (1980), 189. One problem here is that the assurance behind the expression 'on any account' runs into difficulties as soon as one looks at different historical evaluations of eighteenth-century writers. One might well think that Johnson or Hume is central to an understanding of eighteenth-century literary culture until one encounters colleagues who do not teach either writer in any course but prefer to list Elisabeth Carter, Junius, Mary Leapor, Anna Seward, or the trial of Warren Hastings.

25 G. M. Trevelyan, *Illustrated English Social History*, 4 vols. (Harmondsworth: Penguin, 1964), III, 13.

26 I am alluding here to Jacques Derrida's remarks on the topic in his *Positions*, trans. and annotated Alan Bass (Chicago, IL: University of Chicago Press, 1981), 58f.

27 Eveline Cruickshanks, *Political Untouchables: the Tories and the '45* (New York, NY: Holmes and Meier, 1979), 6.

28 *Ibid.*, 70–71.

29 Linda Colley, *In Defiance of Oligarchy: the Tory Party 1714–50* (Cambridge University Press, 1982), 41–42.

30 Paul Kléber Monod, *Jacobitism and the English People 1688–1788* (Cambridge University Press, 1989), 269.

31 I am thinking, in particular, of two reviews of Linda Colley's *In Defiance of Oligarchy*: J. C. D. Clark, 'The Politics of the Excluded: Tories, Jacobites and Whig Patriots 1715–1760', *Parliamentary History*, 2 (1983), 209–22, and Donald Greene, 'What is a Tory?', *The American Scholar*, 52 (1983), 422–27. Also see James J. Sack, *From Jacobite to Conservative: Reaction and Orthodoxy in Britain, c. 1760–1832* (Cambridge University Press, 1993), ch. 3.

32 In this regard see A. J. Youngson, *The Prince and the Pretender: a Study in the Writing of History* (London: Croom Helm, 1985).

33 Quoted by Fritz Stern in his anthology, *The Varieties of History: from Voltaire to the Present* (London: Macmillan, 1956), 55.

34 Philip Schaff, *The Principle of Protestantism as Related to the Present State of the Church*, trans. and intro. John W. Nevin (Chambersburg, PA: Publication Office of the German Reformed Church 1845), 177.

35 In Jacob Burckhardt's major work we read that 'Every period of civilization which forms a complete and consistent whole manifests itself not only in political life, in religion, art and science, but also sets its characteristic stamp of social life', *The Civilization of the Renaissance in Italy*, trans. S. G. C. Middlemore, intro. Peter Burke and notes by Peter Murray (London: Penguin, 1990), 230. Also see Michel Foucault, *The Order of Things: an Archeology of the Human Sciences*, n. trans. (London: Tavistock Publications, 1970), 217.

36 J. M. Robson, ed. *Collected Works of John Stuart Mill*, XXII: *Newspaper Writings December 1822–July 1831* (Toronto: University of Toronto Press, 1986), 228.

All further quotations from Mill will be from this edition.

37 The essay's title was changed in 1760 from 'Of Luxury' to 'Of Refinement in the Arts'. The relevant passage is as follows: 'We cannot reasonably expect, that a piece of woollen cloth will be wrought to perfection in a nation, which is ignorant of astronomy, or where ethics are neglected. The spirit of the age affects all the arts; and the minds of men, being once roused from their lethargy, and put into a fermentation, turn themselves on all sides, and carry improvements into every art and science', David Hume, *Essays Moral, Political, and Literary*, ed. Eugene F. Miller (Indianapolis, IN: Liberty Classics, 1987), 270–71.

38 William Hazlitt, *The Spirit of the Age* (1825; Oxford: Woodstock Books, 1989), 231. I am indebted to M. H. Abrams's essay 'English Romanticism: the Spirit of the Age', in *Romanticism Reconsidered: Selected Papers from the English Institute*, ed. and foreword Northrop Frye (New York, NY: Columbia University Press, 1963).

39 Hugh Blair, 'A Critical Discussion on the Poems of Ossian' (1763), in *The Poems of Ossian and Related Works*, ed. Howard Gaskill and introd. Fiona Stafford (Edinburgh University Press, 1996), 353.

40 Voltaire, *The Age of Louis XIV*, trans. Martyn P. Pollack, preface F. C. Green. Everyman's Library (London: Dent, 1926).

41 Johann Gottfried Herder, *Outlines of a Philosophy of the History of Man*, trans. T. Churchill (London: J. Johnson, 1800), 314.

42 The most significant Victorian study of the philosopher was J. H. Stirling's *The Secret of Hegel* (London: Longman, Green, Longman, Roberts and Green, 1865). Hegel's influence can be felt in later British philosophers, especially F. H. Bradley and Bernard Bosanquet.

43 G. W. F. Hegel, *The Philosophy of History*, trans. J. Sibree and intro. C. J. Friedrich (New York, NY: Dover Publications, 1956), 30.

44 G. H. Lewes reviews Hegel's *Vorlesungen über die Aesthetik* in *British and Foreign Review* 13 (1842), 1–49. Lewes later became highly critical of dialectical idealism.

45 Hegel, *Aesthetics: Lectures on Fine Art*, trans. T. M. Knox, 2 vols. (Oxford: Clarendon Press, 1974), II, 1049.

46 See Peter Gordon and John White, *Philosophers as Educational Reformers: the Influences of Idealism on British Educational Thought and Practice* (London: Routledge and Kegan Paul, 1979).

47 Robson, *Collected Works of John Stuart Mill*, IX: *An Examination of Sir William Hamilton's Philosophy*, 47.

48 Thomas Carlyle, *On Heroes, Hero-Worship, and the Heroic in History*, notes and intro. Michael K. Goldberg, text established by Michael K. Goldberg, Joel J. Brattin and Mark Engel, The Norman and Charlotte Strouse Edition of the Writings of Thomas Carlyle (Los Angeles, CA: University of California Press, 1993), 135.

49 Carlyle, 'On History', *Critical and Miscellaneous Essays*, 5 vols., Centenary Edition of the Works of Thomas Carlyle, ed. H. D. Traill (London:

Chapman and Hall, 1896–99), II, 86; *On Heroes, Hero-Worship, and the Heroic in History*, 26.

50 J. G. Fichte, 'Selections from "On the Nature of the Scholar, and his Manifestations in the Sphere of Freeedom"', in *German Aesthetic and Literary Criticism: Kant, Fichte, Schelling, Schopenhauer, Hegel*, ed. and intro. David Simpson (Cambridge University Press, 1984), 108, 111–12.

51 In *Adventurer* 99 Johnson writes, 'I am far from intending to vindicate the sanguinary projects of heroes and conquerors, and would wish rather to diminish the reputation of their success, than the infamy of their miscarriages...' (Yale II, 433).

52 In *Rambler* 122 Johnson makes a slightly stronger remark, 'The inhabitants of the same country have opposite characters in different ages' (Yale, IV, 289).

53 The expression plainly can be used without such extension in mind. Thus in a letter to Samuel Richardson of 28 March 1754, Johnson also characterises his times as 'this age of dictionaries', Redford, *The Letters of Samuel Johnson*, I, 179.

54 ['Samuel Johnson and his Age'], *Quarterly Review* 159 (1885), 168. It is worth noting that the books reviewed in this article on Johnson are mostly various editions of Boswell's *Life*.

55 Frazer Neimn, ed., *Essays, Letters, and Reviews by Matthew Arnold* (Cambridge, MA: Harvard University Press, 1960), 5.

56 Thomas Seccombe, *The Age of Johnson (1748–1798)*, Handbooks of English Literature (London: George Bell and Sons, 1900), 1. Exactly the same title, *The Age of Johnson*, is used for the relevant volume of the *Cambridge History of English Literature*, ed. A. W. Ward and A. R. Waller (Cambridge University Press, 1913), x. The formulation 'Age of – ' begins to be used quite commonly after J. W. Hales's series. G. B. Hill is one of the first in his reference to 'the age of Pope' in his 1905 edition of the *Lives of the Poets*, III, 98 n. 2.

57 Seccombe, *The Age of Johnson*, 2.

58 *Ibid.*, 163.

59 Augustine Birrell, 'The Transmission of Dr Johnson's Personality', *Johnson Club Papers* by Various Hands (London: T. Fisher Unwin, 1899), 5, 9.

60 Lionel Johnson, 'At the "Cheshire Cheese"', *Johnson Club Papers*, 273. The volume begins with a dedicatory poem by George H. Radford, 'Verses Addressed to the Editors', in which we are told that Boswell's '*Life* remains / (As annotated by our Birkbeck Hill),/ The great Johnsonian mine', vii. I should add, though, that Johnson the author was not universally ignored at the turn of the century. For example, Clement Shorter in his 'To the Immortal Memory of Dr Samuel Johnson', a toast proposed at the Johnson Birthday Celebration of 1906, says, 'As a writer, many will tell you, Dr Johnson is dead. The thing is absurd on the face of it.' And he goes on to insist that 'these three works, *Rasselas*, *The Lives of the Poets*, and the *Prayers and Meditations*, make it quite clear that Johnson still holds his place as one of our

greatest writers', *Immortal Memories* (London: Hodder and Stoughton, 1907), 14, 19.

61 John Bailey, *Dr Johnson and his Circle*, Home University Library of Modern Knowledge (London: Williams and Norgate, 1913), 9, 10, 16.

62 George Saintsbury, *The Peace of the Augustans: a Survey of Eighteenth-Century Literature as a Place of Rest and Refreshment*, intro. Sir Herbert Grierson (1916; rpt. London: Oxford University Press, 1946), 180.

63 Bernard Groom, *A Literary History of England* (London: Longmans, Green and Co., 1929), 203–4.

64 Pat Rogers, *Johnson*, Past Masters (Oxford University Press, 1993), 1.

65 Isaac D'Israeli, *The Literary Character, Illustrated by the History of Men of Genius, Drawn from their Own Feelings and Confessions* (London: John Murray, 1818), 102, 362. The book was first published as *An Essay on the Manners and Genius of the Literary Character* (1795).

66 J. R. Green, *A Short History of the English People*, 4 vols. (1st edn. 1874; London: Macmillan, 1913), I, xxiv.

67 Trevelyan, 'Clio, A Muse' in his *Clio, A Muse: and Other Essays Literary and Pedestrian* (London: Longmans, Green and Co., 1913), 46.

68 I have drawn this distinction from Michel de Certeau's *The Writing of History*, trans. Tom Conley (New York, NY: Columbia University Press, 1988), 3. I am indebted to de Certeau's study.

69 *The Works of John Dryden*, XVII, *Prose 1668–91*, ed. Samuel Holt Monk (Berkeley, CA: University of California Press, 1971), 55, 58.

70 Needless to say, perhaps, expressions like 'the Age of Burke' and 'the Age of Hogarth' continue to circulate. For example, Derek Jarrett claims that 'the England of the 1750s was in a very special sense the England of Hogarth' and that 'Hogarth put into pictorial form the underlying paradox of eighteenth-century English society, the society that claimed to keep each individual Englishman in his proper place and yet could at times be overawed by the spectacle of Englishmen as a whole claiming their ancient birthright of freedom', *England in the Age of Hogarth* (1974; rpt. New Haven, CT: Yale University Press, 1986), 19.

71 Walter Raleigh, *Six Essays on Johnson* (Oxford: Clarendon Press, 1910), 20.

72 W. J. Dawson, *The Makers of Modern Prose: a Popular Handbook to the Greater Prose Writers of the Century* (London: Hodder and Stoughton, 1899), 20.

73 These criticisms are drawn from Nicholas Boyle's *Goethe: The Poet and the Age*, I: *The Poetry of Desire (1749–1790)* (Oxford: Clarendon Press, 1991), 4–7.

74 See William H. Epstein, 'Professing the Eighteenth Century', *Profession* (1985), 10–15.

75 Notice must be taken, though, of Oxford University Press for publishing material on and by Johnson earlier in the century.

76 Max Weber, *On Charisma and Institution Building: Selected Papers*, ed. and intro. S. N. Eisenstadt (Chicago, IL: University of Chicago Press, 1968), 46.

77 See Richard Harries, 'Johnson – A Church of England Saint?', *Transactions of the Johnson Society, 1988*, ed. John D. Austin and Graham Nicholls

(Lichfield, 1989), 4–14. Also see Donald Greene's 'Johnson's "Saintdom": A Reply' in the same issue, and Neil Tomkinson's reply in the 1989 *Transactions*. Harries may have been influenced by the *Times* editorial of 13 December, 1984, 'An English Saint Remembered', in which Johnson is represented as an Anglican saint.

78 *Life*, I, 129. The expression recurs three times: II, 300; IV, 191; V, 20.

79 John Lucas, *England and Englishness: Ideas of Nationhood in English Poetry, 1688–1900* (London: Hogarth Press, 1990), 12.

80 On the question of the London booksellers' intention not only to improve on John Bell's *The Poets of Great Britain Complete from Chaucer to Churchill* (109 vols, 1776–82) but also to compete with it, see Thomas F. Bonnell, 'John Bell's *Poets of Great Britain*: The "Little Trifling Edition" Revisited', *Modern Philology*, 85 (1987–88), 128–52. There is reason to think that Bell rather than Johnson had canonical ambitions. As Bonnell argues, 'if one considers Bell's explicit design, the great size of his undertaking, and his pointed and persistent advertising, then the significance of the *Poets* becomes clear: it was the first serious attempt to publish a comprehensive English literary canon' (130).

81 Lord Rosebery, *Dr Johnson: an Address delivered at the Johnson Bicentenary Celebration, at Lichfield, September 15, 1909* (London: Arthur L. Humphreys, 1909), 18.

82 [Johnson Society of Lichfield], *Dr Samuel Johnson: a Typical Englishman*, 207th Birthday Celebration at Lichfield (18 September 1916), 10. Needless to say, this kind of ideological attention is not restricted to Johnson; it marks the formation of English studies as a whole. For example, in the 1871 *Report* of the Committee of the Early English Text Society Frederick Furnivall underlines the words of Professor Seeley as given in his 'Lecture on English in Schools' *Macmillan's Magazine* (November 1867, 86): 'Classical studies may make a man intellectual, but the study of the native literature has a moral effect as well. *It is the true ground and foundation of patriotism.*' Furnivall goes on to say, 'not dilettante Antiquarianism, but duty to England, is the motive of the Society's workers...', *Early English Text Society: Seventh Report of the Committee* (February 1871), 1–2. I am obliged to David Matthews for drawing my attention to this passage.

83 'Royal Gift to British Prisoners', the London *Times*, Friday, 17 December 1943. Johnson was frequently invoked by English writers during the Second World War. See, for example, the character of Johnson in 'Socrates Asks Why' in Eric Linklater's *The Raft and Socrates Asks Why: Two Conversations* (London: Macmillan and Co., 1944).

84 Bailey, *Dr Johnson and his Circle*, 109–10. See Tinker's strictures against the view that Johnson unites 'in himself the typical traits of the Englishman', *Essays in Retrospect*, 34–35.

3 PROPERTY LINES

1 Edward Young, *Conjectures on Original Composition in a Letter to the Author of Sir*

Charles Grandison (London: n.p., 1759), 54.

2 Redford, ed. *The Letters of Samuel Johnson*, I, 94–97.

3 Locke, *Two Treatises of Government*, 306.

4 It should be underlined, however, that few writers in the eighteenth century made large sums from the sale of copyright. Exceptions include George Lyttelton who in 1767 received £3,000 for the six volumes of his *History of Henry II*, and William Robertson who in 1769 was paid £4,500 for the three volumes of his *Charles V*. See A. S. Collins, *Authorship in the Days of Johnson: being a Study of the Relation Between Author, Patron, Publisher and Public, 1726–1780* (London: Robert Holden, 1927), 34. Nor did the case of *Donaldson v. Becket* have the consequence that authors were well paid for their copyright. In 1777 Thomas Lowndes offered Frances Burney twenty guineas (£20 in the printed account) for *Evelina*. In the wake of her novel's success, Burney was offered – by another bookseller – £250 for *Cecilia*. See Fanny Burney, *Evelina: Or the History of a Young Lady's Entrance into the World*, ed. and intro. Edward A. Bloom with the assistance of Lillian D. Bloom, The World's Classics (Oxford University Press, 1982), x, xii. James Raven offers a thorough account of relations between booksellers, authors and markets in his *Judging New Wealth*, ch. 3. However, as Raven notes, 'detailed study of copyright transaction is restricted to the first two-thirds of the century', 27 n. 20.

5 The point is nicely made with respect to Johnson by Alvin Kernan: 'copyright, we might say, encouraged Johnson to think of the writer as the *author* of his work in the fullest and most explicit sense of that word', *Samuel Johnson and the Impact of Print* (Princeton, NJ: Princeton University Press, 1987), 101. The book was first published under the title of *Printing, Technology, Letters, and Samuel Johnson*.

6 Donald W. Nicol draws attention to Arthur Murphy's role in these cases in 'Arthur Murphy's Law', *Times Literary Supplement*, 19 April 1996, 15–16.

7 See Rose, *Authors and Owners* ch. 6 and 7.

8 Also see in this regard Johnson's letter to William Strahan of 7 March 1774, *The Letters of Samuel Johnson*, II, 129–31.

9 Aaron Hill, *The Muses in Mourning: An Opera*, in *The Dramatic Works of Aaron Hill, Esq.*, 2 vols. (London: T. Lowndes, 1760), II.

10 *Monthly Review*, 51 (1774), 81. In *Rambler* 145 (Yale, v) Johnson notes that in *Tale of a Tub* Swift computes the authors of London to number several thousands. As the number of authors increased so too did the number of readers. It is worth recalling the bookseller James Lackington's observation, 'In short, all ranks and degrees now READ. But the most rapid increase of the sale of books has been since the termination of the late war', *Memoirs of the Forty-Five First Years of the Life of James Lackington*, 7th edn (London: Printed for the Author, 1794), 243.

11 Although the number of printers in London increased only slightly from forty-one to forty-four over the period 1735–40 to 1770–75, it seems that the size of the establishments grew. Also, the number of printers outside

London over the same period increased very significantly, from thirty-seven to seventy-seven. See J. A. Cochrane, *Dr Johnson's Printer: the Life of William Strahan* (London: Routledge and Kegan Paul, 1964), 4–5. The population of London grew from about 575,000 in 1700 to 675,000 in 1750 and 900,000 in 1800. Its growth was much faster than Paris. See E. A. Wrigley, 'A Simple Model of London's Importance in Changing English Society and Economy 1650–1750', in *Aristocratic Government and Society in Eighteenth-Century England: the Foundations of Stability*, ed. and intro. Daniel A. Baugh (New York, NY: Franklin Watts, 1975), 62.

12 For example, Captain Alexander Smith's *Compleat History of the Lives and Robberies of the Most Notorious Highwaymen, Foot-Pads, Shop-Lifts and Cheats* (1713) was very popular in the first three decades of the eighteenth century, going through several editions and reprints.

13 Thomas Sprat, 'An Account of the Life and Writings of Mr Abraham Cowley Written to Mr M. Clifford', in *The Works of Mr Abraham Cowley* (London: J.M. for Henry Herringman, 1668), n.p.

14 W. S. Lewis, ed. *The Yale Edition of Horace Walpole's Correspondence*, 48 vols (New Haven, CT: Yale University Press, 1995), XXVIII, 184–85.

15 In addition to those already listed, these can be added: William Winstanley, *Lives of the Most Famous English Poets, or the Honour of Parnassus* (1687), Gerard Langbaine, *Account of the English Dramatic Poets* (1691), Giles Jacob, *The Poetical Register: or, the Lives and Characters of the English Dramatick Poets* (1719), Theophilus Cibber [Robert Shiels], *Lives of the Poets of Great Britain and Ireland* (1753), Horace Walpole, *A Catalogue of the Royal and Noble Authors of England, Scotland, and Ireland* (1758), John Berkenhout, *Biographia Literaria* (1777), and – the most interesting of all contemporary literary histories next to Johnson's *Lives of the Poets* – Thomas Warton, *History of English Poetry* (1774–81).

16 'The Life of Sir Thomas Browne', *Early Biographical Writings of Dr Johnson*, ed. and intro. J. D. Fleeman (Farnborough, Hants: Gregg International Publishers, 1973), 452.

17 My judgement concerns biographies. Towards the end of the century there were of course collections of details and stories concerning artists, authors, ecclesiastics, politicians and royalty. See for example, William Seward, *Anecdotes of Some Distinguished Persons, Chiefly of the Present and Two Preceding Centuries* (London: T. Cardell and W. Davies, 1795–97), 4 vols.

18 Malone helped Boswell very extensively with the passage of the *Tour* through the press. See, for example, *The Correspondence of James Boswell with David Garrick, Edmund Burke, and Edmond Malone*, ed. Peter S. Baker, The Yale Editions of the Private Papers of James Boswell, Research Edition, Correspondence (New York, NY: McGraw-Hill, 1987), IV, 198, 199. An account of Malone's involvement with page layout, type size and italics is given by Ian McGowan in his 'Boswell at Work: the Revision and Publication of *The Journal of a Tour to the Hebrides*', in *Tradition in Transition: Women Writers, Marginal Texts and the Eighteenth-Century Canon*, eds. Alvaro Ribeiro, SJ and James G. Basker (Oxford: Clarendon Press, 1996), 127–42.

19 See Lustig and Pottle, eds. *Boswell: The Applause of the Jury*. 312.

20 David Erskine Baker, 'Mr Samuel Johnson, M.A.', in *The Early Biographies of Samuel Johnson*, eds. O. M. Brack, Jr and Robert E. Kelley (Iowa City, IA: University of Iowa Press, 1974), 5. The same phrase was recycled in other early biographies of Johnson in 1774 and 1782.

21 See 'The Life of Dr Sydenham', in Fleeman's *Early Biographical Writings of Dr Johnson*, 189.

22 The point is well made by Cafarelli in her *Prose in the Age of Poets*.

23 See, for example, Baker, *Correspondence of James Boswell with David Garrick, Edmund Burke, and Edmond Malone*, 294, 326, 351; 327–31, 395–96; 413–14; 371–75, 417–20. Also see Boswell's journals: *Boswell: the English Experiment 1785–1789*, ed., Irma S. Lustig and Frederick A. Pottle (New York, NY: McGraw-Hill, 1986), 96–97, 126, 221, 226–27, 287; *Boswell: The Great Biographer 1789–1795*, eds. Danziger and Brady, 5, 12, 16–17, 18–23. A full account of Malone's part in the composition of the *Life* is given by Peter Martin, *Edmond Malone, Shakespearean Scholar: a Literary Biography* (Cambridge University Press, 1995), ch. 8.

24 Charlotte Barrett, ed. *Diaries and Letters of Madame d'Arblay (1778–1840)*, with preface and notes by Austin Dobson, 6 vols. (London: Macmillan and Co., 1905), IV, 432–33.

25 J. W. Croker, ed. 'Preface to This Edition', James Boswell, *The Life of Samuel Johnson, Including A Journal of a Tour to the Hebrides* (London: John Murray, 1831), I, v.

26 Percy Fitzgerald, ed. *The Life of Samuel Johnson, LL.D.* with *A Journal of a Tour to the Hebrides*, by James Boswell. A reprint of the first edition with James Boswell's corrections and additions, edited with new notes, 3 vols. (London: Bickers and Son, 1874), x.

27 Austin Dobson, 'Boswell's Predecessors and Editors' in his *Eighteenth Century Studies*, The Wayfarer's Library. (London: J. M. Dent and Sons, [1914]), 146.

28 Fitzgerald, *A Critical Examination of Dr G. Birkbeck Hill's 'Johnsonian' Editions* (London: Bliss, Sands and Co., 1898), 12, 13, 56. Fitzgerald recalls Napier here. In the preface to his edition of 1884, Napier complains that Croker's 'notes are excessive in number, without being conspicuous for their utility', *Life of Samuel Johnson*, 5 vols., I, xvii. Also see Fitzgerald's strictures on Croker's editorial principles in his *Croker's Boswell and Boswell: Studies in the 'Life of Johnson'* (London: Chapman and Hall, 1880), chs. 3 and 4.

The question as to what constitutes a good footnote is taken up by G. W. Bowersock in 'The Art of the Footnote', *The American Scholar* (Winter, 1983/84), 54–62. The following passage makes several judicious points: 'The text is a continuous thing – everything in it has a context; but the footnote is more or less free. It is connected, obviously, to what stands above it, and yet its contents need not fit seamlessly into a fabric of sentences. It is like a variation on a theme. The composer offers a new perspective on what he or someone else has already expressed. The footnote looks neither backward nor forward' (55).

29 In recent years the question has been re-set with intentionality rather than originality being the focus. See for example Ian Small's essay 'The Editor as Annotator as Ideal Reader' in *The Theory and Practice of Text-Editing: Essays in Honour of James T. Boulton*, eds. Marcus Walsh and Ian Small (Cambridge University Press, 1991), 186–209. Also see Marcus Walsh's discussion of historically opposed understandings of commentary in his *Shakespeare, Milton and Eighteenth-Century Literary Editing* (Cambridge University Press, 1997), 24–25.

30 Quoted by George Rudé in his *Paris and London in the Eighteenth Century: Studies in Popular Protest* (London: Collins, 1970), 268.

31 F. A. Pottle, *The Literary Career of James Boswell, Esq.* (Oxford: Clarendon Press, 1929), 192.

32 In 'The Visiting Scholar', an essay on visiting Four Oaks Library, L. F. Powell talks of the library's 'unique feature, the Grangerised copies of Dr Birkbeck Hill's editions of Boswell's *Life of Johnson, Letters of Johnson, Johnsonian Miscellanies, In the Footsteps of Dr Johnson, Dr Johnson and the Fair Sex*, and *Johnsoniana* in 60 volumes', *Four Oaks Library*, ed. Gabriel Austin (Somerville, NJ: Donald and Mary Hyde, 1967), 121. Powell cites Hill's remarks on this phenomenon in his essay 'Boswell's Proof Sheets', and when one reads this paper it is clear that the Grangerising was not done by Hill: 'whoever was mentioned in the text or in the notes of either of these works, from Burke and Reynolds, Goldsmith and Garrick, downwards, of him, if they could be found, a likeness and an autograph letter had been procured', *Johnson Club Papers* (London: T. Fisher Unwin, 1899), 53.

33 Henry Francis Cary, *Lives of English Poets, from Johnson to Kirke White, Designed as a Continuation of Johnson's 'Lives'* (London: Henry G. Bohn, 1846), 92–93.

34 C. E. Vulliamy, *Ursa Major: a Study of Dr Johnson and His Friends* (London: Michael Joseph, 1946), 314.

35 Clifford, *Young Samuel Johnson*, 310.

36 Hester Thrale presents the meeting as accidental: 'meeting him however accidentally in the Shop, Boswell resolved to introduce himself...', *Thraliana: the Diary of Mrs Hester Lynch Thrale (later Mrs Piozzi), 1776–1809*, ed. Katherine C. Balderston (Oxford: Clarendon Press, 1942), 2 vols, I, 62. Boswell recounts another 'accidental meeting' in the *Life*, IV, 72.

37 See Aristotle's *Metaphysics*, 1025a.

38 Ralph H. Isham, Joseph Wood Krutch, Mark van Doren, 'Boswell: the Life of Johnson', in *The New Invitation to Learning*, ed. Mark Van Doren (New York, NY: New Home Library, 1944), 288.

39 The change of emphasis can be seen in James L. Clifford and Donald Greene, *Samuel Johnson: a Survey and Bibliography of Critical Studies* (Minneapolis, MN: University of Minnesota Press, 1970). Also see its successor volume: Donald Greene and John A. Vance, *A Bibliography of Johnsonian Studies, 1970–1985*. ELS Monograph Series 39, 1987.

40 Donald Greene, 'Reflections on a Literary Anniversary', *Queen's Quarterly* 70: 2 (1963), 198, 208. All further references to this essay will be incorporated

into the body of the text.

41 Boswell mentions meeting Hume several days before in a letter to William Johnson Temple dated 29 July 1758. See *The Correspondence of James Boswell and William Johnson Temple 1756–1795*, 2 vols., ed. Thomas Crawford (Edinburgh University Press, 1997; New Haven, CT: Yale University Press, 1997), I, 6.

42 Like similar groupings, the line between 'Johnsonians' and 'Boswellians' shifts and on occasion is partly erased or wholly denied. James L. Clifford and William L. Payne present David Nichol Smith's sense of the division in the following way: 'he makes clear the distinction between Boswellians and Johnsonians. Not that he or any of us would imply there is anything antagonistic between the two. Many of us are ardent admirers of both Boswell and Johnson. But he does insist that true Johnsonians regard the *Life* as supplementing what can be learned from Johnson's own writings. Boswellians, on the other hand, may read and reread the *Life* but have little acquaintance with "The Vanity of Human Wishes", "Rasselas", "The Rambler" or "The Lives of the Poets"', 'Johnsonians and Boswellians', *Johnsonian News Letter*, 10: 2 (1950), 4. Six years later, Clifford and a new co-editor, John H. Middendorf, concede that some people draw firm lines between the two writers: 'if you can take Boswell at all, and some benighted souls, we know, find it difficult to do so', 'Boswell in Search of a Wife', *Johnsonian News Letter*, 16: 3 (1956), 1. Ten years later, with more acquaintance with Boswell, the same co-editors observe that 'regardless of one's personal estimation of Boswell – his continual self-indulgence and self-contemplation are alone enough to force most of us to one or the other side – we soon found moral judgement giving way before simple energy', 'Boswell', *Johnsonian News Letter*, 26: 2 (1966), 2. There are of course contemporary scholars who decline to be labelled 'Johnsonian' or 'Boswellian', but unfortunately one still hears appeals to these groupings.

43 To 'Reflections on a Literary Anniversary' one can add the following related essays by Greene: 'The Uses of Autobiography in the Eighteenth Century', *Essays in Eighteenth-Century Biography*, ed. Philip B. Daghlian (Bloomington, IN: Indiana University Press, 1968), 43–66; 'Do We Need a Biography of Johnson's "Boswell" Years?', *Modern Language Studies*, 9: 3 (1979), 128–36; ''Tis a Pretty Book, Mr Boswell, But –', *Boswell's 'Life of Johnson': New Questions, New Answers*, ed. John A. Vance (Athens, GA: University of Georgia Press, 1985), 110–46; 'Boswell's Life as "Literary Biography"', *ibid.*, 161–171; 'Samuel Johnson', *The Craft of Literary Biography*, ed. Jeffrey Meyers (New York, NY: Schocken, 1985), 9–32; 'Preface to the Second Edition', *The Politics of Samuel Johnson*, 2nd edn (Athens, GA: University of Georgia Press, 1990); 'The *Logia* of Samuel Johnson and the Quest for the Historical Johnson', *The Age of Johnson*, 3 (1990), 1–33.

44 On Greene's understanding the *Tour* passes muster as biography, though presumably it would fall victim to his first argument, namely that it cannot be both art and biography.

45 Greene, "'Tis a Pretty Book, Mr Boswell, But –', 128.

46 This line is argued by William C. Dowling in his *Language and Logos in Boswell's 'Life of Johnson'* (Princeton, NJ: Princeton University Press, 1981).

47 Greene, "'Tis a Pretty Book, Mr Boswell, But –', 122.

48 Greene, 'The *Logia* of Samuel Johnson', 15. See 'The Gospel According to Dr Johnson' in Augustine Birrill, *Self-Selected Essays* (London: Thomas Nelson, 1916).

49 Greene indicates his preparatory work on this biography in his essay, 'Do We Need a Biography of Johnson's "Boswell" Years?', 128.

50 Greene, "'Tis a Pretty Book, Mr Boswell, But – ', 122.

51 James L. Clifford, 'Introduction' to his *Twentieth Century Interpretations of Boswell's 'Life of Johnson'* (Englewood Cliffs, NJ: Prentice-Hall, 1970), 1.

52 Greene, 'The *Logia* of Samuel Johnson', 3.

53 Not all of Greene's attempts at form criticism are equally persuasive, as Philip Edward Baruth argues in his 'Recognizing the Author-Function: Alternatives to Greene's Black-and-Red Book of Johnson's *Logia*', *The Age of Johnson*, 5 (1992), 35–60.

54 Greene, 'The *Logia* of Samuel Johnson', 19. Cf. *Rambler* 14 (Yale, III, 79–80).

55 Roberts, *Memoirs of the Life of Mrs Hannah More*, I, 313.

56 'Sheet omitted in B——'s Life of Johnson', *The Looker-On, a Periodical Paper*, by the Reverend Simon Olivebranch, no. 80, 3rd edn (London: G. G. and J. Robinson, 1795), IV, 110–14.

57 Frederick W. Hilles, ed., *Portraits by Sir Joshua Reynolds* (London: Heinemann, 1952), 67. One might also cite Mrs James Harris, wife of '*Hermes*' Harris, who thought Boswell to be 'a low-bred kind of being' and who was scarcely favourable to Johnson, when she testified in 1775 that his 'conversation is the same as his writing' (*Life*, II, 520). Similar remarks are made by Frances Burney and Thomas Tyers. In the September of 1778 Burney observes that 'I could not help remarking how very like Dr Johnson is to his writing; & how much the same thing it was to *hear*, or to *read* him ... "Very true", said Mrs Thrale, he *writes* & *talks* with the same ease, & in the same manner.' *The Early Journals and Letters of Fanny Burney*, Troide and III, p. 153–54. And Thomas Tyers in his 'A Biographical Sketch of Dr Samuel Johnson' claims that 'His conversation, in the judgement of several, was thought to be equal to his correct writings', *The Early Biographies of Samuel Johnson*, 79. Then there is the testimony of Ozias Humphry in a letter to his brother that 'every thing he [Johnson] says is as *correct* as a *second edition*', *Johnsonian Miscellanies*, II, 401. Finally, it may be felt as an irony that it is Boswell who runs counter to this general line, '... he owned he sometimes talked for victory; he was too conscientious to make errour permanent and pernicious, by deliberately writing it', *Tour*, v, 17.

58 I take the expression from John A. Vance, *Samuel Johnson and the Sense of History* (Athens, GA: The University of Georgia Press, 1984), 171.

4 SUBORDINATION AND EXCHANGE

1 The charge that Boswell falsified material in the *Life*, adding remarks purportedly by Johnson which are not recorded in the journal, is frequently made by Donald Greene. See, for example, his 'The Uses of Autobiography in the Eighteenth Century', in Daghlian's *Essays in Eighteenth-Century Biography* 56–57; 'Preface to the Second Edition', *The Politics of Samuel Johnson*, xlv; and 'The *Logia* of Samuel Johnson', 1–5, 20–22 and *passim*. Howard Erskine-Hill also points out that Boswell made certain remarks by Johnson appear earlier than they could possibly have been. See his 'The Political Character of Samuel Johnson', in *Samuel Johnson: New Critical Essays*, ed. Isobel Grundy (London: Vision, 1984),112–13.

2 The lack of law enforcement was noted by visitors to England. César de Saussure noted that 'London does not possess any watchmen, either on foot or on horseback as in Paris, to prevent murder and robbery...', *A Foreign View of England in the Reigns of George I and George II*, trans. and ed. Madame van Muyden (London: John Murray, 1902), 68. It is only much later in the century that we find coherent plans for a police force. See Patrick Colquhoun, *A Treatise on the Police of the Metropolis*, 6th edn (1795; London: Joseph Mawman, 1800).

3 Johnson, Review of [William Tytler], *An Historical and Critical Enquiry into the Evidence Produced by the Earls of Moray and Morton against Mary, Queen of Scots with an Examination of the Rev. Fr Robertson's Dissertation and Mr Hume's History with Respect to That Evidence*, *Gentleman's Magazine*, October 1760, 453.

4 Horace Walpole, *Memoirs of the Reign of King George the Third*, ed. Denis Le Merchant, 4 vols. (London: Richard Bentley, 1845), IV, 297.

5 John Buchan, *Midwinter* (New York, NY: Grosset and Dunlap, 1923), 181–82, 311.

6 Boswell goes on to speculate, 'He no doubt had an early attachment to the House of Stuart; but his zeal had cooled as his reason strengthened', *Life*, I, 498. Boswell appears to overreach in the 'no doubt'.

7 See James Clifford, *Young Sam Johnson* (New York, NY: McGraw-Hill, 1955), Aleyn Llyll Reade's *Johnsonian Gleanings* (rpt. New York, NY: Octagan Books, 1968), esp. I, 3–6, 10, and Kaminksi, *The Early Career of Samuel Johnson* (1987).

8 Donald Greene makes the point admirably in his 'Preface to the Second Edition', *The Politics of Samuel Johnson*, xxxii.

9 Erskine-Hill, 'The Political Character of Samuel Johnson', 121; and 'The Political Character of Samuel Johnson: *The Lives of the Poets* and a Further Report on *The Vanity of Human Wishes*', in Eveline Cruikshanks and Jeremy Black, eds., *The Jacobite Challenge* (Edinburgh: John Donald, 1988), 161. Erskine-Hill is joined by J. C. D. Clark in regarding Johnson as a likely Jacobite. See J. C. D. Clark's *Samuel Johnson: Literature, Religion and English Cultural Politics from the Restoration to Romanticism* (Cambridge University Press, 1994), especially his discussion of *Marmor* in ch. 6. Also see Clark's 'The Politics of Samuel Johnson', *The Age of Johnson*, 7 (1996), 27–56; 'The

Cultural Identity of Samuel Johnson', *The Age of Johnson*, 8 (1997), 15–70; and 'Religious Affiliation and Dynastic Allegiance in Eighteenth-Century England: Edmund Burke, Thomas Paine and Samuel Johnson', *ELH*, 64 (1997), 1029–67. The positive influence of Erskine-Hill's account of Johnson can readily be seen in Murray G. H. Pittock's brief outline of Johnson's writings in his *Poetry and Jacobite Politics in Eighteenth-Century Britain and Ireland* (Cambridge University Press, 1994), 128–32.

10 Howard Erskine-Hill, 'Johnson the Jacobite?', *The Age of Johnson*, 7 (1996), 11.

11 *Ibid.*, 10.

12 'The Speech of David Morgan, Esquire', *The Lyon in Mourning*, collated by Robert Forbes, preface by Henry Paton, Scottish History Society 20–22 (Edinburgh, 1895–6), 20, 1, 43.

13 See Bruce Lenman, *The Jacobite Risings in Britain 1689–1746* (London: Eyre Methuen, 1980), 161.

14 Eveline Cruickshanks offers a list of 176 persons 'expected to declare for a restoration' that was given to James Butler, Louis XV's Master of the Horse, in 1743. See her *Political Untouchables*, Appendix I. The second appendix gives an even higher number of persons likely to support a Stuart restoration. Also see Linda Colley's strictures on these lists in her *In Defiance of Oligarchy*, 35–36.

15 Clark, *Samuel Johnson*, 7, 175, 189.

16 'This is a bloody Jacobitical pamphlet . . .', *The Monthly Review*, 53 (1775), 360.

17 According to Monod, 'Between 1714 and 1754, a consistent third of Tory M.P.'s showed some definite sign of attachment to Jacobitism', *Jacobitism and the English People 1688–1788*, 270.

18 See David Greenwood, *William King: Tory and Jacobite* (Oxford: Clarendon Press, 1969), 75, 235.

19 The best summation of Oxford Toryism is by Paul Langford, and I quote at length: 'The truth is that Oxford's Toryism was much like the nation's, or rather the gentry's toryism. It included some authentic Jacobites, and some authentic Hanoverians. But it consisted largely of those in the middle, who were occasionally brought, sentimentally, to contemplate the possibility of a returned Stuart line prepared to respect the Church of England, but who certainly did not think of acting themselves . . . Oxford's record was of a kind which makes it possible to claim both that there was a basic acceptance of the Hanoverian line while it prospered and at the same time substantial dissatisfaction with the personnel and policies of Hanoverian rule', 'Tories and Jacobites 1714–1751', *The History of the University of Oxford*, vol. v: *The Eighteenth Century*, eds. L. S. Sunderland and L. G. Mitchell (Oxford: Clarendon Press, 1986), 126.

20 Hester Thrale, writing a character of Johnson in 1777, does not cast the Johnson she knows as a Jacobite. Her shading is carefully done: 'He is a Tory in what he calls the truest sense of the Word; and is strongly attached to the notion of Divine & Hereditary Right inherent in Kings: he was therefore a *Jacobite* while *Jacob* existed, or any of his Progeny was likely to sit

on the Throne: he is now however firmly attached to the present Royal Family; not from change of Principles, but difference of Situations, and he is as zealous that *this* King should maintain his Prerogatives, as if he belonged to the exiled Family', *Thraliana*, I, 192. William Burke's representation of Johnson's politics in 1777 converges with Mrs Thrale's, although it is given in a less friendly light. Writing to the Duke of Portland in 1779, Burke quotes Johnson as saying 'in Company' 'about two years agoe [*sic*]', that 'various circumstances move us to an acquiescence in what *is*, without abandoning our opinions of what *ought to be*'. The difference between Mrs Thrale and William Burke is that the former calls him 'a Tory' and the latter 'that Levianthan Jacobite'. See William Burke to Portland, 26 July 1779, Portland Papers, Hallward Library, University of Nottingham (Pw F 2149). It is relevant to note that several pages later in *Thraliana* Mrs Thrale observes that Johnson's 'Zeal for Subordination [was] warm even to Bigotry', I, 207.

21 The point is made by Lenman, *The Jacobite Risings in Britain 1689–1746*, 196.

22 Johnson, 'Preface' to *A General Index to the First Twenty Volumes of the Gentleman's Magazine* (1753), in L. F. Powell, 'An Addition to the Canon of Johnson's Writings', *Essays and Studies* (London) 28 (1942), 40. It is clear that Johnson wrote most of this preface and revised all of it. I regard it is extremely unlikely that Johnson would have allowed so sharp a judgement of the Forty-Five to remain were he a Jacobite of any colour.

23 Donald Greene offers a long attack, on textual grounds, on the view of Johnson as Jacobite. See his 'Preface to the Second Edition', *The Politics of Samuel Johnson*; 'Johnson: The Jacobite Legend Exhumed: a Rejoinder to Howard Erskine-Hill and J. C. D. Clark', *The Age of Johnson*, 7 (1996), 57–135; and 'Jonathan Clark and the Abominable Cultural Mind-Set', *The Age of Johnson*, 8 (1997), 71–88.

24 See Ragnhild Hatton's discussion of this in *George I, Elector and King* (London: Thames and Hudson, 1978), 72–76.

25 Mary Cowper, *Diary of Mary Countess Cowper, Lady of the Bedchamber to the Princess of Wales, 1714–1720* (London: John Murray, 1864), 4, 5.

26 In 'Taxation No Tyranny' (1775) Johnson argues that while there can be 'limited royalty' there cannot be 'limited government', for 'there must in every society be some power or other from which there is no appeal, which admits no restrictions, which pervades the whole mass of the community, regulates and adjusts all subordination, enacts laws or repeals them, erects or annuls judicatures, extends or contracts privileges, exempts itself from question or control, and bounded only by physical necessity' (Yale, x, 423).

27 Danziger and Brady, *Boswell: The Great Biographer*, 39.

28 'The retreat of Gaelic into its Highlands habitat can be dated to around the late fourteenth century. From that period, the Highlands were recognised not simply as a distinct cultural province within Scotland, but alien and distant in every sense', Charles W. J. Withers, *Gaelic in Scotland 1698–1981: the Geographical History of a Language*, foreword by Derick S. Thomson (Edinburgh: John Donald Publishers, 1984), 3.

29 *Lives of the Poets*, III, 243.
30 John Butt, ed. *The Poems of Alexander Pope* (London: Methuen, 1968), 512.
31 Johnson's review is reprinted by Richard B. Schwartz in his *Samuel Johnson and the Problem of Evil* (Madison, WI: University of Wisconsin Press, 1975), 305. My references are to the original page numbers in the *Literary Review*. All further references to this review will be incorporated into the body of the text.
32 *Gentleman's Magazine*, XII (1742), 668. All further references to this debate will be incorporated into the body of the text.
33 W. J. Bate, *Samuel Johnson* (New York, NY: Harcourt Brace Jovanovich, 1975), 195.
34 Allen T. Hazen, ed., *Samuel Johnson's Prefaces and Dedications* (New Haven, CT: Yale University Press, 1937), 187.
35 Johnson does not take every opportunity to criticise unregulated trade. See, for example, his observation on unconstrained trade on Skye, *Journey*, 45. When reading Johnson's remarks on trade John H. Middendorf's acture observation should be kept in mind: 'When Johnson praised commerce he was generally thinking of it as the abstract distribution of goods rather than as an activity of individual traders', 'Johnson on Wealth and Commerce', *Johnson, Boswell and their Circle: Essays Presented to Lawrence Fitzroy Powell in Honour of his Eighty-Fourth Birthday* (Oxford: Clarendon Press, 1965), 58. For an account of Johnson's debts to mercantilism in his thoughts about economics, see Middendorf's essay 'Dr Johnson and Mercantilism', *Journal of the History of Ideas*, 21: 1 (1960), 66–83.
36 David Loch, *Essays on the Trade, Commerce, Manufactures and Fisheries of Scotland*, 3 vols. (Edinburgh: W. and T. Ruddiman, 1778–79), III, 44.
37 See John Mason, 'Conditions in the Highlands after the 'Forty-five', *The Scottish Historical Review*, 26 (1947), 134–46. In order not to overvalue the impact of the Forty-Five, Charles Camic's remarks should be kept in mind: 'From the 1740s onward, however, better access to English and colonial markets and related changes stimulated a substantial growth in the linen, cattle, and particularly the entrepot tobacco trade, and this trade in turn made way for the later and more radical transformation of the Scottish economy', *Experience and Enlightenment: Socialization for Cultural Change in Eighteenth-Century Scotland* (Chicago, IL: University of Chicago Press, 1983), 96.
38 *The Acts of the Parliament of Scotland*, vol. VIII, *1670–1686* (1820), 238–39.
39 *Ibid.*, 348.
40 The point is argued fully by George Pratt Insh, *The Scottish Jacobite Movement: a Study in Economic and Social Forces* (Edinburgh: The Moray Press, 1952), Books I and II. David Loch pointed out several years after Johnson had travelled through Scotland that, as a part of the Act of Union, England was to give Scotland £2000 a year for seven years 'to the promoting and encouraging of our Manufactures and Fisheries' but that nothing was done about this until 1725. See his *Essays on the Trade, Commerce, Manufactures, and Fisheries of Scotland*, III, 43.

41 In an anonymous response to Johnson's *Journey*, particular exception is taken to his defence of the Tacksman. The passage is worth quoting at length: 'The Tacksman has for these twenty years, been the pest of the north of Scotland; he is generally *a bastard of nature, adopted by fortune*; one who has obtained wealth, not by merit, but by accident, or by crimes; he takes the advantage of that thrift of money, which a taste for extravagance and modern refinement has introduced among the Scotch gentry; by overbidding, he joins the possessions of the old tenants, who must either become tenants to him, or seek new possessions in the wilds of America', *Remarks on a Voyage to the Hebrides in a Letter to Samuel Johnson, LL.D.* (London: George Kearsly, 1775), 18. To put the last point into perspective it should be noted that while emigration from the Highlands to America started in the last quarter of the eighteenth century, very large numbers of emigrants can be found only in the nineteenth century, after the potato famine. Charles Withers cites estimates of 800 leaving the north Highlands in 1801, and nearly 3250 in 1802, *Gaelic in Scotland 1698–1981*, 4.

42 Defoe observes that 'Commerce is naturally an encourager of Learning, and has by its correspondence been the greatest assistance to human knowledge', and 'Trade thriving, Arts always Flourish; Commerce is a friend to Learning', *The History of the Principal Discoveries and Improvements in the Several Arts and Sciences: Particularly the Great Branches of Commerce, Navigation and Plantation, in All Parts of the Known World* (London: W. Mears, 1727), 80, 92.

43 Georg Simmel confirms Johnson's point, maintaining that 'money economy and the domination of the intellect stand in the closest relationship to one another', 'The Metropolis and Mental Life', in his *On Individuality and Social Forms: Selected Writings*, ed. and intro. Donald N. Levine (Chicago, IL: University of Chicago Press, 1971), 326.

44 Edward Gibbon, *The Decline and Fall of the Roman Empire*, ed. David Womersley, 3 vols. (London: Allen Lane, 1994), I, 237.

45 See for example the Everyman edition published by Dent in 1910. The first edition of the *Decline and Fall* has 'factitious', and the *OED* cites this very sentence when illustrating the third sense of the adjective: 'Got up, made up for a particular occasion or purpose; arising from custom, habit, or design; not natural or spontaneous; artificial, conventional'.

46 Not only is money a convention but also there were conventions relating to money in the seventeenth and eighteenth centuries. Promissory notes, tokens and tallies were frequently given in lieu of gold and silver.

47 The view that 'among trading and polite nations . . . money must be such as hath an intrinsic value, and thence, an universal esteem among those they traffic with' is underlined by Joseph Harris in his *An Essay Upon Money and Coins*, Part I: *The Theories of Commerce, Money, and Exchanges* (London: G. Hawkins, 1757), 42. Also relevant is Michel Foucault's illuminating discussion of this point in *The Order of Things*, I: 6.

48 See Pierre Vilar, *A History of Gold and Money: 1450 to 1920*, trans. Judith White (1976; rpt. London: Verso, 1991), 219. Also see Patrick Hyde Kelly's

valuable introduction to *Locke on Money*, 2 vols., The Clarendon Edition of the Works of John Locke (Oxford: Clarendon Press, 1991), 1. I am indebted to Kelly and Vilar.

49 John Butt, ed. *The Poems of Alexander Pope*, 572.

50 'Trade, without enlarging the *British* Territories, has given us a kind of additional Empire: It has multiplied the Number of the Rich, made our Landed Estates infinitely more Valuable than they were formerly, and added to them an Accession of other Estates as valuable as the Lands themselves', Joseph Addison, *The Spectator*, 19 May, 1711.

51 Pope's lines on luxury reveal a debt to Bernard Mandeville's *The Fable of the Bees: or, Private Vices, Publick Benefits* (1714). Yet where Pope's lines indicate a distrust of luxury, Johnson – at least in conversation – saw no reason to condemn occasional luxuries. Johnson's appreciation and critique of Mandevillian economics is recorded in the *Life*, III, 292. Not only does Johnson disagree with Mandeville about the economic virtues of vice but also, as we have seen, he is far from being a wholehearted supporter of the *laissez-faire* economics that is foreshadowed in the *Fable*. See, for example, Cleomenes' claim in the 'The Sixth Dialogue' that 'due Proportion is the Result and natural Consequence of the difference there is in the Qualification of Men, and the Vicissitudes that happen among them, so it is never better attained to, or preserv'd, than when no body meddles with it. Hence we may learn, how the short-sighted Wisdom, of perhaps well-meaning People, may rob us of a Felicity, that would flow spontaneously from the Nature of every large Society, if none were to divert or interrupt the Stream', *The Fable of the Bees: or Private Vices, Publick Benefits*, ed. F. B. Kaye. (1924; rpt. Indianapolis, IN: Liberty Classics, 1988), 2 vols., 2, 353.

52 Donald MacNicol argues that several Bards and Seanachies existed at the time of the tour, and that many more existed in the previous generation. See his *Remarks on Dr. Samuel Johnson's Journey to the Hebrides* (1779; rpt. New York, NY: Garland Publishing Inc., 1974), 363.

53 MacNicol also takes Johnson to task for claiming that there were no written records in Scotland. He argues that from the institution of the monasteries letters were known in seminaries, and that much was written in Gaelic. See his *Remarks*, 206, 307.

5 CULTURAL PROPERTIES

1 The London journal was sent with a letter by weekly posts to John Johnston of Grange. Each morning Boswell wrote memoranda which would guide his daily activities. This is referred to as *London Journal* in the text.

2 Boswell says of Macheath, 'This is one of the Characters, in which Mr *Digges*, the *Roscius* of our Stage, was universally acknowledged to shine with distinguished Lustre', *A View of the Edinburgh Theatre During the Summer Season, 1759*, intro. David W. Tarbet (1760; rpt. Los Angeles, CA: The Augustan Reprint Society, 1976), 20. Boswell dedicates the booklet to Digges. On 19

May, 1763, Boswell sang '*Youth's the Season . . .*' while in the company of 'two very pretty little girls' and thought himself Captain Macheath, *London Journal*, 263–64. His enthusiasm for the play continued for many years. On 29 November 1776 Boswell records in his journal, 'I thought tonight of publishing an edition of it with notes . . . and then there would be in libraries and shops and catalogues *Boswell's Beggar's Opera*', *Boswell in Extremes 1776–1778*, ed. Charles McC. Weiss and Frederick A. Pottle (New York, NY: McGraw-Hill, 1970), 62.

3 John Gay, *Dramatic Works*, ed. John Fuller, 2 vols. (Oxford: Clarendon Press, 1983), II, 27.

4 Baker, ed. *The Correspondence of James Boswell with David Garrick, Edmund Burke, and Edmond Malone*, 53, 54.

5 I quote from a UNESCO document: 'the term "cultural property" means property which, on religious or secular grounds, is specifically designated by each State as being of importance for archeology, prehistory, history, literature, art or science . . .', 'UNESCO Convention on the Illicit Movement of Art Treasures', *International Legal Materials*, 10 (1971), 289.

6 See Frederick A. Pottle, ed. *Boswell's London Journal 1762–1763. Together With Journal of My Jaunt Harvest 1762* (London: Heinemann, 1951), 74.

7 *Letters between the Honorourable Andrew Erskine, and James Boswell, Esq.* (London: W. Flexney, 1763), 58, 62.

8 The Ossianic poems, along with all early English and Celtic poems, were frequently regarded as monumental in the mid to late eighteenth century. Thomas Innes, for example, writes of the recent discovery 'of so many monuments of antiquity', *A Critical Essay on the Ancient Inhabitants of the Northern Parts of Britain, or Scotland*, 2 vols. (London: W. Innys, 1729), I, iv. John Macpherson refers to Ossian's poems as 'a monument of the poetical merit of the ancient Bards', *Critical Dissertations on the Origin, Antiquities, Language, Government, Manners and Religion, of the Ancient Caledonians* (London: J. Becket and P. A. De Hondt, 1768), 217. Thomas Warton does not reflect on early English or Celtic poetry, yet maintains that 'the first monuments of composition in every nation are those of the poet', *The History of English Poetry from the Close of the Eleventh to the Commencement of the Eighteenth Century*, 3 vols. (London: J. Dodsley *et al.*, 1775), I, iii.

9 'A Tour to the Hebrides. Bossy Bounce Preparing for the Scotch Professors to Kiss', published by S. W. Fores, 19 April 1786. A reproduction may be found in *Reynolds*, ed. Nicholas Penny (New York. NY: Harry N. Abrams, 1986), 385.

10 I am indebted to Ross Chambers for this distinction. See his *Story and Situation: Narrative Seduction and the Power of Fiction* (Minneapolis, MN: University of Minnesota Press, 1984), 50–55.

11 John Halliday, *The Life of William Late Earl of Mansfield* (London: P. Elmsly *et al.*, 1797), 149.

12 The act was in force until 1830, although it was in fact superseded by 2 Geo. 2, c. 25 (1729).

13 Blackstone, *Commentaries on the Laws of England*, IV, 246.
14 Sir Robert Chambers, *A Course of Lectures on the English Law Delivered at the University of Oxford 1767–1773 and Composed in Association with Samuel Johnson*, ed. Thomas M. Curley, 2 vols. (Madison, WI: University of Wisconsin Press, 1986), I, 422. Curley points out that while serving on the Calcutta bench during the Nandakumar trial of 1775 Sir Robert argued that while forgery may be a capital offence in Britain it need not be considered so in Bengal where less wealth is embodied in bills. See 'Editor's Introduction', 57–58.
15 See Frank McLynn, *Crime and Punishment in Eighteenth-Century England* (London: Routledge, 1989), ch. 8. Radzinowicz details the relevant laws in his *The Movement for Reform*, 642–50.
16 Quoted by Mark Rose, *Authors and Owners*, 129.
17 The long title of Cap. LXXIX runs as follows: 'An Act for the more effectual preventing of the forging of the Notes and Bills of the Governor and Company of the Bank of England; and for the preventing the obtaining a false Credit, by the Imitation of the Notes or Bills of the said Governor and Company.' See Great Britain, *The Statutes at Large*, 20 vols. (London: George Eyre and Andrew Strahan, 1811), XIII (1768–1774), 580.
18 The Vinerian lectures discuss the relations of forging money and treason. See Chambers, *A Course of Lectures on the English Law*, I, 355–56, 363–65, 369–70.
19 In 1773 James Macpherson published not only a new two-volume edition of *The Poems of Ossian*, but also his translation of *The Iliad* and the third edition of his *An Introduction to the History of Great Britain and Ireland*.
20 Malcolm Laing, ed. *The Poems of Ossian*, 2 vols. (London: W. Strahan and T. Beckett, 1773), II, 573.
21 John Home and Hugh Blair encouraged Macpherson to translate from the Gaelic. See Fiona J. Stafford, *The Sublime Savage: a Study of James Macpherson and the Poems of Ossian* (Edinburgh University Press, 1988), 78–79. It is likely that Macpherson's imagination was sparked by reading Jerome Stone's version of a Gaelic poem in the *Scots Magazine* for January 1756.
22 Three volumes of Allan Ramsay's *The Tea-Table Miscellany*, containing 'choice songs, Scots and English', including some by Ramsay and his contemporaries, were issued by A. Donaldson in 1724, 1725 and 1727. There is a fourth volume in the series, published in 1732, but it is doubtful whether Ramsay had any hand in it. He also published the two volumes of *The Ever Green* (Edinburgh: A. Ramsay, 1724) which contained Scots poems before 1600, as well as 'The Vision' which, though disguised, is by Ramsay. Ambrose Philips published *A Collection of Old Ballads*, 3 vols. (London: J. Roberts and D. Leach, 1723–25), and from David Herd we have *The Ancient and Modern Scots Songs, Heroic Ballads, &c* (Edinburgh: Martin and Wotherspoon, 1769), which was expanded to two volumes in 1776. George Paton is sometimes credited for work on the earlier collection. There are several Scottish ballads in Thomas Evans's *Old Ballads, Historical and Narrative, with*

Some of Modern Date, 2 vols. (London: T. Evans, 1777). A four volume edition appeared in 1784. John Pinkerton published *Scottish Tragic Ballads* (London: J. Nichols, 1781) which was expanded to become *Select Scottish Ballads*, 2 vols. (London: J. Nichols, 1783), although he later admitted to composing a number of the poems himself. His *Scotish Poems, Reprinted from Scarce Editions*, 3 vols. (London: J. Nichols, 1792) is more reliable.

23 J. Logie Robertson, ed. *The Complete Poetical Works of James Thomson* (London: Oxford University Press, 1965), 263.

24 Joseph Warton, *An Essay on the Genius and Writings of Pope*, 2 vols. (1756; rpt. London: W. J. and J. Richardson, *et al.*, 1806), I, 349.

25 According to Derick S. Thomson, Macpherson was carrying 'to its logical conclusion a tendency which was already becoming apparent' though, to be sure, he carried it 'far beyond anything which appears in available contemporary sources'. See his *The Gaelic Sources of Macpherson's 'Ossian'* (1952; rpt. Folcroft, PA: Folcroft Library Editions, 1973), 10–12. On the Irish reactions to Macpherson's translations, see Clare O'Halloran, 'Irish Recreations of the Gaelic Past: the Challenge of Macpherson's Ossian', *Past and Present*, 124 (1989), 69–95.

26 William Shaw, *An Enquiry into the Authenticity of the Poems Ascribed to Ossian* (London: J. Murray, 1781), 34.

27 James Macpherson, *The Poems of Ossian and Related Works*, ed. Howard Gaskill, intro. Fiona Stafford (Edinburgh University Press, 1996), 450 n. 33.

28 Macpherson, 'Preface' to the *Fragments, The Poems of Ossian and Related Works*, 6. The preface was composed by Hugh Blair after conversations with James Macpherson.

29 The influence of Thomas Blackwell, a Greek scholar at the University of Aberdeen, on James Macpherson has been long noted. In recent years it has been underlined by Josef Bysveen, who attends to the relation between genius and primitive, in his *Epic Tradition and Innovation in James Macpherson's 'Fingal'*, Studia Anglistica Ubsaliensia S. Academiae 44 (Uppsala, 1982), 35–39, and by Stafford who explores the possible influence of Blackwell's historical criticism on the poet in her *The Sublime Savage*, 28–37.

30 Thomas Blackwell makes the following points about the father of Greek poetry: '*Homer* drew his *Mythology* from these *three* Sources: First, from the *Form of Worship* already established in his Country: Secondly, from the *traditional Doctrines* of *Orpheus* and *Meampus*, who first formed the *Grecian Ceremonies*, and gave that People a Notion of *Immortality*: And lastly, which was the Parent of the other two, from the *Egyptian Learning*', 'What we have seen is sufficient to convince us that *Homer* owed most of those Tales that raise our Wonder in the *Odyssey*, to his converse with the PHENICIANS', *An Enquiry into the Life and Writings of Homer* (1736; rpt. Hildesheim: Georg Olms Verlag, 1976), 179, 286–87. Blackwell later makes it plain that his *Enquiry* is a demystification of Homer. See the sixth letter of his *Letters Concerning Mythology* (1748; rpt. New York, NY: Garland Publishing Inc., 1976).

31 William Duff, for example, made a point of arguing for Ossian as an individual and a genius. 'It is very remarkable however, that in the earliest and most uncultivated periods of society, Poetry is by one great effort of nature, in one age, and by one individual, brought to the highest perfection to which human Genius is capable of advancing it; not only when the other Arts and Sciences are in a languishing state, but when they do not so much as exist. Thus HOMER wrote his *Iliad* and *Odyssey*, when there was not a single picture to be seen in *Greece*; and OSSIAN composed *Fingal* and *Temora*, when none of the Arts, whether liberal or mechanical, were known in his country', *An Essay on Original Genius; and Its Various Modes of Exertion in Philosophy and the Fine Arts, Particularly in Poetry* (London: Edward and Charles Dilly, 1767), 264.

It is worth noting that Herder, who helped to promote Ossian's role in Scottish cultural nationalism, was indebted to Blackwell's study of Homer. See Eugene E. Reed, 'Herder, Primitivism and the Age of Poetry', *The Modern Language Review*, 60: 4 (1965), 557.

32 Macpherson, *The Poems of Ossian and Related Works*, 36, 479.

33 Macpherson, 'Advertisement' (preceding the first edition of *Fingal*), *The Poems of Ossian and Related Works*, 33.

34 For the influence of Ossian in France, see Paul Van Tieghem, *Ossian en France*, 2 vols. (Paris: F. Rieder, 1917) and 'Ossian et l'ossianisme' in *Le Préromantisme*, 3 vols. (Paris: F. Rieder, 1924–30), I, 195–285. A more general survey is offered by Howard Gaskill in '*Ossian* in Europe', *Canadian Review of Comparative Literature*, 21 (1994), 643–78.

35 Macpherson, *The Poems of Ossian and Related Works*, 9.

36 Little of critical interest has been written on Johnson's attitude to romance. Eithne Henson's *'The Fictions of Romantick Chivalry': Samuel Johnson and Romance* (Rutherford, NJ: Fairleigh Dickinson University Press, 1992) marks the beginning of what promises to be a rewarding area of study.

37 For Johnson's stress on the importance of historical knowledge, see his 'Preface' to *The Preceptor*, in Hazen's *Samuel Johnson's Prefaces and Dedications*, 182–3. This should be read alongside the following passage from Johnson's review of the *Account of the Conduct of the Duchess of Malborough*. Of the student of history we are told that 'distrust quickens his discernment of different degrees of probability, animates his search after evidence, and, perhaps, heightens his pleasure at the discovery of truth; for truth, though not always obvious, is generally discoverable . . .', *The Works of Samuel Johnson, LL.D.* 16 vols. (Cambridge, MA: Harvard Cooperative Society, 1903), XIII, 165.

38 Psalmanazar acknowledged his deceit in 1728 and thereafter lived a pious life. Johnson found his conduct edifying. In a posthumous declaration he condemned 'the base and shameful imposture of passing upon the world for a native of Formosa, and a convert to Christianity, and backing it with a fictitious account of that island, and of my own travels, conversion, &c. all or most of it hatched in my own brain, without regard to truth and honesty', *Memoirs of * * *. Commonly Known by the Name of George Psalmanazar, a Reputed*

Native of Formosa. Written by Himself in order to be Published after his Death (London: R. Davis *et al.*, 1765), 5.

39 Johnson dictated an apology to Lauder, the *Letter to the Reverend Mr Douglas* (1750). It is worth noting that, shortly before his death, Johnson was troubled by several of his parliamentary reports, where the truth may have been stretched beyond the flexible limits he allowed himself.

40 The quotation is from the sermon that Johnson composed for William Dodd, 'The Convict's Address to his Unhappy Brethren'. sermon 40, Yale XIV.

41 Johnson, *Lives of the Poets*, III, 242.

42 Howard Gaskill clarifies the discussion very considerably in his introduction to *Ossian Revisited* (Edinburgh University Press, 1991).

43 It is important to keep in mind that Donald MacNichol's *Remarks* were very likely retouched by James Macpherson before publication. For an account of the amendments and additions see Robert F. Metzdorf, 'M'Nicol, Macpherson, and Johnson', *Eighteenth-Century Studies in Honour of Donald F. Hyde*, ed. W. H. Bond (New York, NY: The Grolier Club, 1970), 45–61.

In his *Remarks* Donald MacNichol – or, more likely, James Macpherson – indicated that John Mackenzie had 'some of Ossian's poems'. On reading this William Shaw visited Mr Mackenzie and inspected the manuscripts. 'They are manuscripts written in the Irish dialect and character, on the subject of Irish and Highland genealogy', *An Enquiry into the Authenticity of the Poems Ascribed to Ossian*, 84. John Clark, who himself had counterfeited Gaelic poems in his *Works of Caledonian Bards. Translated from the Gaelic* (1778), replied to Shaw as follows. 'The manuscripts left in the possession of Mr Mackenzie, were not placed in his hands, as containing any of the originals of Ossian's poems. They were only intended to prove, that Mr McNicol had shown to the public, that there still exist Gaelic manuscripts written many centuries ago, in contradiction to Dr Johnson, who precipitately averred, that there is not a manuscript in the Highlands a hundred years old', *An Answer to Mr Shaw's Inquiry into the Authenticity of the Poems Ascribed to Ossian* (Edinburgh: C. Elliot, 1781), 24. In his *Reply to Mr Clark's Answer* Shaw retaliates, 'Dr Johnson never denied the existence of Galic MSS. for the term Galic, perhaps, he did not know; he only said there were no Earse MSS. and so far as yet appears he was right in saying so; for the MSS. yet produced as not Earse; they are Galic, but not Scotch Galic', *Enquiry into the Authenticity of the Poems Ascribed to Ossian with a Reply to Mr Clark's Answer*, 2nd edn (London: J. Murray, 1783), 65. As a final twist, it should be mentioned that Johnson had a hand in writing the *Reply to Mr Clark's Answer*. See Thomas M. Curley, 'Johnson's Last Word on Ossian: Ghostwriting for William Shaw', *Aberdeen and the Enlightenment: Proceedings of a Conference held at the University of Aberdeen*, ed. Jennifer J. Carter and Joan H. Pittock (Aberdeen University Press, 1987), 375–94.

44 Lord Kames reports of Macpherson that 'the translator saw, in the Isle of Sky, the first four books of the poem Fingal, written in a fair hand on

vellum, and bearing date in the year 1403', 'Critical Observations on the Poems of Ossian', in *Poems of Ossian, the Son of Fingal* by James Macpherson, 2 vols. (New York, NY: Evert Duyckink and James and Thomas Ronalds, 1806), II, 289.

On the question of Macpherson and the Book of the Dean see Thomson, *The Gaelic Sources of Macpherson's 'Ossian'*, 74, 83. Thomson directs us to Donald T. Mackintosh's paper 'James Macpherson and the Book of the Dean of Lismore', *Scottish Gaelic Studies* 6 (1949), 11–20, for evidence that (as Thomson puts it) 'the nineteen MSS handed over by John MacKenzie, secretary to the Highland Society, in 1803, were the same as those deposited by Macpherson in the shop of Becket, his publisher, in 1762. Among them was the Book of the Dean, whose preservation we thus owe in part to Macpherson', 74.

45 Howard Gaskill argues convincingly against Donald Mackintosh's claim that the Book of the Dean was deposited with Becket. I agree with his conclusion that in all likelihood Macpherson deposited transcripts, not manuscripts. See his article, 'What did James Macpherson really leave on Display at his Publisher's Shop in 1762?', *Scottish Gaelic Studies* 16 (1990), 67–89. Gaskill also reminds us that Macpherson was 'careful to stress, in print at least, that only a small part of the compositions translated by him derives from written sources', 'Ossian in Europe', 645.

46 Paget Toynbee and Leonard Whibley, eds., *Correspondence of Thomas Gray*, with corrections and additions by H. W. Starr, 3 vols. (Oxford: Clarendon Press, 1971), II, 680.

47 J. Y. T. Greig, ed. *The Letters of David Hume*, 2 vols. (Oxford: Clarendon Press, 1932), I, 329, 330. All further references will be incorporated into the text.

48 Thomson shows that *Fingal* draws on twelve Gaelic sources, *Temora* on just one, *The Gaelic Sources of Macpherson's 'Ossian'*, 3.

49 Hume may well have been recalling his earlier support of another Scottish epic, William Wilkie's *The Epigoniad* (1757), a poem which failed to muster literary interest south of the Tweed and from which Hume gradually distanced himself.

50 David Hume, 'Essay on the Genuineness of the Poems', reprinted as an appendix to John Hill Burton, *Life and Correspondence of David Hume*, 2 vols. (1846; rpt. New York, NY: Burt Franklin, 1967), I, 471–80. Hume observed to Boswell that 'if fifty barea—d Highlanders should say that *Fingal* was an ancient poem, he would not believe them', *Boswell: the Ominous Years 1774–1776*, eds. Charles Ryskamp and Frederick A. Pottle (New York, NY: McGraw-Hill, 1963), 73.

51 David Hume, *A Treatise of Human Nature*, ed. L. A. Selby-Bigge, 2nd edn revised P. H. Nidditch (Oxford: Clarendon Press, 1978), 97–98.

52 See Barbara Luttrell, *The Prim Romantic: a Biography of Ellis Cornelia Knight, 1758–1837*, intro. Roger Fulford (London: Chatto and Windus, 1965), 90.

53 Marjorie Levinson, *The Romantic Fragment Poem: a Critique of a Form* (Chapel

Hill, NC: The University of North Carolina Press, 1986), 35–36.

54 Donald MacNichol, *Remarks*, 9–10. Lord Kames makes a similar argument. 'Supposing the author of Ossian, to be a late writer, adorned with every refinement of modern education; yet, even upon that supposition, he is a miracle, far from being equalled by any other author ancient or modern', 'Critical Observations on the Poems of Ossian', 291. Also see Andrew Henderson, 'Had any person intended to pass a compliment on James McPherson, he could not have thought of a nobler than that of stiling him the author of Fingal', *A Letter to Dr Samuel Johnson on his Journey to the Western Isles* (London: J. Henderson *et al.*, 1775).

55 Anon., *Remarks on a Voyage to the Hebrides* 30.

56 The argument from internal evidence was first made by Hugh Blair. 'The compositions of Ossian are so strongly marked with characters of antiquity, that although there were no external proofs to support that antiquity, hardly any reader of judgement and taste, could hesitate in referring them to a very remote era', 'A Critical Discussion on the Poems of Ossian, Son of Fingal', 433.

57 Ferdinando Warner, *Remarks on the History of Fingal, and Other Poems of Ossian: Translated by Mr Macpherson in a Letter to the Lord L—* (London: H. Payne and W. Cropley, 1762), 25, 31.

58 Macpherson replies to the charges made by Warner in the 'Advertisement' to the third edition of *The Works of Ossian*. See *The Poems of Ossian and Related Works*, 201–2. For Macpherson's claim about the Irish appropriation of Ossian, see the 'Dissertation' which opens that edition, reprinted in *The Poems of Ossian and Related Works*, 223.

59 Hugh Trevor-Roper documents this in his 'The Invention of Tradition: The Highland Tradition of Scotland', in *The Invention of Tradition*, ed. Eric Hobsbawm and Terence Ranger (Cambridge University Press, 1983), 16–18. I am indebted to his analysis.

60 John Macpherson, *Critical Dissertations*, vi, 96.

61 Quoted by Bertrand H. Bronson in 'Ritson's "Bibliographia Scotia"', *PMLA* 52 (1937), 134.

62 Ritson calls this book 'a publication in which history, fact and truth are, universally, sacrific'd to system, fable and falsehood', *ibid.*, 134.

63 John Macpherson, *Critical Dissertations*, 216.

64 James Macpherson, *An Introduction*, 7, 52.

65 *Ibid.*, 150. Macpherson maintains that 'Bede borrowed his account of the Scots from the Irish', 124.

66 Gibbon, *The Decline and Fall of the Roman Empire*, I, 997, n. 110. Gibbon refers us to John Macpherson's *Critical Dissertations* and to James Macpherson's *Introduction to the History of Great Britain and Ireland*.

67 Warner uncovers many of Macpherson's historical errors in his *Remarks on the History of Fingal*.

68 Perhaps the most important reading of Ossian in terms of cultural nationalism was that of Herder. For his account of Ossian's poems as *Volkspoesie*, see

his 'Extracts from a Correspondence on Ossian's poems and the Songs of Ancient Peoples', *German Aesthetic and Literary Criticism: Wincklemann, Lessing, Hamann, Herder, Schiller, Goethe*, ed. and intro. H. B. Nisbet (Cambridge University Press, 1985), 154–161, esp. 155.

69 See John Telfer Dunbar, *History of Highland Dress* (Edinburgh: Oliver and Boyd, 1962), 12–14. The 'Highland Clothes' were proscribed in 1746 in the act of 19 Geo. II, c. 39 which was repealed in 1782.

70 Story related by Anna Seward in *Letters of Anna Seward: Written Between the Years 1784 and 1807*, 6 vols. (Edinburgh: George Ramsay, 1811), v, 272.

71 I quote from Boswell's letter to the *Public Advertiser*, 8 April 1779, *Boswell: Laird of Auchinleck 1778–1782*, ed. Joseph W. Reed and Frederick A. Pottle (New York, NY: McGraw-Hill, 1977), 66.

72 *Boswell on the Grand Tour: Germany and Switzerland, 1764*, ed. Frederick A. Pottle (London: Heinemann, 1953), 84–85.

73 On 12 May 1783 Boswell spoke of 'Scots partiality, the oatmeal in the blood', *Boswell: the Applause of the Jury 1782–1785*, Lustig and Pottle 138. When travelling in Germany with Lieutenant Lauchlan Macpherson, Boswell imagines the two of them being 'like two immense Highlanders', and later the two dress up as Highlanders 'and a fine frolic did we make of it' in the company of the Earl of Marischal, *Boswell on the Grand Tour: Germany and Switzerland, 1764*, 24, 84.

74 In his preface to *Fingal* (1761–62), James Macpherson writes, 'the idea of meanness, which is now connected with a narrow fortune, had its rise after commerce had thrown too much property into the hands of a few', *The Poems of Ossian and Related Works*, 36.

75 *Boswell in Extremes, 1776–1778*, 347.

76 [Boswell], *A Letter to Robert Macqueen Lord Baxfield, on His Promotion to be one of the Judges of the High Court of Justiciary* (Edinburgh: Sold by all the Booksellers, 1780), 13; Boswell, *The Ominous Years*, 158.

77 Dennis Todd lists a number of monsters, including many fakes, in his study of Mary Toft, who gave birth to seventeen rabbits in 1726. See his *Imagining Monsters: Miscreations of the Self in Eighteenth-Century England* (Chicago, IL: University of Chicago Press, 1995), 5, 144–48.

78 Edward Topham, *Letters from Edinburgh, 1774–75* (London: J. Dodsley, 1776), 138.

79 Thomas Crawford, ed. *The Correspondence of James Boswell and William Johnson Temple*, i, 364, 372. The supplement consists of a commentary on Johnson's *Journey* running to ten manuscript pages. It is now held in the Hyde Collection.

80 Bourdieu casts a useful light here. 'The artistic field is a *universe of belief*', he argues. 'Cultural production distinguishes itself from the production of the most common objects in that it must produce not only the object in its materiality, but also the value of this object, that is, the recognition of artistic legitimacy', *The Field of Cultural Production*, 164. We can see Boswell in Scotland producing Johnson in the sense of enticing him up north as well

as, once there, charging his friend with values.

81 As Hugo M. Reichard points out, 'Boswell's Johnson is more guided than guiding', 'Boswell's Johnson, the Hero made by a Committee', *PMLA*, 95: 2 (1980), 227.

82 Boswell discussed with David Hume the possibility of writing a history of the Union. See *Boswell: The Ominous Years*, 29–30. Boswell defended the Union in his *A Letter to the People of Scotland on the Alarming Attempt to Infringe the Articles of the Union and Introduce a Most Pernicious Innovation, by Diminishing the Number of the Lords of Session* (London: C. Dilly, 1785).

83 Pottle, *Boswell on the Grand Tour*, 61. Boswell later imagines the Union as a marriage: 'I assimilated the Union between England and Scotland – the stronger and the weaker country – to a contract of marriage, and I mentioned (as I sometimes look into old books) a curious pamphlet, published about the time of the Union, *On the Marriage of Fergusia and Heptarchus*', *Boswell: Laird of Auchinleck*, 123–24.

84 *Boswell: The English Experiment*, Lustig and Pottle, 140.

85 For a complementary reading of this point, see Gordon Turnbull's '"Generous Attachment": The Politics of Biography in the *Tour to the Hebrides*', in *Dr Samuel Johnson and James Boswell*, ed. and intro. Harold Bloom (New York, NY: Chelsea House, 1988).

86 Malcolm Laing, 'Dissertation on the Supposed Authenticity of Ossian's Poems', in his *The History of Scotland from the Union of the Crowns on the Accession of James VI to the Throne of England, to the Union of the Kingdoms in the Reign of Queen Anne*. 3rd edn. 4 vols. (London: J. Maurman *et al.*, 1819), IV, 429.

87 Henry Mackenzie, ed., *Report of the Committee of the Highland Society of Scotland, Appointed to Inquire into the Nature and Authenticity of the Poems of Ossian* (Edinburgh: Archibald Constable and Co., 1805), 152. This argument, which presupposes a unified 'original composition', was taken up by Patrick Graham. He maintains that Macpherson 'has suppressed, or lost, many beauties in the Gaelic, both in expression and in imagery; whilst he has unwarrantably added images and expressions, which are not there to be found; additions which, without contributing to the beauty of the poem, deprive it of its air of simplicity and antiquity, and give it the appearance of a modern and sophisticated poem', *Essay on the Authenticity of the Poems of Ossian* (Edinburgh: Peter Hill *et al.*, 1807), 276.

88 Gaskill, '*Ossian* in Europe', 646.

89 William Mason, *An Epistle to Dr Shebbeare: to which is added an Ode to Sir Fletcher Norton* (London: J. Almon, 1777), 25–27.

6   EVERYDAY LIFE IN JOHNSON

1 See for example E. S. F. Gow, 'Dr Johnson's Household', *The Empire Review*, 45 (1927), 23–32, Cecil S. Emden, 'Dr Johnson's Ménage', *Quarterly Review* (London), 649 (1966), 281–87, and Lyle Larsen, *Dr Johnson's Household* (Hamden, CT: Archon Books, 1985).

2 The article first appeared in the *St James Chronicle* and a corrected version was published in the *Gentleman's Magazine*. We owe the identification to Edmond Malone who enquired of the matter to John Nichols in 1803. Sir John Hawkins quotes the piece in his discussion of Levett in *The Life of Samuel Johnson, LL.D.*, 396–401.

3 David Fleeman, ed. *Early Biographical Writings of Dr Johnson* (Farnborough, Hants: Gregg, 1993), 452.

4 I take the phrase from Gloria Sybil Gross, *This Invisible Riot of the Mind: Samuel Johnson's Psychological Theory* (Philadelphia, PA: University of Pennyslvania Press, 1992), 82.

5 Elizabeth Burton, *The Georgians at Home, 1714–1830* (London: Longmans, 1967), André Parreaux, *Daily Life in England in the Reign of George III*, trans. Carola Congreve (London: George Allen and Unwin, 1969), Richard B. Schwartz, *Daily Life in Johnson's London* (Madison, WI: University of Wisconsin Press, 1983). The list could be extended to include these and many others: E. N. Williams, *Life in Georgian England* (London: B. T. Batsford Ltd., 1962) and Robert W. Malcolmson, *Popular Recreations in English Society 1700–1850* (Cambridge University Press, 1973).

6 William Shenstone, *Works in Verse and Prose*, 2 vols. (London: J. Dodsley, 1765), II, 163.

7 Johnson, *Lives of the Poets*, III, 412.

8 For Boswell's animadversions on Piozzi's *Anecdotes* see, *Life*, IV, 340–46.

9 Hesther Lynch Piozzi, *Anecdotes of the Late Samuel Johnson, LL.D., during the Last Twenty Years of his Life*, ed. and intro. S. C. Roberts (Westport, CT: Greenwood Press, 1971), 127.

10 Paul Langford suggests that about this time tradesmen were valued for their everyday knowledge, something that gentlemen often did not have. See his *Public Life*, 257. Hester Thrale used the word 'everyday' unselfconsciously in her diary: 'I understand from my Maid – who knows ten Gossiping Tales for my one – that the Ladies when here spoke openly with great Disrespect of Mr Piozzi, a Circumstance I should not have been led to suspect from their ostensible & common everyday Behaviour', *Thraliana*, II, 956.

11 Samuel Kinser, 'Everday Ordinary', *Diacritics* 22: 2 (1992), 79, 80.

12 John Gay, *Poetry and Prose*, ed., Vinton A. Dearing and assisted by Charles E. Beckwith, 2 vols. (Oxford: Clarendon Press, 1974), I, 143–44.

13 *Ibid.*, I, 166.

14 Consider for example the Reverend John Mill's journal, set for the most part in Shetland. There is a good deal of repetition recorded, but no sense of what one would call the everyday. See Gilbert Goudie, ed. and intro., *The Diary of the Rev. John Mill, Minister of the Parishes of Dunrossness, Sandwick and Cunningsburgh in Shetland 1740–1803*, Scottish Historical Society (Edinburgh University Press, 1889).

15 On this point see Stuart Sherman, *Telling Time: Clocks, Diaries, and English Diurnal Form, 1660–1785* (Chicago, IL: University of Chicago Press, 1996), xi.

16 I cite items 24, 33, 42 and 124 in J. D. Fleeman, ed. and intro., *The Sale Catalogue of Samuel Johnson's Library: a Facsimile Edition*, *ELS* Monograph Series, 2 (1975).

17 Maurice Blanchot, 'Everyday Speech', in his *The Infinite Conversation*, trans. and foreword Susan Hanson (Minneapolis, MN: University of Minnesota Press, 1993), 238, 242.

18 See for example Erving Goffmann, *The Presentation of Self in Everyday Life* (New York, NY: Anchor Books, 1959) and Paul J. Korshin, 'The Typology of the Everyday' in his *Typologies in England 1650–1820* (Princeton, NJ: Princeton University Press, 1982).

19 Michel de Certeau, *The Practice of Everyday Life*, trans. Steven Rendall (Berkeley, CA: University of California Press, 1984), 109.

20 I take the phrases from Samuel Kinser's characterisation of Michel de Certeau's account of the everyday. See Kinser's 'Everyday Ordinary', 73.

21 Johnson, *Life of Savage*, ed. Clarence Tracy (Oxford: Clarendon Press, 1971), 97.

22 Friedman, ed. *Collected Works of Oliver Goldsmith*, IV, 269.

23 Martin Heidegger, *Being and Time*, trans. John Macquarrie and Edward Robinson (Oxford: Basil Blackwell, 1973), 422 (H 370).

24 Kristin Ross finds this distinction in Maurice Blanchot's criticism. It is likely that Blanchot, who read *Sein und Zeit* shortly after it was published, is continuing a theme he found in Heidegger. See Ross's 'Two Versions of the Everyday', *L'Esprit Créateur*, 24: 3 (1984), 29–37.

25 For this point and for a stimulating discussion of the everyday in Heidegger I am indebted to Michel Haar, 'The Enigma of Everydayness', trans. Michael B. Naas and Pascale-Anne Brault, in *Reading Heidegger: Commemorations*, ed. John Sallis (Bloomington, IN: Indiana University Press, 1993), 20–28.

26 On the philosophical differences of Marx and Heidegger in their doctrine of human being see Agnes Heller, *Everyday Life*, trans. G. L. Campbell (London: Routledge and Kegan Paul, 1984), 256–58, and Henri Lefebvre, *Critique de la vie quotidienne*, III: *De la modernité au modernisme (Pour une métaphilosophie du quotidian)* (Paris: L'Arche, 1981), 23–25. More generally, see Lefebvre, *The Production of Space*, trans. Donald Nicholson-Smith (Oxford: Blackwell, 1991), 164–65. I am indebted to both authors.

27 Karl Marx, 'Economic and Philosophic Manuscripts of 1844', in Karl Marx and Frederick Engels *Collected Works*, vol. III *Marx and Engels: 1843–44* (New York, NY: International Publishers, 1975), 299–300.

28 I follow the formulation proposed by Heller and used throughout her study *Everyday Life*.

29 Secord, *Defoe's Review*, V, 631b.

30 Lefebvre's examples of dominated space are 'military architecture, fortification and ramparts, dams and irrigation systems', and to exemplify non-dominated space he asks us to imagine 'an igloo, an Oriental straw hut or a Japanese house', *The Production of Space*, 164, 165.

31 Heller, *Everyday Life*, 86–87. Lefebvre maintains that style reduces the everyday, even to the point of eliminating it. On his account there have been societies with no everyday life: for example, the Incas, the Aztecs, the Greeks and the Romans. See his *Everyday Life in the Modern World*, trans. Sacha Rabinovitch, intro. Philip Wander (London: Transaction Books, 1984), 29. In the 1960s the Internationale Situationniste developed Lefebvre's thoughts in their own ways. Raoul Vaneigem, for one, argued that social theory should be derived directly from a lived experience of everyday life. Inevitably, then, 'The construction of everyday life and the realisation of history are henceforward one and the same project', *The Revolution of Everyday Life*, trans. Donald Nicholson-Smith (London: Rebel Press/Left Bank Books, 1994), 221.

32 W. H. Auden, 'Young Boswell', *The New Yorker*, 25 November 1950, 148.

33 Thomas Haywood, ed. *The Diary of Rev. Henry Newcome* (Chetham Society Publications 18, 1849).

34 Boswell, *London Journal*, 211 n. 4.

35 Frederick A. Pottle, 'The Life of James Boswell', *The Yale Review*, 35 (1946), 445.

36 Boswell, *Ominous Years*, 265.

37 Boswell, *The Hypochondriack*, II, 259.

38 Peter Steele, *The Autobiographical Passion: Studies in the Self on Show* (Melbourne: Melbourne University Press, 1989), 5.

39 Boswell, *London Journal*, 94.

40 Butt, ed. *The Poems of Alexander Pope*, 211.

41 Paul K. Alkon, 'Boswellian Time', *Studies in Burke and His Time*, 14: 3 (1973), 246. The disjunction is inclusive on Alkon's interpretation.

42 Croker, *Life of Samuel Johnson, LL.D.*, I, xii, n. 1.

43 P. A. W. Collins observes that 'Croker's figures must be some of the most-quoted inaccurate "facts" in English Literary studies' and maintains that Boswell met Johnson on 'about 425 days in all', 'Boswell's Contact with Johnson', *Notes and Queries*, 201 (1956), 164. Donald Greene offers another calculation in 'Do We Need a Biography of Johnson's "Boswell" Years?', 128–36.

44 Alkon, 'Boswellian Time', 249.

CONCLUSION: 'PROPERTY, CONTRACT, TRADE AND PROFITS'

1 Lewis Namier, *England in the Age of the American Revolution* (London: Macmillan, 1930), 36.

2 Burke, *Reflections on the Revolution in France*, 74.

3 Wolcot, *The Works of Peter Pindar, Esq.* (London: J. Walker, 1794), I, 316.

4 See Greene, ''Tis a Pretty Book, Mr. Boswell, But –', 134.

5 Carlyle, *On Heroes, Hero-Worship, and the Heroic in History*, 133.

Bibliography

JOHNSON

A Dictionary of the English Language. 2 vols. London: J. and P. Knapton, *et al.*, 1755.

A Journey to the Western Isles of Scotland. Ed. J. D. Fleeman. Oxford: Clarendon Press, 1985.

Early Biographical Writings of Dr Johnson. Ed. J. D. Fleeman. Farnborough, Hants: Gregg International Publishers, 1973.

Johsoniana: or supplement to Boswell, being anecdotes and sayings of Dr Johnson. London: J. Murray, 1836.

Johnsonian Gleanings. Ed. Aleyn Llyll Reade. 11 vols. 1909–52. Rpt. New York, NY: Octagan Books, 1968.

Johnsonian Miscellanies. Ed. George Birkbeck Hill. 2 vols. Oxford: Clarendon Press, 1897.

Life of Savage. Ed. Clarence Tracy. Oxford: Clarendon Press, 1971.

Lives of the English Poets. Ed. George Birkbeck Hill. 3 vols. Oxford: Clarendon Press, 1905.

Review of [William Tytler], *An Historical and Critical Enquiry into the Evidence Produced by the Earls of Moray and Morton against Mary, Queen of Scots with an Examination of the Rev. Fr Robertson's Dissertation and Mr Hume's History with Respect to That Evidence, Gentleman's Magazine,* October 1760, 453–56.

Samuel Johnson's Prefaces and Dedications. Ed. Allen T. Hazen. New Haven, CT: Yale University Press, 1937.

The Letters of Samuel Johnson. Ed. Bruce Redford. 5 vols. Princeton, NJ: Princeton University Press, 1992.

The Plan of a Dictionary of the English Language. London: J. and P. Knapton, *et al.*, 1747.

The Works of Samuel Johnson, LL.D. 16 vols. Cambridge, MA: Harvard Cooperative Society, 1903.

THE YALE EDITION OF THE WORKS OF SAMUEL JOHNSON

I   *Diaries, Prayers, and Annals.* Eds E. L. McAdam, Jr with Donald and Mary Hyde, 1985.
II   *The Idler* and *The Adventurer.* Eds. W. J. Bate, J. M. Bullit and L. F. Powell, 1963.
III–V   *The Rambler.* Eds. W. J. Bate and Albrecht B. Strauss, 1969.
VI   *Poems.* Eds. E. L. McAdam, Jr, with George Milne, 1964.
VII–VIII   *Johnson on Shakespeare.* Ed. Arthur Sherbo. Intro. Bertrand H. Bronson, 1968.
X   *Political Writings.* Ed. Donald J. Greene, 1977.
XIV   *Sermons.* Eds. Jean Hagstrum and James Gray, 1978.
XV   *A Voyage to Abyssinia.* Ed. Joel J. Gold, 1985.
XVI   *Rasselas and Other Tales.* Ed. Gwin J. Kolb, 1990.

These works are referred to in the text as Yale *followed by the number shown beside the title in the list above.*

BOSWELL

THE YALE EDITIONS OF THE PRIVATE PAPERS OF JAMES BOSWELL

Boswell's London Journal, 1762–1763. Ed. Frederick A. Pottle. London: Heinemann, 1950.
Boswell's London Journal, 1762–1763 together with Journal of my Jaunt, Harvest, 1762. Ed. Frederick A. Pottle. London: Heinemann, 1951.
Portraits by Sir Joshua Reynolds. Ed. Frederick W. Hilles. London: Heinemann, 1952.
Boswell on the Grand Tour: Germany and Switzerland, 1764. Ed. Frederick A. Pottle. London: Heinemann, 1953.
Boswell: the Ominous Years, 1774–1776. Eds. Charles Ryskamp and Frederick A. Pottle. New York, NY: McGraw-Hill, 1963.
Boswell in Extremes 1776–1778. Eds. Charles McC. Weiss and Frederick A. Pottle. New York, NY: McGraw-Hill, 1970.
Boswell, Laird of Auckinleck, 1778–1782. Eds. Joseph W. Reed and Frederick A. Pottle. London: Heinemann, 1977.
Boswell: the Applause of the Jury, 1782–1785. Eds. Irma S. Lustig and Frederick A. Pottle. London: Heinemann, 1982.
Boswell: the English Experiment, 1785–1789. Eds. Irma S. Lustig and Frederick A. Pottle. New York, NY: McGraw-Hill, 1982.
Boswell: the Great Biographer, 1789–1795. Eds. Marlies K. Danziger and Frank Brady. New York, NY: McGraw-Hill, 1989.

YALE (RESEARCH) EDITIONS OF THE PRIVATE PAPERS OF JAMES
BOSWELL: CORRESPONDENCE

The Correspondence and Other Papers of James Boswell, Relating to the Making of the 'Life of Johnson'. Ed. Marshall Waingrow. Research Edition of the Correspondence, vol. II. New York, NY: McGraw-Hill, 1969.

The Correspondence of James Boswell with David Garrick, Edmund Burke, and Edmond Malone. Ed. Peter S. Baker. Research Edition of the Correspondence, vol. IV. New York, NY: McGraw-Hill, 1987.

The General Correspondence of James Boswell, 1766–1769. Eds. Richard C. Cole with Peter S. Baker and Rachel McClellan, and assistant James J. Caudle. 2 vols. Vol. I: *1766–1767.* Research Edition, Correspondence, vol. V. New Haven, CT: Yale University Press, and Edinburgh University Press, 1993.

The Correspondence of James Boswell and William Johnson Temple 1756–1777. Ed. Thomas Crawford. 2 vols. Vol. I: *1756–1777.* Research Edition, Correspondence, vol. VI. New Haven, CT: Yale University Press, and Edinburgh University Press, 1997.

James Boswell's 'Life of Johnson': an Edition of the Original Manuscript in Four Volumes. Ed. Marshall Waingrow. Research Edition, *Life of Johnson,* vol. I: *1709–1765.* New Haven, CT: Yale University Press, 1994.

OTHER WORKS BY JAMES BOSWELL

A Letter to Robert Macqueen Lord Braxfield, on His Promotion to be one of the Judges of the High Court of Justiciary. Edinburgh: Sold by all the Booksellers, 1780.

A Letter to the People of Scotland on the Alarming Attempt to Infringe the Articles of the Union and Introduce a Most Pernicious Innovation, by Diminishing the Number of the Lords of Session. London: C. Dilly, 1785.

A View of the Edinburgh Theatre During the Summer Season, 1759. Intro. David W. Tarbet. 1760; rpt. Los Angeles, CA: The Augustan Reprint Society, 1976.

Letters Between the Honourable Andrew Erskine and James Boswell, Esq. London: W. Flexney, 1763.

The Hypochondriack: Being the Seventy Essays by the Celebrated Biographer James Boswell, Appearing in the 'London Magazine', from November 1777 to August 1783 and Here First Reprinted. Ed. Margery Bailey. 2 vols. Stanford, CA: Stanford University Press, 1928.

The Life of Johnson, Together with Boswell's Journal of a Tour to the Hebrides and Johnson's Diary into North Wales. Ed. George Birkbeck Hill. Revised and enlarged L. F. Powell. 6 vols. Oxford: Clarendon Press, 1934–64.

The Life of Samuel Johnson, LL.D. with A Journal of a Tour to the Hebrides. Ed. Percy Fitzgerald. Reprint of 1st edn. with Boswell's corrections and additions. Edited with new notes. 3 vols. London: Bickers and Son, 1874.

The Life of Samuel Johnson, Including A Journal of a Tour to the Hebrides. Ed. J. W. Croker. London: John Murray, 1831.

GENERAL

Abrams, M. H. 'English Romanticism: the Spirit of the Age', in *Romanticism Reconsidered: Selected Papers from the English Institute*. Ed. and foreword Northrop Frye. New York, NY: Columbia University Press, 1963.

Addison, Joseph, Sir Richard Steele, *et al. The Spectator*. Ed. Gregory Smith, intro. Peter Smithers. 4 vols. Everyman's Library. London: Dent, 1945.

Agutter, William. *On the Difference Between the Deaths of the Righteous and the Wicked, Illustrated in the Instance of Dr Samuel Johnson, and David Hume, Esq.* London: J. Richardson, 1800.

Alkon, Paul K. 'Boswellian Time'. *Studies in Burke and His Time* 14: 3 (1973), 239–56.

Allan, D. G. C. and John L. Abbott, eds. *The Virtuoso Tribe of Arts and Sciences: Studies in the Eighteenth-Century Work and Membership of the London Society of Arts.* Athens, GA: University of Georgia Press, 1992.

Anon. *An Ode on the Much Lamented Death of Dr Samuel Johnson.* London: J. Rozea, 1784.

Anon. *Johnson's Laurel: or, Contest of the Poets.* London: S. Hooper, 1785.

Anon. *Remarks on a Voyage to the Hebrides in a Letter to Samuel Johnson, LL.D.* London: George Kearsly, 1775.

Anon. ['Samuel Johnson and his Age'], *Quarterly Review*, 159 (1885), 147–74.

Auden, W. H. 'Young Boswell', *The New Yorker*, 25 November 1950, 148.

Austin, Gabriel, ed. *Four Oaks Library.* Somerville, NJ: Donald and Mary Hyde, 1967.

Austin, John D. and Graham Nicholls. *Transactions of the Johnson Society, 1988.* Lichfield, 1989.

Aylmer, G. E. 'The Meaning and Definition of "Property" in Seventeenth-Century England'. *Past and Present* 86 (1980), 87–97.

Bailey, John. *Dr Johnson and his Circle.* Home University Library of Modern Knowledge. London: Williams and Norgate, 1913.

Balderston, Katherine C., ed. *Thraliana: the Diary of Mrs Hester Lynch Thrale (later Mrs Piozzi), 1776–1809.* 2 vols. 2nd edn Oxford: Clarendon Press, 1951.

Barnouw, Jeffrey. 'Johnson and Hume Considered as the Core of a New "Period Concept" of the Enlightenment', *Studies on Voltaire and the Eighteenth Century* 190 (1980), 189–96.

Barrett, Charlotte, ed. *Diaries and Letters of Madame d'Arblay (1778–1840)*, preface and notes by Austin Dobson. 6 vols. London: Macmillan and Co., 1905.

Baruth, Philip Edward. 'Recognizing the Author-Function: Alternatives to Greene's Black-and-Red Book of Johnson's *Logia*', *The Age of Johnson* 5 (1992), 35–60.

Bate, W. J. *Samuel Johnson.* New York, NY: Harcourt Brace Jovanovich, 1975.

Birrell, Augustine. 'The Transmission of Dr Johnson's Personality'. *Johnson Club Papers.* By Various Hands. London: T. Fisher Unwin, 1899, 3–16.

. *Self-Selected Essays.* London: Thomas Nelson, 1916.

Blackstone, William. *Commentaries on the Laws of England.* 4 vols. Oxford: Clarendon Press, 1765–69.

Blackwell, Thomas. *An Enquiry into the Life and Writings of Homer.* 1736; rpt. Hildesheim: Georg Olms Verlag, 1976.

Letters Concerning Mythology. 1748; rpt. New York, NY: Garland Publishing Inc., 1976.

Blair, Hugh, 'A Critical Dissertation on the Poems of Ossian, Son of Fingal', in *The Works of Ossian, the Son of Fingal*, 2 vols. Trans. from the Gaelic by James Macpherson. 2nd edn. London: T. Becket and P. A. De Hondt, 1765.

Sermons. 5 vols. London: T. Cadell and W. Davies, 1815.

Blanchot, Maurice, *The Infinite Conversation.* Trans. and foreword Susan Hanson. Minneapolis, MN: University of Minnesota Press, 1993.

Bloom, Harold, ed. and intro. *Dr Samuel Johnson and James Boswell.* New York, NY: Chelsea House, 1988.

Bonnell, Thomas F. 'John Bell's *Poets of Great Britain*: the "Little Trifling Edition" Revisited', *Modern Philology* 85 (1987–88), 128–52.

Boorstin, Daniel J. *The Mysterious Science of the Law: an Essay on Blackstone's 'Commentaries'.* 1941; rpt. Gloucester, MA: Peter Smith, 1973.

Bourdieu, Pierre. *The Field of Cultural Production: Essays on Art and Literature.* Ed. and intro. Randal Johnson. London: Polity Press, 1993.

Bowersock, G. W. 'The Art of the Footnote', *The American Scholar*, Winter 1983/84, 54–62.

Boyle, Nicholas. *Goethe: the Poet and the Age*, 1: *The Poetry of Desire (1749–1790).* Oxford: Clarendon Press, 1991.

Brack, O M Jr. and Robert E. Kelley, eds. *The Early Biographies of Samuel Johnson.* Iowa City, IA: University of Iowa Press, 1974.

Braudy, Leo. *The Frenzy of Renown: Fame and its History.* New York, NY: Oxford University Press, 1986.

Bronson, Bertrand H. 'Ritson's "Bibliographia Scotia"', *PMLA* 52 (1937), 122–59.

Johnson Agonistes and Other Essays. Berkeley, CA: University of California Press, 1965.

Buchan, John. *Midwinter.* New York, NY: Grosset and Dunlap, 1923.

Burckhardt, Jacob. *The Civilization of the Renaissance in Italy.* Trans. S. G. C. Middlemore. New introduction by Peter Burke. Notes by Peter Murray. London: Penguin, 1990.

Burke, Edmund. *Reflections on the Revolution in France and on the Proceedings in Certain Societies in London Relative to that Event. In a Letter to have been Sent to a Gentleman in Paris.* London: J. Dodsley, 1790.

Burke, William. [Letter to Portland, 26 July 1779] Portland Papers, Hallward Library, University of Nottingham.

Burney, Fanny. *Evelina: or the History of a Young Lady's Entrance into the World.* Ed. and intro. Edward A. Bloom with the assistance of Lillian D. Bloom. The World's Classics. Oxford: Oxford University Press, 1982.

Burton, Elizabeth. *The Georgians at Home, 1714–1830.* London: Longmans, 1967.

Burton, John Hill, ed. *Life and Correspondence of David Hume.* 2 vols. 1846; rpt. New York, NY: Burt Franklin, 1967.

Butt, John. ed. *The Poems of Alexander Pope*. London: Methuen, 1968.
Bysveen, Josef. *Epic Tradition and Innovation in James Macpherson's 'Fingal'*. Studia Anglistica Upsaliensia 44 (Uppsala, 1982).
Cafarelli, Annette Wheeler. *Prose in the Age of Poets: Romanticism and Biographical Narrative from Johnson to De Quincey*. Philadelphia, PA: University of Pennsylvania Press, 1990.
Camic, Charles. *Experience and Enlightenment: Socialization for Cultural Change in Eighteenth-Century Scotland*. Chicago, IL: University of Chicago Press, 1983.
Carlyle, Thomas. *Critical and Miscellaneous Essays*. 5 vols., Centenary Edition of the Works of Thomas Carlyle. Ed. H. D. Traill. London: Chapman and Hall, 1896–99.
   On Heroes, Hero-Worship, and the Heroic in History, notes and intro. Michael K. Goldberg, text established by Michael K. Goldberg, Joel J. Brattin and Mark Engel. The Norman and Charlotte Strouse Edition of the Writings of Thomas Carlyle. Los Angeles, CA: University of California Press, 1993.
Carpenter, Edward. ed. *A House of Kings: the History of Westminster Abbey*. London: John Baker, 1966.
Cary, Henry Francis. *Lives of English Poets, from Johnson to Kirke White, Designed as a Continuation of Johnson's 'Lives'*. London: Henry G. Bohn, 1846.
Chalmers, Alexander, ed. *The Works of the English Poets, from Chaucer to Cowper; Including the Series Edited, with Prefaces, Biographical and Critical, by Dr Samuel Johnson: and the Most Approved Translations*. 21 vols. London: J. Johnson *et al.*, 1810.
Chambers, Alexander, ed. *The British Essayists, with Prefaces Historical and Biographical*. London: C. and J. Rivington, *et al.*, 1823.
Chambers, Sir Robert. *A Course of Lectures on the English Law Delivered at the University of Oxford 1767–1773 and Composed in Association with Samuel Johnson*. Ed. Thomas M. Curley. 2 vols. Madison, WI: University of Wisconsin Press, 1986.
Chambers, Ross. *Story and Situation: Narrative Seduction and the Power of Fiction*. Minneapolis, MN: University of Minnesota Press, 1984.
Christie, Ian R. *Wilkes, Wyvill and Reform: the Parliamentary Reform Movement in British Politics, 1760–1785*. London: Macmillan, 1962.
   British 'non-élite' MPs, 1715–1820. Oxford: Clarendon Press, 1995.
Clark, J. C. D. 'The Politics of the Excluded: Tories, Jacobites and Whig Patriots 1715–1760', *Parliamentary History* 2 (1983), 209–22.
   Samuel Johnson: Literature, Religion and English Cultural Politics from the Restoration to Romanticism. Cambridge University Press, 1994.
   'The Politics of Samuel Johnson', *The Age of Johnson* 7 (1996), 27–56.
   'The Cultural Identity of Samuel Johnson', *The Age of Johnson* 8 (1997), 15–70.
   'Religious Affiliation and Dynastic Allegiance in Eighteenth-Century England: Edmund Burke, Thomas Paine and Samuel Johnson', *ELH*, 64 (1997), 1029–67.
Clark, John. *An Answer to Mr Shaw's Inquiry into the Authenticity of the Poems ascribed to Ossian*. Edinburgh: C. Elliot, 1781.

Enquiry into the Authenticity of the Poems Ascribed to Ossian with a Reply to Mr Clark's Answer. 2nd edn. London: J. Murray, 1783.

Clarke, Charles Cowden, ed. *The Poetical Works of Edmund Waller and Sir John Denham*. Edinburgh: James Nichol, 1862.

Clifford, James L. *Young Samuel Johnson*. London: Heinemann, 1955, also published as *Young Sam Johnson* (New York, NY: McGraw-Hill, 1955).

Clifford, James L., ed. *Twentieth Century Interpretation of Boswell's 'Life of Johnson'*. Englewood Cliffs, NJ: Prentice-Hall, 1970.

Clifford, James L. and Donald Greene. *Samuel Johnson: a Survey and Bibliography of Critical Studies*. Minneapolis, MN: University of Minnesota Press, 1970.

Clifford, James L. and John H. Middendorf. 'Boswell in Search of a Wife', *Johnsonian News Letter* 16: 3 (1956), 1.

'Boswell', *Johnsonian News Letter* 26: 2 (1966), 2–3.

Clifford James L. and William L. Payne. 'Johnsonians and Boswellians', *Johnsonian News Letter* 10: 2 (1950), 3–4.

Cochrane, J. A. *Dr Johnson's Printer: the Life of William Strahan*. London: Routledge and Kegan Paul, 1964.

Colley, Linda. *In Defiance of Oligarchy: the Tory Party 1714–50*. Cambridge University Press, 1982.

Britons: Forging the Nation 1707–1837. New Haven, CT: Yale University Press, 1992.

Collins, A. S. *Authorship in the Days of Johnson: being a Study of the Relation between Author, Patron, Publisher and Public, 1726–1780*. London: Robert Holden, 1927.

Collins, P. A. W. 'Boswell's Contact with Johnson', *Notes and Queries* 201 (1956), 163–66.

Colquhoun, Patrick. *A Treatise on the Police of the Metropolis*. 6th edn (1795 first edn.) London: Joseph Mawman, 1800.

Courtney, W. P. and D. Nichol Smith, *A Bibliography of Samuel Johnson*. 1915; rpt. Oxford: Clarendon Press, 1951.

Cowper, Mary. *Diary of Mary Countess Cowper, Lady of the Bedchamber to the Princess of Wales, 1714–1720*. London: John Murray, 1864.

Cruickshanks, Eveline. *Political Untouchables: the Tories and the '45*. New York, NY: Holmes and Meier, 1979.

Cruickshanks, Eveline and Jeremy Black, eds. *The Jacobite Challenge*. Edinburgh: John Donald, 1988.

Curley, Thomas M. 'Johnson's Last Word on Ossian: Ghostwriting for William Shaw', *Aberdeen and the Enlightenment: Proceedings of a Conference held at the University of Aberdeen*. Ed. Jennifer J. Carter and Joan H. Pittock. Aberdeen University Press, 1987, 375–94.

Daghlian, Philip B., ed. *Essays in Eighteenth-Century Biography*. Bloomington, IN: Indiana University Press, 1968.

Davis, Herbert, ed. *The Prose Writings of Jonathan Swift*. 14 vols. Oxford: Basil Blackwell, 1973.

Davis, Lennard, J., '"Upon Mouldering Stone"': Swift's Politics of Language', *The Age of Johnson* 2 (1989), 39–64.

Dawson, W. J. *The Makers of Modern Prose: a Popular Handbook to the Greater Prose Writers of the Century.* London: Hodder and Stoughton, 1899.

De Certeau, Michel. *The Practice of Everyday Life.* Trans. Steven Rendall. Berkeley, CA: University of California Press, 1984.

The Writing of History. Trans. Tom Conley. New York, NY: Columbia University Press, 1988.

Defoe, Daniel. *The Original Power of the Collective Body of the People of England, Examined and Asserted.* London: R. Baldwin, 1769.

The History of the Principal Discoveries and Improvements in the Several Arts and Sciences: Particularly the Great Branches of Commerce, Navigation, and Plantation, in All Parts of the Known World. London: W. Mears, 1727.

DeMaria, Robert Jr., *Johnson's Dictionary and the Language of Learning.* Chapel Hill, NC: The University of North Carolina Press, 1986.

The Life of Samuel Johnson: a Critical Biography. Oxford: Basil Blackwell, 1993.

Samuel Johnson and the Life of Reading. Baltimore, MD: The Johns Hopkins University Press, 1997.

Derrida, Jacques. *Positions.* Trans. Alan Bass. Chicago, IL: University of Chicago Press, 1981.

Du droit à la philosophie. Paris: Galilée, 1990.

Dickinson, H. T. *Liberty and Property: Political Ideology in Eighteenth-Century Britain.* New York, NY: Holmes and Meier, 1977.

The Politics of the People in Eighteenth-Century Britain. New York, NY: St Martin's Press, 1995.

D'Israeli, Issac. *The Literary Character, Illustrated by the History of Men of Genius, Drawn from their Own Feelings and Confessions.* London: John Murray, 1818.

Dobson, Austin. *Eighteenth Century Studies.* The Wayfarer's Library. London: J. M. Dent and Sons, [1914].

Dowling, William C. *Language and Logos in Boswell's 'Life of Johnson'.* Princeton, NJ: Princeton University Press, 1981.

Dryden, John. *The Poems of John Dryden.* Ed. James Kinsley. 4 vols. Oxford: Clarendon Press, 1958.

Duff, William. *An Essay on Original Genius; and Its Various Modes of Exertion in Philosophy and the Fine Arts, Particularly in Poetry.* London: Edward and Charles Dilly, 1767.

Dunbar, John Telfer. *History of Highland Dress.* Edinburgh: Oliver and Boyd, 1962.

Emden, Cecil S. 'Dr Johnson's Ménage', *Quarterly Review* (London) 649 (1966), 281–87.

Engell, James, ed. *Johnson and His Age.* Harvard English Studies, 12. Cambridge, MA: Harvard University Press, 1984.

Epstein, William H. 'Professing the Eighteenth Century', *Profession* (1985), 10–15.

Erskine-Hill, Howard. 'Johnson the Jacobite? A Response to the New Introduction to Donald Greene's *The Politics of Samuel Johnson'*, *The Age of Johnson* 7 (1996), 3–26.

Fitzgerald, Percy. *Croker's Boswell and Boswell: Studies in the 'Life of Johnson'*. London: Chapman and Hall, 1880.

A Critical Examination of Dr G. Birkbeck Hill's 'Johnsonian' Editions. London: Bliss, Sands and Co., 1898.

Fleeman, J. D., ed. and intro. *The Sale Catalogue of Samuel Johnson's Library: a Facsimile Edition*. *ELS* Monograph Series, 2 (1975).

Foote, Samuel. *The Englishman in Paris: a Comedy in Two Acts. As it is performed at the Theatre-Royal in Covent-Garden*. London: Paul Vaillant, 1753.

The Englishman Returned from Paris: being the sequel to The Englishman in Paris: A Farce in Two Acts. As it is performed at the Theatre-Royal at Covent-Garden. London: Paul Vaillant, 1756.

Forbes, Robert, ed. *The Lyon in Mourning*. Preface by Henry Paton. Scottish History Society 20–22. Edinburgh, 1895–96.

Foucault, Michel. *The Order of Things: an Archeology of the Human Sciences*. Unknown translator. London: Tavistock Publications, 1970.

Friedman, Arthur, ed. *Collected Works of Oliver Goldsmith*. 5 vols. Oxford: Clarendon Press, 1966.

Frye, Northrop. 'Towards Defining an Age of Sensibility', *ELH* 23: 2 (1956), 144–52.

Furnivall, Frederick. *Early English Text Society: Seventh Report of the Committee*. N.p: February 1871.

Gaskill, Howard. 'What did James Macpherson really leave on Display at his Publisher's Shop in 1762?', *Scottish Gaelic Studies* 16 (1990), 67–89.

Ossian Revisited. Edinburgh: Edinburgh University Press, 1991.

'*Ossian* in Europe', *Canadian Review of Comparative Literature* 21 (1994), 643–78.

Gaskell, Howard, ed. *The Poems of Ossian and Related Works*. Intro. Fiona Stafford. Edingburgh: Edinburgh University Press, 1996.

Gay, John. *Poetry and Prose*. Ed. Vinton A. Dearing, assisted by Charles E. Beckwith. 2 vols. Oxford: Clarendon Press, 1974.

Dramatic Works. Ed. John Fuller. 2 vols. Oxford: Clarendon Press, 1983.

Gibbon, Edward. *The History of the Decline and Fall of the Roman Empire*. Ed. David Womersley. 3 vols. London: Allen Lane, 1994.

Gibson's Three Pastoral Letters. Horne's Letters on Infidelity, and to Adam Smith. New York, NY: New York Protestant Episcopal Press, 1831.

Goffman, Erving. *The Presentation of Self in Everyday Life*. New York, NY: Anchor Books, 1959.

Gordon, Peter and John White. *Philosophers as Educational Reformers: the Influence of Idealism on British Educational Thought and Practice*. London: Routledge and Kegan Paul, 1979.

Goudie, Gilbert, ed. and intro. *The Diary of the Rev. John Mill, Minister of the Parishes of Dunrossness, Sandwick and Cunningsburgh in Shetland 1740–1803*. Scottish Historical Society. Edinburgh: Edinburgh University Press, 1889.

Gow, E. S. F. 'Dr Johnson's Household', *The Empire Review* 45 (1927), 23–32.

Graham, Patrick. *Essay on the Authenticity of the Poems of Ossian*. Edinburgh: Peter Hill *et al.*, 1807.

Green, J. R., *A Short History of the English People*. 4 vols. 1874; rpt. London: Macmillan, 1913.

Greene, Donald, J. 'The Development of the Johnson Canon', *Restoration and Eighteenth-Century Literature: Essays in honour of Alan Dugald McKillop*. Chicago, IL: University of Chicago Press, 1963, 407–27.

'Reflections on a Literary Anniversary', *Queen's Quarterly* 70: 2 (1963), 198–208.

'The Uses of Autobiography in the Eighteenth Century', in Daghlian, *Essays in Eighteenth-Century Biography*, 1968.

'The Study of Eighteenth-Century Literature: Past, Present and Future', in Harth, *New Approaches to Eighteenth-Century Literature*, 1974.

'Do We Need a Biography of Johnson's "Boswell" Years?', *Modern Language Studies* 9: 3 (1979), 128–36.

'What is a Tory?', *The American Scholar* 52 (1983), 422–27.

'Boswell's Life as "Literary Biography"', in Vance, *Boswell's 'Life of Johnson'*, 1985.

'Samuel Johnson', in Meyers, *The Craft of Literary Biography*, 1985.

"'Tis a Pretty Book, Mr Boswell, But—', in Vance, *Boswell's 'Life of Johnson'*, 1985.

'The *Logia* of Samuel Johnson and the Quest for the Historical Johnson', *The Age of Johnson* 3 (1990), 1–33.

The Politics of Samuel Johnson, 2nd edn. Athens, GA: University of Georgia Press, 1990.

'Johnson: The Jacobite Legend Exhumed: a Rejoinder to Howard Erskine-Hill and J. C. D. Clark', *The Age of Johnson*, 7 (1996), 57–135.

'Jonathan Clark and the Abominable Cultural Mind-Set', *The Age of Johnson* 8 (1997), 71–88.

Greene, Donald J. and John A. Vance. *A Bibliography of Johnsonian Studies, 1970–1985*. *ELS* Monograph Series 39, 1987.

Greenwood, David. *William King: Tory and Jacobite*. Oxford: Clarendon Press, 1969.

Greig, J. Y. T., ed. *The Letters of David Hume*. 2 vols. Oxford: Clarendon Press, 1932.

Groom, Bernard. *A Literary History of England*. London: Longmans, Green and Co., 1929.

Gross, Gloria Sybil. *This Invisible Riot of the Mind: Samuel Johnson's Psychological Theory*. Philadelphia, PA: University of Pennsylvania Press, 1992.

Grundy, Isobel, ed. *Samuel Johnson: New Critical Essays*. London: Vision, 1984.

Haar, Michel. 'The Enigma of Everydayness', trans. Michael B. Naas and Pascale-Anne Brault. In *Reading Heidegger: Commemorations*. Ed. John Sallis. Bloomington, IN: Indiana University Press, 1993, 20–28.

Halliday, John. *The Life of William Late Earl of Mansfield*. London: P. Elmsly *et al.*, 1797.

Harrington, James. *The Commonwealth of Oceana and a System of Politics.* Ed. J. G. A. Pocock. Cambridge University Press, 1992.

Harris, Joseph. *An Essay upon Money and Coins.* Part I: *The Theories of Commerce, Money, and Exchanges.* London: G. Hawkins, 1757.

Harth, Phillip, ed. *New Approaches to Eighteenth-Century Literature: Selected Papers from the English Institute.* New York, NY: Columbia University Press, 1974.

Hatton, Ragnhild. *George I, Elector and King.* London: Thames and Hudson, 1978.

Hawkins, Sir John, *The Life of Samuel Johnson, LL.D.,* 2nd edn. London: J. Buckland *et al.,* 1787.

Hay, Douglas, Peter Linebaugh, John G. Rule, E. P. Thomson and Cal Winslow. *Albion's Fatal Tree: Crime and Society in Eighteenth-Century England.* New York, NY: Pantheon Books, 1975.

Haywood, Thomas, ed. *The Diary of Rev. Henry Newcome.* Chetham Society Publications 18, 1849.

Hazlitt, William. *The Spirit of the Age.* 1825; rpt. Oxford: Woodstock Books, 1989.

Hegel, G. W. F. *The Philosophy of History.* Trans. J. Sibree and intro. C. J. Friedrich. New York, NY: Dover Publications, 1956.

Aesthetics: Lectures on Fine Art. Trans. T. M. Knox. 2 vols. Oxford: Clarendon Press, 1974.

Heidegger, Martin. *Being and Time.* Trans. John Macquarrie and Edward Robinson. Oxford: Basil Blackwell, 1973.

Heller, Agnes. *Everyday Life.* Trans. G. L. Campbell. London: Routledge and Kegan Paul, 1984.

Henderson, Andrew. *A Letter to Dr Samuel Johnson on his Journey to the Western Isles.* London: J. Henderson *et al.,* 1775.

Henson, Eithne. *'The Fictions of Romantick Chivalry': Samuel Johnson and Romance.* Rutherford, NJ: Fairleigh Dickinson University Press, 1992.

Herder, J. G. *Outlines of a Philosophy of the History of Man.* Trans. T. Churchill. London: J. Johnson, 1800.

'Extracts from a Correspondence on Ossian and the Songs of Ancient Peoples', in *German Aesthetic and Literary Criticism: Wincklemann, Lessing, Hamann, Herder, Schiller, Goethe.* Ed. and intro. H. B. Nisbet. Cambridge University Press, 1985, 154–61.

Hill, Aaron. *The Dramatic Works of Aaron Hill, Esq.* 2 vols. London: T. Lowndes, 1760.

Hilles, Frederick W., ed. *The Age of Johnson: Essays Presented to Chauncey Brewster Tinker.* New Haven, CT: Yale University Press, 1949.

Hobsbawm, Eric and Terence Ranger, eds. *The Invention of Tradition.* Cambridge University Press, 1983.

Hume, David. *A Treatise of Human Nature.* Ed. L. A. Selby-Bigge. 2nd edn. revised P. H. Nidditch. Oxford: Clarendon Press, 1978.

Essays Moral, Political, and Literary. Ed. Eugene F. Miller. Indianapolis, IN: Liberty Classics, 1987.

Innes, Thomas. *A Critical Essay on the Ancient Inhabitants of the Northern Parts of*

Britain, or Scotland. 2 vols. London: W. Innys, 1729.

Insh, George Pratt. *The Scottish Jacobite Movement: a Study in Economic and Social Forces.* Edinburgh: The Moray Press, 1952.

Isham, Ralph H., Joseph Wood Krutch and Mark van Doren. 'Boswell: the Life of Johnson', in *The New Invitation to Learning.* Ed. Mark van Doren. New York, NY: New Home Library, 1944.

Jabès, Edmond, *The Book of Resemblances.* Trans. Rosemarie Waldrop. 3 vols. Hanover, NH: Wesleyan University Press, 1991.

Jarrett, Derek. *England in the Age of Hogarth.* 1974; rpt. New Haven, CT: Yale University Press, 1986.

Johnson Club Papers. By Various Hands London: T. Fisher Unwin, 1899.

[Johnson Society of Lichfield], *Dr Samuel Johnson: a Typical Englishman.* 207th Birthday Celebration at Lichfield, 18 September 1916.

Jonson, Ben. *Poems.* ed. Ian Donaldson. Oxford University Press, 1975.

Kames, Lord. 'Critical Observations on the Poems of Ossian', in *Poems of Ossian, the Son of Fingal* by James Macpherson. 2 vols. New York, NY: Evert Duyckink and James and Thomas Ronalds, 1806, II, 289–315.

Kaminksi, Thomas. *The Early Career of Samuel Johnson.* New York, NY: Oxford University Press, 1987.

Kearsley, George, ed. *The Poetical Works of David Garrick.* 2 vols. London: George Kearsley, 1785.

Kelly, Patrick Hyde, ed. and intro. *Locke on Money.* 2 vols. The Clarendon Edition of the Works of John Locke. Oxford: Clarendon Press, 1991.

Kernan, Alvin. *Samuel Johnson and the Impact of Print.* Princeton, NJ: Princeton University Press, 1987.

Kinser, Samuel. 'Everyday Ordinary', *Diacritics* 22: 2 (1992), 70–82.

Knapp, Lewis, M., ed. *The Letters of Tobias Smollett.* Oxford: Clarendon, 1970.

Korshin, Paul J. *Typologies in England 1650–1820.* Princeton, NJ: Princeton University Press, 1982.

Korshin, Paul J., ed. *The Age of Johnson: A Scholarly Annual.* New York, NY: AMS Press, 1987, I v–vi.

Lackington, James. *Memoirs of the Forty-Five First Years of the Life of James Lackington.* 7th edn. London: Printed for the Author, 1794.

Laing, Malcolm. *The History of Scotland from the Union of the Crowns on the Accession of James VI to the Throne of England, to the Union of the Kingdoms in the Reign of Queen Anne.* 3rd edn. 4 vols. London: J. Maurman *et al.*, 1819.

Laing, Malcolm, ed. *The Poems of Ossian.* 2 vols. London: W. Strahan and T. Beckett, 1773.

Langford, Paul. *A Polite and Commercial People: England 1727–1783.* Oxford: Clarendon Press, 1989.

Public Life and the Propertied Englishman 1689–1798. Oxford: Clarendon Press, 1991.

Larkin, Paschal. *Property in the Eighteenth Century with Special Reference to England and Locke.* 1930; rpt. with new introduction. New York, NY: Howard Fertig, 1969.

Larsen, Lyle. *Dr Johnson's Household*. Hamden, CT: Archon Books, 1985.

Lefebvre, Henri. *Critique de la vie quotidienne*, III: *De la modernité au modernisme (Pour une métaphilosophie du quotidien)*. Paris: L'Arche, 1981.

    Everyday Life in the Modern World. Intro. Philip Wander. Trans. Sacha Rabinovitch. New Brunswick, NJ: Transaction Books, 1984.

    The Production of Space. Trans. Donald Nicholson-Smith. Oxford: Basil Blackwell, 1991.

Lenman, Bruce. *The Jacobite Risings in Britain 1689–1746*. London: Eyre Methuen, 1980.

Levinson, Marjorie. *The Romantic Fragment Poem: a Critique of a Form*. Chapel Hill, NC: The University of North Carolina Press, 1986.

Lewes, G. H. 'Hegel's Aesthetics', *British and Foreign Review*, 13 (1842), 1–49.

Lewis, W. S., *et al.*, eds. *The Yale Edition of Horace Walpole's Correspondence*. 48 vols. New Haven, CT: Yale University Press, 1995.

Linebaugh, Peter. *The London Hanged: Crime and Civil Society in the Eighteenth Century*. Cambridge University Press, 1992.

Linklater, Eric. *The Raft and Socrates Asks Why: Two Conversations*. London: Macmillan and Co., 1944.

Loch, David. *Essays on the Trade, Commerce, Manufactures and Fisheries of Scotland*. 3 vols. Edinburgh: W. and T. Ruddiman, 1778–79.

Locke, John. *Two Treatises of Government*. Ed. Peter Laslett. Cambridge University Press, 1967.

Lucas, John. *England and Englishness: Ideas of Nationhood in English Poetry, 1688–1900*. London: Hogarth Press, 1990.

Luttrell, Barbara. *The Prim Romantic: a Biography of Ellis Cornelia Knight, 1758–1837*. Intro. Roger Fulford. London: Chatto and Windus, 1965.

Macaulay, Thomas B. 'Essay on Boswell's "Life of Johnson"', *Edinburgh Review* 54 (September 1831), 1–38.

Mackenzie, Henry, ed. *Report of the Committee of the Highland Society of Scotland, Appointed to Inquire into the Nature and Authenticity of the Poems of Ossian*. Edinburgh: Archibald Constable and Co., 1805.

Mackintosh, Donald T. 'James Macpherson and the Book of the Dean of Lismore', *Scottish Gaelic Studies*, 6 (1949), 11–20.

Mackintosh, R. J., ed. *Memoirs of the Life of the Right Honourable Sir James Mackintosh*. 2 vols. 1835; rpt. Boston, MA: Little, Brown and Co., 1853.

MacNicol, Donald. *Remarks on Dr Samuel Johnson's Journey to the Hebrides*. 1779; reprinted New York, NY: Garland Publishing Inc., 1974.

Macpherson, C. B. *The Political Theory of Possessive Individualism: Hobbes to Locke*. Oxford: Oxford University Press, 1962.

Macpherson, C. B., ed. and intro. *Property: Mainstream and Critical Positions*. Toronto: University of Toronto Press, 1978.

Macpherson, James. *An Introduction to the History of Great Britain and Ireland*. London: T. Becket and P. A. de Hondt, 1771.

    The Poems of Ossian and Related Works. ed. Howard Gaskill, intro. Fiona Stafford. Edinburgh: Edinburgh University Press, 1996.

Macpherson, John. *Critical Dissertations on the Origin, Antiquities, Language, Government, Manners and Religion, of the Ancient Caledonians.* London: J. Becket and P. A. De Hondt, 1768.

Malcolmson, Robert W. *Popular Recreations in English Society 1700–1850.* Cambridge University Press, 1973.

Mandelbaum, Maurice. *The Anatomy of Historical Knowledge.* Baltimore, MD: The Johns Hopkins University Press, 1977.

Mandeville, Bernard. *The Fable of the Bees: Or, Private Vices, Publick Benefits.* Ed. F. B. Kaye. 2 vols. 1924; rpt. Indianapolis, IN: Liberty Classics, 1988.

Martin, Peter. 'Edmond Malone, Sir Joshua Reynolds, and Dr Johnson's Monument in St Paul's Cathedral', *The Age of Johnson* 3 (1990), 331–51.

   Edmond Malone, Shakespearean Scholar: a Literary Biography. Cambridge University Press, 1995.

Martin, Samuel. *An Epistle in Verse, Occasioned by the Death of James Boswell, Esquire, of Auchinleck. Addressed to the Rev. Dr T. D.* Edinburgh: Mundell and Son, 1795.

Marx, Karl. 'Economic and Philosophic Manuscripts of 1844', in Karl Marx and Frederick Engels, *Collected Works*, vol. III: *Marx and Engels: 1843–44.* New York, NY: International Publishers, 1975.

Mason, John. 'Conditions in the Highlands after the 'Forty-five', *The Scottish Historical Review* 26 (1947), 134–46.

Mason, William. *An Epistle to Dr Shebbeare: to which is added an Ode to Sir Fletcher Norton.* London, J. Almon, 1777.

McElderry, B. R. Jr., 'Boswell in 1790–91: Two Unpublished Comments', *Notes and Queries*, 9: 7 ns (1962), 266–68.

McGowan, Ian. 'Boswell at Work: the Revision and Publication of *The Journal of a Tour to the Hebrides*', in Ribeiro, SJ and Booker, *Tradition in Transition.*

McGuffie, Helen Louise. *Samuel Johnson in the British Press, 1749–1784: a Chronological Checklist.* New York, NY: Garland, 1976.

McLynn, Frank. *Crime and Punishment in Eighteenth-Century England.* London: Routledge, 1989.

Metzdorf, Robert F. 'M'Nicol, Macpherson, and Johnson', *Eighteenth-Century Studies in Honour of Donald F. Hyde.* Ed. W. H. Bond. New York, NY: The Grolier Club, 1970, 45–61.

Meyers, Jeffrey, ed. *The Craft of Literary Biography.* New York, NY: Schocken, 1985.

Middendorf, John H. 'Dr Johnson and Mercantilism', *Journal of the History of Ideas* 21: 1 (1960), 66–83.

   'Johnson on Wealth and Commerce', in his *Johnson, Boswell and their Circle: Essays Presented to Lawrence Fitzroy Powell in Honour of his Eighty-Fourth Birthday.* Oxford: Clarendon Press, 1965, 47–64.

Monk, Samuel Holt, ed. *The Works of John Dryden*, XVII, *Prose 1668–91.* Berkeley, CA: University of California Press, 1971.

Monod, Paul Kléber. *Jacobitism and the English People 1688–1788.* Cambridge University Press, 1989.

Murphy, Arthur. 'An Essay on the Life and Genius of Samuel Johnson LL.D.', in his *The Works of Samuel Johnson, LL.D.*, 6 vols. Dublin: Luke White, 1793.

Namier, Lewis. *England in the Age of the American Revolution*. London: Macmillan, 1930.

Nangle, Benjamin Christie. *The Monthly Review, First Series, 1749–1789: Indexes of Contributors and Articles*. Oxford: Clarendon Press, 1934.

Neimn, Frazer, ed. *Essays, Letters, and Reviews by Matthew Arnold*. Cambridge, MA: Harvard University Press, 1960.

Nicol, Donald, W. 'Arthur Murphy's Law', *Times Literary Supplement*, April 19 1996, 15–16.

O'Halloran, Clare. 'Irish Recreations of the Gaelic Past: the Challenge of Macpherson's Ossian', *Past and Present* 124 (1989), 69–95.

Oldmixon, John. *Reflections on Dr Swift's Letter to the Earl of Oxford about the English Tongue*. 1712; rpt. Los Angeles, CA: Augustan Reprint Society, 1948.

Olivebranch, Simon. 'Sheet omitted in B———'s Life of Johnson'. *The Looker-On, a Periodical Paper*. 3rd edn. London: G. G. and J. Robinson, 1795, IV, 110–14.

Parreaux, André. *Daily Life in England in the Reign of George III*. Trans. Carola Congreve. London: George Allen and Unwin, 1969.

Paulson, Ronald. *Breaking and Remaking: Aesthetic Practice in England, 1700–1820*. New Brunswick, NJ: Rutgers University Press, 1989.

Penny, Nicholas, ed. *Reynolds*. New York, NY: Harry N. Abrams, 1986.

Piozzi, Hesther Lynch. *Anecdotes of the Late Samuel Johnson, LL.D., during the Last Twenty Years of his Life*. Ed. and intro. S. C. Roberts. 1925; rpt. Westport, CT: Greenwood Press, 1971.

Pittock, Murray G. H. *Poetry and Jacobite Politics in Eighteenth-Century Britain and Ireland*. Cambridge University Press, 1994.

Pottle, Frederick A. *The Literary Career of James Boswell, Esq*. Oxford: Clarendon Press, 1929.

'The Life of James Boswell', *The Yale Review* 35 (1946), 445–60.

Pride and Negligence: The History of the Boswell Papers. New Haven, CT: Yale University Press, 1982.

Powell, L. F. 'An Addition to the Canon of Johnson's Writings'. *Essays and Studies* (London) 28 (1942), 38–41.

Psalmanazar, George. *Memoirs of ****. Commonly known by the Name of George Psalmanazar, A Reputed Native of Formosa. Written by Himself in order to be Published after his Death*. London: R. Davis *et al.*, 1765.

Radzinowicz, Leon. *A History of the English Criminal Law and its Administration from 1750*, vol. I: *The Movement for Reform*. Foreword by Lord Macmillan. London: Stevens and sons, 1948.

Raleigh, Walter. *Six Essays on Johnson*. Oxford: Clarendon Press, 1910.

Raven, James. *Judging New Wealth: Popular Publishing and Responses to Commerce in England, 1750–1800*. Oxford: Clarendon Press, 1992.

Rawson, Claude. 'The Night I Didn't Get Drunk'. Review of *Boswell: The English Experiment 1785–1789*, *London Review of Books* (7 May 1989).

Reddick, Allen. *The Making of Johnson's Dictionary, 1746–1773.* Cambridge University Press, 1990.

Reed, Eugene R. 'Herder, Primitivism and the Age of Poetry', *The Modern Language Review* 60: 4 (1965), 553–67.

Reichard, Hugo M. 'Boswell's Johnson, the Hero made by a Committee', *PMLA* 95: 2 (1980), 225–33.

Reynolds, Sir Joshua. 'A Journey to Flanders and Holland', in his *Literary Works*. Ed. Henry William Beechey, new and improved edn Bohn's Standard Library. 2 vols. London: Henry G. Bohn, 1852.

Ribeiro, Alvaro, SJ and James G. Basker, eds. *Tradition in Transition: Women Writers, Marginal Texts and the Eighteenth-Century Canon.* Oxford: Clarendon Press, 1996.

Roberts, William. *Memoirs of the Life of Mrs Hannah More.* 2 vols. London: R. B. Seeley and W. Burnside, 1836.

Robertson, J. Logie, ed. *The Complete Poetical Works of James Thomson.* London: Oxford University Press, 1965.

Robson, J. M., ed. *Collected Works of John Stuart Mill*, vol. XXII: *Newspaper Writings December 1822–July 1831.* Toronto: University of Toronto Press, 1986.

Rogers, Pat. *Johnson.* Past Masters. Oxford: Oxford University Press, 1993.

Rose, Mark. *Authors and Owners: the Invention of Copyright.* Cambridge, MA: Harvard University Press, 1993.

Rosebery, Lord. *Dr Johnson: an Address delivered at the Johnson Bicentenary Celebration, at Lichfield, September 15, 1909.* London: Arthur L. Humphreys, 1909.

Ross, Kristin. 'Two Versions of the Everyday', *L'Esprit Créateur* 24: 3 (1984), 29–37.

Rudé, George. *Paris and London in the Eighteenth Century: Studies in Popular Protest.* London: Collins, 1970.

Sack, James J. *From Jacobite to Conservative: Reaction and Orthodoxy in Britain, c. 1760–1832.* Cambridge University Press, 1993.

Saintsbury, George. *The Peace of the Augustans: a Survey of Eighteenth Century Literature as a Place of Rest and Refreshment.* Intro. Sir Herbert Grierson. 1916; rpt. London: Oxford University Press, 1946.

Saussure, César de. *A Foreign View of England in the Reigns of George I and George II.* Trans. and ed. Madame van Muyden. London: John Murray, 1902.

Schaff, Philip. *The Principle of Protestantism as Related to the Present State of the Church.* Trans. and intro. John W. Nevin. Chambersburg, PA: Publication Office of the German Reformed Church, 1845.

Schwartz, Richard B. *Samuel Johnson and the Problem of Evil.* Madison, WI: University of Wisconsin Press, 1975.

   Daily Life in Johnson's London. Madison, WI: University of Wisconsin Press, 1983.

Seccombe, Thomas. *The Age of Johnson (1748–1798).* Handbooks of English Literature. London: George Bell and Sons, 1900.

Secord, Arthur Wellesley, ed. *Defoe's Review.* 22 vols. New York, NY: Facsimile Text Society by Columbia University Press, 1938.

Seward, Anna. *Letters of Anna Seward: Written Between the Years 1784 and 1807.* Edinburgh: George Ramsay, 1811.

Seward, William. *Anecdotes of Some Distinguished Persons, Chiefly of the Present and Two Preceding Centuries.* 4 vols. London: T. Cardell and W. Davies, 1795–97.

Shaw, William. *An Enquiry into the Authenticity of the Poems Ascribed to Ossian.* London: J. Murray, 1781.

Shell, Marc. *The Economy of Literature.* Baltimore, MD: The Johns Hopkins University Press, 1978.

Money, Language, and Thought: Literary and Philosophic Economies from the Medieval to the Modern Era. Berkeley, CA: University of California Press, 1982.

Shenstone, William. *Works in Verse and Prose.* 2 vols. London: J. Dodsley, 1765.

Sherman, Stuart. *Telling Time: Clocks, Diaries, and English Diurnal Form, 1660–1785.* Chicago, IL: University of Chicago Press, 1996.

Shorter, Clement. *Immortal Memories.* London: Hodder and Stoughton, 1907.

Simmel, Georg. *On Individuality and Social Forms: Selected Writings.* Ed. and intro. Donald N. Levine. Chicago, IL: University of Chicago Press, 1971.

Simpson, David, ed. and intro. *German Aesthetic and Literary Criticism: Kant, Fichte, Schelling, Schopenhauer, Hegel.* Cambridge University Press, 1984.

Solomon, Harry M. *The Rise of Robert Dodsley: Creating the New Age of Print.* Carbondale, IL: Southern Illinois University Press, 1996.

Sprat, Thomas. 'An Account of the Life and Writings of Mr Abraham Cowley written to Mr M. Clifford', in *The Works of Mr Abraham Cowley.* London: J. M. for Henry Herringman, 1668.

Stafford, Fiona J. *The Sublime Savage: a Study of James Macpherson and the Poems of Ossian.* Edinburgh: Edinburgh University Press, 1988.

Steele, Peter. *The Autobiographical Passion: Studies in the Self on Show.* Melbourne: Melbourne University Press, 1989.

Stern, Fritz. ed. *The Varieties of History: from Voltaire to the Present.* London: Macmillan, 1956.

Stirling, J. H. *The Secret of Hegel.* London: Longman, Green, Longman, Roberts and Green, 1865.

Stone, Lawrence. *The Family, Sex and Marriage in England, 1500–1800.* New York, NY: Harper and Row, 1977.

Sunderland, L. S. and L. G. Mitchell, eds. *The History of the University of Oxford,* vol. v: *The Eighteenth Century.* Oxford: Clarendon Press, 1986.

Thomson, Derick S. *The Gaelic Sources of Macpherson's 'Ossian'.* 1952; rpt. Folcroft, PA: Folcroft Library Editions, 1973.

[The *Times*]. 'An English Saint Remembered'. Editorial. 13 December 1984, 15, 'Royal Gifts to British Prisoners'. Friday, 17 December 1943.

Tinker, Chauncey Brewster, ed. *Letters of James Boswell.* 2 vols. Oxford: Clarendon Press, 1924.

Essays in Retrospect: Collected Articles and Addresses. New Haven, CT: Yale University Press, 1948.

Todd, Dennis. *Imagining Monsters: Miscreations of the Self in Eighteenth-Century England.* Chicago, IL: University of Chicago Press, 1995.

Topham, Edward. *Letters from Edinburgh, 1774–75*. London: J. Dodsley, 1776.

Toynbee, Paget and Leonard Whibley, eds. *Correspondence of Thomas Gray*. With corrections and additions by H. W. Starr. 3 vols. Oxford: Clarendon Press, 1971.

Trevelyan, G. M. *Clio, A Muse: and Other Essays Literary and Pedestrian*. London: Longmans, Green and Co., 1913.

History of England. 1st edn 1926. London: Longmans, 1956.

Illustrated English Social History. 4 vols. Harmondsworth: Penguin, 1964.

Troide, Lars E. ed. *The Early Journals and Letters of Fanny Burney*. 3 vols. Oxford: Clarendon Press, 1988–94.

Turberville, A. S. *English Men and Manners in the Eighteenth Century*. 1st edn., 1926; New York, NY: Oxford University Press, 1957.

Turberville, A. S., ed. *Johnson's England: an Account of the Life and Manners of his Age*. 2 vols. Oxford: Clarendon Press, 1933.

'UNESCO Convention on the Illicit Movement of Art Treasures', *International Legal Materials* 10 (1971), 289–93.

Van Tieghem, Paul. *Ossian en France*. 2 vols. Paris: F. Rieder, 1917.

'Ossian et l'ossianisme', in *Le Préromantisme*. 3 vols. Paris: F. Rieder, 1924–30.

Vance, John A. *Samuel Johnson and the Sense of History*. Athens, GA: University of Georgia Press, 1984.

Vance, John A., ed. *Boswell's 'Life of Johnson': New Questions, New Answers*. Athens, GA: University of Georgia Press, 1985.

Vaneigem, Raoul. *The Revolution of Everyday Life*. Trans. Donald Nicholson-Smith. London: Rebel Press/Left Bank Books, 1994.

Vilar, Pierre. *A History of Gold and Money: 1450 to 1920*. Trans. Judith White 1976; rpt. London: Verso, 1991.

Voltaire. *The Age of Louis XIV*. Trans. Martyn P. Pollack, preface by F. C. Green. Everyman's Library. London: Dent, 1926.

Vulliamy, C. E., *Ursa Major: a Study of Dr Johnson and His Friends*. London: Michael Joseph, 1946.

Wain, John, ed. and intro. *Johnson on Johnson: a Selection of the Personal and Auobiographical Writings of Samuel Johnson (1709–1784)*. Everyman's Library. London: Dent, 1976.

Walpole, Horace. *Memoirs of the Reign of King George the Third*. Ed. Denis Le Merchant. 4 vols. London: Richard Bentley, 1845.

Walsh, Marcus. *Shakespeare, Milton and Eighteenth-Century Literary Editing*. Cambridge University Press, 1997.

Walsh, Marcus and Ian Small, eds. *The Theory of Practice of Text-Editing: Essays in Honour of James T. Boulton*. Cambridge University Press, 1991.

Ward, A. W. and A. R. Waller, eds. *Cambridge History of English Literature*. Cambridge University Press, 1913.

Warner, Ferdinando. *Remarks on the History of Fingal and other Poems of Ossian: Translated by Mr Macpherson in a Letter to the Lord L—*. London: H. Payne and W. Cropley, 1762.

Warton, Joseph. *An Essay on the Genius and Writings of Pope.* 2 vols. 1756; rpt. London: W. J. and J. Richardson *et al.*, 1806.

Warton, Thomas. *The History of English Poetry from the Close of the Eleventh to the Commencement of the Eighteenth Century.* 3 vols. London: J. Dodsley *et al.*, 1774–81.

Weber, Max. *On Charisma and Institution Building: Selected Papers.* Ed. and intro. S. N. Eisenstadt. Chicago, IL: University of Chicago Press, 1968.

Weinbrot, Howard D. *Britannia's Issue: the Rise of British Literature from Dryden to Ossian.* Cambridge University Press, 1995.

Williams, E. N. *Life in Georgian England.* London: B. T. Batsford Ltd, 1962.

Withers, Charles W. J. *Gaelic in Scotland 1698–1981: the Geographical History of a Language.* Foreword by Derick S. Thomson. Edinburgh: John Donald Publishers, 1984.

Wolcot, John. *The Works of Peter Pindar, Esq.* 3 vols. London: J. Walker, 1794.

Wright, H. Bunker and Monroe K. Spears, eds. *The Literary Works of Matthew Prior.* 2 vols. Oxford: Clarendon Press, 1959.

Wrigley, E. A. 'A Simple Model of London's Importance in Changing English Society and Economy 1650–1750', in *Aristocratic Government and Society in Eighteenth-Century England: the Foundations of Stability.* Ed. and intro. Daniel A. Baugh. New York, NY: Franklin Watts, 1975.

Young, Edward, *Conjectures on Original Composition in a Letter to the Author of Sir Charles Grandison.* London: n.p., 1759.

Youngson, A. J. *The Prince and the Pretender: a Study in the Writing of History.* London: Croom Helm, 1985.

Index of persons

Arnold, Matthew 59–60, 63

Birrill, Augustine 60–61
Blackstone, William 1–2, 134
Blackwell, Thomas 138–39, 213 n. 29
Blair, Hugh 54, 143–44, 146, 190 n. 40, 217 n. 56
Boswell, James
  as diarist 174–76
  as social negotiator 150–53
  as supplement 7, 152, 154
  biographical style 8, 36–38
  narrative space 25–29
  Works
    Journal of a Tour 101–3, 133–34, 151–52
    Life of Johnson 24–33, 78–79, 173, 177
    London Journal 129–31
    No Abolition of Slavery 110
Bronson, Bertrand H. 6–7, 32, 98
Burke, Edmund 3, 153
Burney, Frances 16, 41, 79–80

Carlyle, Thomas 56–59, 62, 66, 70, 78, 91, 182
Cary, Henry Francis 89–90
Certeau, Michel de 165–68
Chambers, Robert 134–35
Chesterfield, Lord 12, 71
Clark, J. C. D. 51, 107
Croker, J. W. 81–86, 178

Defoe, Daniel 4–5, 87, 121, 171–72
Dryden, John 42–43, 46, 64, 103

Erskine-Hill, Howard 105–6

Fichte, J. G. 56–57, 72
Fitzgerald, Percy 81–86, 93

Garrick, David 12, 181
Gay, John 130, 163–64
Gibbon, Edward 121–23, 148

Goethe, J. W. von 16, 57, 64–65, 139
Goldsmith, Oliver 11, 13, 29–30, 110–11, 168
Gray, Thomas 19, 142–43
Greene, Donald 51, 91–100, 181

Hamilton, William 34–35, 44
Harrington, James 2
Hawkins, Sir John 11, 15, 39–40
Hazlitt, William 54
Hegel, G. W. F. 55–56
Heidegger, Martin 169–70
Herder, J. G. 55, 63
Hervey, James 30
Hill, G. B. 82–88, 172
Hollis, Thomas 3–4
Hume, David 40, 50, 91, 142–45

Jenyns, Soame 113
Johnson, Samuel
  as Classic 13, 40–41
  as 'Dr Johnson' 18, 48–49, 108
  as hero 12, 15, 24, 79, 84, 89
  as Jacobite 105–8, 110
  as Mr Rambler 13
  as monster 26, 150
  as monument 13, 16–18, 20, 58
  as property 8, 77, 132, 181
  as Romantic 79
  as saint 66–67
  as spectacle 20, 133, 150
  as Tory 78, 107–8, 110, 206 n. 20
  death of 33–35, 39–41, 170
  double tradition of 6–7, 32, 98
  fame of 12, 13, 25, 33, 41–42
  statues of 14–15, 191 n. 52
  Works
    'Debates' 115–16
    Dictionary 20–24
    Journey to the Western Islands 112–13, 118–28, 140
    Lives of the Poets 67, 75–76

Index of subjects